MW00617274

On the Great Wall

On the
Great Wall

Penny Peng

Bamboo Books
Arlington, Virginia

First Printing January, 2004

Cover design by John A. Pino, Kiry Yin, and Carolina Cid
Chinese calligraphy by Weiming Yao
Edited by John H. Wills

Typography & interior design by Books AtoZ (Seattle, Washington)

ISBN: 0-9722610-2-8

Published in English by:
Bamboo Books Inc.
2111 Wilson Boulevard, Suite 700
Arlington, Virginia   22201
www.bamboobooks.com

Manufactured in the United States of America

Cover photo: main characters on the Great Wall at Shanhaiguan.

To Tung-ping

*Tung-ping in Aachen, Germany
shortly before returning to China.*

Contents

Foreword xi

Author's Note xiii

1. Meeting My Prince 1
2. A Proposal with Conditions 8
3. The Man Born in the "Year of the Dog" 18
4. Marry First, Fall in Love Afterwards 27
5. Candles in the Wind 37
6. Chop Suey? What's That? 50
7. Chasing Sparrows on the Rooftop 60
8. Catch up with the Yankees 71
9. A Month's Pay for One Chicken 79
10. Our Second Wedding Chamber 87
11. A Most Famous Seaside Resort 100
12. A Crouching Tiger Blocking the Way 109
13. Helsinki, Finland 119
14. Our Little Buddha 126
15. A White-Beard Project 136
16. Madame Mao – the Blue Apple 141
17. You're Great, *Baba*! 150
18. Pretty Apricot 164

19. Stop! Stop! No More Reciting 171
20. Open the Door! 181
21. "Good-bye! My Darling" 189
22. Rage of the Heavens 197
23. Where Are You? 204
24. Four Days in Purgatory 212
25. Sending Charcoal in the Snows 219
26. A Scarlet "X" 229
27. My Letter to Premier Zhou Enlai 239
28. My Ninth Cousin 246
29. Ping-Pong Diplomacy 256
30. The Year of the Dragon 262
31. A Visitor from Germany 270
32. Crossing Over the Pacific 279
33. Meet in the Ninth Heaven 288
Epilogue 297

Foreword

THIS IS A STORY about a man and a woman. About their paths in China, America, Great Britain, and Germany. It is a story about their love, their happiness, their sufferings, and their sorrows.

The man was born in the "Year of the Dog." He's loyal, faithful, loving, with every virtue of the dog. He is on an important quest. The woman was born in the "Year of the Horse." After you read this book you will find out all about her.

This is also a story about a time when a great country went through chaos, a time when thunderbolts split open the sky and rain washed away so many stories untold.

Map of China

(c) Bamboo Books, Inc. 2003

Author's Note

WHEN MY BOOK *In Love with Space* was published in China in 1993, Mia Turner suggested to me, "Why don't you put the story into English?" Several years later, I said to myself, "Why not?"

Just about that time, Bill Steig and his beautiful wife, Jennifer Ling, invited me to their lovely apartment in Beijing. Both of them were moved by my story. Bill said, "Wow, it's just like a TV series." He helped me expand my English manuscript and make it more accessible to Western readers.

After Tom Dwyer read my manuscript he said, "Penny, I think it is like a Chinese version of *Love Story*." His wife even read some of the humorous incidents in the manuscript to their whole family during dinner.

My thanks to Susan Lawrence, Shirley and Bob Hayes, Claire Zhu, Michela Fontana, Mark Kolakowski and some friends who are still in China for their help and encouragement.

I would also like to thank my editor John H. Wills. We worked for weeks in Arlington, Virginia and Seattle, Washington and e-mailed each other back and forth across the Pacific for months. We went over the text sentence by sentence in order to bring out the best possible way of telling the story.

Finally, my special thanks to Nien Cheng, Merle Goldman, and Carolyn Wakeman for reviewing my manuscript.

The Chinese calligraphy in this book was done by my daughter Weiming. My youngest daughter Carolyn helped me with some precious memories about her father.

For reasons of privacy, I have changed the names of some people in the text. Most of the Chinese names and places appear in the *pinyin* system (which China uses today). The names of two main characters, Chieh-ching and Tung-ping, however appear according to the older Wade-Giles system. Two letters in *pinyin* have a different pronunciation than you may be used to: Q is pronounced as "ch"; X as "sh."

1

Meeting my Prince

W<small>HEN</small> I <small>RETURNED</small> to China in the fall of 1957 after ten years away, it was not the homeland I had remembered. Men and women now dressed alike in blue or gray uniforms and black cotton-cloth shoes. Wearing the latest western dress and leather shoes, I felt like a stranger among my own people.

For the previous five years I had worked in Chicago, the Windy City. The blustery gray of Beijing was another story. I had forgotten what it was like to see streets filled with bicycles, shopkeepers cooking noodles, and a sea of heads everywhere.

Tucked away in a *hutong*, the old-fashioned alleys one still finds in Beijing, was a simple gray building. The Chinese government had turned this two-story building into a hostel for overseas Chinese students returning to China. Here lived more than twenty people just like me. This was the first "gate" we all had to pass through on our return to the motherland.

The name of the hostel was Yong-An. In Chinese, this means "Forever Safe." I rather liked the name. I craved a peaceful and secure life after fleeing Hunan on boats, trains and trucks as a girl during Japan's invasion of China — seeing my family scatter like sparrows. Somehow, I had a premonition something important might happen to me at Yong-An.

While I had just come from the United States, I met people who had lived for years in university towns in Great Britain, France, Japan, West Germany, and Holland. Each person had a fascinating story to tell. Some were married with kids, but most were single men. There were also two other single lady students. And we all hoped to serve our motherland.

All of us lived in single rooms on the second floor. Each room was furnished with a wash basin, a hard bed, a writing desk, and two wooden chairs. The entire floor shared one bathroom.

On the first floor were the offices of the hostel staff members. At the back was the most joyful room for us students: the canteen. We'd gather there three times a day for meals. When a round table was filled up with ten people, the attendants would bring out the food. We'd pass around bowls of red-cooked pork, fried fish or steamed tofu. Chinese greens were served everyday, often with red or white-skinned turnips cooked by themselves or in salads. Our food was a lot better than that of most Chinese families. One overseas student who had returned a few years earlier said to us, "You guys might as well enjoy this high standard of living while you're here. Once you start to work, you'll find life quite different."

Our drinking water was boiled, so the attendants would bring two thermoses up to each room daily. I was accustomed to the cool clean water from American faucets, so this was one of many adjustments I would have to make. I didn't like hot water or tea (even though my father had owned a tea shop!), so I'd always pour the water into glasses and let it cool off.

When the officials at the hostel asked us to write out a list of what we needed to buy, each of us put down three Mao uniforms — two for summer and a cotton-padded one for Beijing's cold winters. (These uniforms sported two breast pockets plus two

2

pockets lower down.) Although it was the late 1950s, you needed coupons to buy anything made of cloth — whether bed sheets or socks. Here in Beijing, each citizen was granted coupons for just three yards per year. I was unaware of this situation while in the United States, so I hadn't brought back to China the necessary things. Besides the uniforms, we each listed quilt covers, pillowcases, and warm cotton underwear. Luckily, we were granted more coupons than other Beijing residents.

You also needed ration coupons to buy foodstuffs — including cooking oil, sugar, eggs, meat, fish — as well as soap, cigarettes and matches.

Despite living conditions that were extremely different from our previous homes abroad, I heard few complaints. The only real complaint was waiting for job assignments. In China, the government assigned all work. Those who had studied science or engineering usually waited only a couple of months before getting assigned.

It was a different story if your specialty was in the liberal arts — especially philosophy, economics, or literature. China did not need such "bourgeois" ideology. Anyone in these fields had to wait a long time or was assigned to teach.

This was the situation for a couple who had come to the hostel from Japan. The man was a Chinese lawyer, his wife a native Japanese who did not speak any Chinese. There was no "official" need for any lawyers in the People's Republic of China then, so they ended up staying in the hostel for more than a year. They even had a baby while they waited. The man was eventually assigned to teach Japanese. Partly for this reason — and partly because many returnees would become the "object of the revolution" during political campaigns — when China's doors opened after 1972, this couple was among those who applied for exit permits.

Of course, none of us at that time were even contemplating

leaving China again. We had just returned. Or in a few cases, coming here for the very first time. Mr. Wang was one such person. He had been born in Vietnam, then brought up and educated in Paris. He was a civil engineer. As a matter of fact, he had a very good job with an engineering company in Paris. He had decided to come "back" to China out of a sense of patriotism, even though he had never been to his "motherland" before. He could speak French fluently, but whenever he tried to speak Chinese, he would stutter. So we usually conversed in English.

Life in the hostel centered around political study sessions. Six days a week, mornings and afternoons, we gathered to study Chairman Mao's Works or newspaper articles. It could get pretty dull.

To give our lives some seasoning that fall, a group of overseas students decided to hold a dance on the night of the "August Moon". This Festival is always held on the 15th day of the 8th moon (according to the lunar calendar) and is a major family gathering. People linger outdoors, drinking jasmine tea and eating moon cakes, roasted sunflower seeds, dried apricots and dates. Family members relax and chat, while kids run around under the full moon.

Moon cakes are closely associated with this festival. These delicious little cakes (shaped round like the moon) come with all sorts of fillings: sweet red-bean sauce, lotus-seed sauce, date sauce. If you prefer salted fillings, there is also minced pork, ham, and salted duck-egg yolk. But there is another ingredient as well — history.

Long ago China was under the control of the Mongols. The Chinese fought back against these aggressors without success. Finally, a revolt was planned. The date was set for the 15th day of the 8th moon. Because of the iron rule of the Mongols, the Chinese decided to conceal this date on slips of paper inside small round cakes and pass them around as if exchanging gifts. This way, the message was spread without attracting the Mongols' attention.

The Mongol invaders were driven out, and the commander of the rebel forces, Zhu Yuanzhang, donned a golden-yellow silk robe embroidered with dragons (the color and symbol of royalty). He proclaimed himself the first emperor of the Ming dynasty (1368–1644). From then on, the Chinese have kept the tradition of eating little round cakes on that lunar date. But there are no longer messages inside. Whenever I go to a Chinese restaurant abroad, the waiter usually serves almond cookies at the end of the meal, with a slip of fortune-telling paper tucked inside. I guess they borrowed this custom from their ancestor country.

When the students held another dance on New Year's Eve, the canteen in Yong-An Hostel was turned into a ballroom. The tables were pushed out of the way and chairs lined the walls. Candy, roasted sunflower seeds, peanuts and jasmine tea were all set out. Since the room was illuminated by bare bulbs hanging from the ceiling, we also hung bright paper rings of red, green, yellow and blue. Some people brought their kids along. The children soon had their hands full of goodies and were chasing one another around the room.

I had been coaxed by friends to attend the party. That night, I chose to wear a white blouse, an ankle-length skirt in navy blue over a pair of navy pumps. Fair-skinned and slender, I was somewhat delicate in appearance. I sat on a chair at the far end of the room, facing the entrance. Hands folded in my lap as I was taught at St. Francis College, I began to enjoy the holi-

The author in 1957

day atmosphere. A record player had been set up playing some Western music, and a few couples were dancing.

The tall stranger at the dance

Then I saw him. A tall man in his thirties, slim, dark and good-looking. He was wearing horn-rimmed glasses. I noticed his thick black hair and unconsciously touched my own thin, brownish hair. Well-dressed in a navy jacket and gray trousers, his graceful carriage and very manner made him stand out from the others he was with.

I kept my eyes on him. I couldn't help it. Then he approached. I crossed my fingers. To make doubly sure, I crossed my ankles. And it worked! He walked straight my way and introduced himself. He told me his name was Yao Tung-ping and he had just returned from Aachen, West Germany. "Glad to meet you. I am Peng Chieh-ching from Chicago." At that moment, the music started and he asked me to dance. I was so happy. I even blushed.

We stepped toward the dance floor. "The Blue Danube" was playing on the record player. A waltz! That was great! In Chicago, I had taken dance lessons at Arthur Murray Dancing School. My teacher had praised me highly for my waltzing. I took a deep breath and off we went. This fellow Tung-ping whirled me around and around, nimble and sure. I hung on as best I could, mesmerized by this smiling stranger. The song ended, but we stayed together. We danced some more. We talked. I told him about my childhood, my days at the College of St. Francis in Joliet, Illinois and my graduate student life at New York University.

I told him everything about myself. Tung-ping was a good listener. He only put in a sentence or two. We talked and danced, with scarcely a rest. He didn't ask anyone else to dance that night.

At one point, as the party was winding down, we walked over to the man spinning the records. "Can you play 'The Blue Danube' again?" I asked. I turned to smile at Tung-ping. He smiled back.

We'd known each other for only a couple of hours, and already we had our own song. We skipped lightly back onto the floor and danced again — this time, comfortable in each other's arms and sure of our steps. We danced until the party ended. Deep in my heart, I wished time would stand still so that we could be together forever.

Tung-ping told me he felt something special would happen to him here at Yong-An Hostel. "And so it did," he said. As for me, it was '*yi jian zhong qing*' (love at first sight). And I thought to myself, it would be love till the end of time.

2

A Proposal With Conditions

———————— ✺ ————————

THE DAY WE MOVED into the Yong-An Hostel, the officials took away our passports. This was because they had been issued by the Kuomintang government, the "Nationalist" regime that had been driven to Taiwan by the Communists in 1949. China was now our home.

Our first assignment at the hostel was to write an autobiography, starting from the age of seven, when we entered primary school. We had to describe what kind of family we came from and list all its members, including grandparents, parents, siblings, in-laws, distant relatives and close friends.

We had to detail our education, work experience abroad, political background and religious beliefs. We were also told to list any family members who still lived abroad, especially in Hong Kong or Taiwan. These *"hai wai guan xi"* — overseas relations — required detailed information submissions. If you had any *hai wai guan xi*, usually you weren't trusted for important jobs.

This autobiography was forwarded to your *danwei* (work unit). In China, everyone belonged to a *danwei*. And everyone had a personal file. Besides what you wrote, this file contained matters your *danwei* would periodically add. Whatever accomplishments or mistakes you made would be recorded. Wherever you went, the file followed you, until death.

While living at the hostel and waiting for work assignments, our primary activity was political study. We would gather in the large room with big windows on the second floor, where the newspapers and magazines were kept. People would also come here every day from their rooms down the hall to read newspapers.

The first day I walked into this room, I made a big discovery. In the United States I was used to big thick newspapers like the *Chicago Tribune* as well as magazines like *Time* or *Newsweek*, packed with articles. I especially remembered the heft of the *New York Times* on Sundays — to read everything would take more than a day. So when I picked up *People's Daily* on the table there, I asked, "Who took the rest of *People's Daily*?"

Someone looked up. "Isn't that it in your hand?"

"There are only four pages," I said. "Where is the rest?"

"Don't you know?" came the answer. "There are only four pages in *People's Daily*. There is no more."

I looked at the flimsy sheets of newsprint in my hand. I wondered what my eldest brother — whom I had not seen for ten years — would think. He had been a journalist for the Central News Agency in Nanking (today called Nanjing) before the People's Republic was established and later for the *Central Daily News* in Taipei. He had once told me, "When a dog bites a man, it's not news; when a man bites a dog, it's news." Besides hard news, he liked to see some human-interest stories.

Things were different in China in 1957. The newspapers' purpose was to educate people ideologically, so that everyone would know the Communist Party's policy and follow its rules and regulations. There was very little that could be described as "human interest." When you opened the newspaper, you saw such news as: "Output of steel increased thirty percent as workers work all night long." Stories fell into three main categories:

- Articles about how deeply people loved Chairman Mao, how diligently they studied his Works, and how much the lives of the workers and peasants had changed.
- Pictures of Chairman Mao or other leaders receiving foreign guests — evidence of China's great power and of foreigners' love and respect for Mao.
- Articles about encouraging developments in the construction of a socialist country. Current campaigns such as "Wiping Out the Four Pests" were highlighted. (One photo showed an old peasant woman holding up scores of dead rats by their tails.)

A political study meeting usually went like this: One person would read an article aloud from beginning to end. (The articles all came from *People's Daily* or *Guangming Daily* — both government-owned, like all newspapers.) Then he or she would read each paragraph again, asking others for their opinions. It seemed ludicrous, and it was. But none of us dared say so. Although we were new to the political climate, we had been coached by relatives to repeat whatever the paragraph said, just changing a few words.

It was really very boring.

We looked forward to the days when we got to go on field trips. Tiananmen Square was our first destination. We were informed that Tiananmen Square was much bigger than Red Square in Moscow. A senior cadre from the hostel said, "Some of you people from the United States probably know that Times Square has no comparison to our Tiananmen Square."

It was true. Tiananmen Square is huge.

Mao Zedong's portrait hangs up high on the Tiananmen rostrum at the north end. It was and still is flanked on both sides by red slogans with big white Chinese characters that say: "Long live the worldwide unity of the people!" and "Long live the People's Republic of China!"

Tiananmen Square is the southern portal to the Forbidden City, the palace where emperors of the Ming and Qing dynasties once lived. Following Chinese tradition, the emperor's throne usually faced south. The emperor sat on his throne every morning and the high officials would kowtow to him and shout long live to his majesty before they were allowed to stand up and do whatever reporting they had.

When our group visited Tiananmen, there were four other portraits in the square facing Chairman Mao's. The portraits were along the street, much lower than Mao's. I asked Tung-ping, "Who's the man with the long mustache?"

"Which one?"

"Second one from the left."

"Oh," he said. "That's Engels. Don't you know?"

"Engels? How do you spell it?" He spelled it for me in Roman letters.

"Oh. I've seen pictures of Marx, Lenin and Stalin, but never of Engels. I've never even heard of him."

I looked around. It seemed to me there was a portrait missing of the man who had overthrown the Qing dynasty (1645-1911) and established a republic in China in 1911. The man whom I was taught was the father of modern China. Someone to regard as Americans regard George Washington.

"How come they don't have Dr. Sun Yat-sen's portrait?" I asked Tung-ping. "Isn't he the father of our country?"

He nudged me. "No, the founder of the People's Republic is Chairman Mao."

"Oooh…" a political blunder.

Later, I was told that Dr. Sun Yat-sen's portrait was displayed, but only during holidays. Since the Cultural Revolution, all the portraits have been taken down except Mao's.

⁂

Beijing was new to both Tung-ping and me. We both enjoyed these trips immensely. The place we liked best was the Great Wall. We hiked up the pine-covered mountains to its base, then climbed more steps to the top of the wall itself. From there, we could see forever, the blue sky merging with the horizon. It was a grand sight.

Tung-ping was inspired.

"What do you think," he mused. "Don't you think we should be proud that our ancestors made this thousands of years ago? Just think, how could they move all those rocks and make all of this by hand."

He gazed into the distance. He was speaking not only to me, but to himself as well.

"Perhaps," he continued, "we can do something for our motherland so that China will catch up in science and technology with Western countries."

This was Tung-ping — always thinking how to devote his study to the advancement of China. I didn't say anything. I was simply enchanted by the beauty and grandeur of the Great Wall. And to be next to the man I loved.

Another place we adored was Tiantan Park. Inside this vast park ground stood the Temple of Heaven, where the emperors used to worship heaven. In some parks in China, instead of seeing scenery, all you see is other people. Tiantan was different, not as crowded. It became our favorite retreat.

At the southern end of this impressive collection of Ming temples and altars is the circular Echo Wall. I would stand at one end of the Echo Wall and Tung-ping would stand at the other.

"*Ni hao*, Tung-ping. Can you hear what I just said?"

"Yes, very clearly. Just like a telephone."

Every time we went, we'd affectionately repeat the same thing, and we never got tired of it.

Whenever we went on group excursions, a cadre from the hostel usually acted as our guide. He liked to pepper his remarks with political insights. One day as we were soaking up the incredible scenery of the Great Wall, the hostel cadre came over and announced, "Do you know it was all a wreck here once? Now it's so nice because our Party and our government restored it after the liberation."

We heard a similar message when we were out paddling small boats around Kunming Lake in the Summer Palace. The cadre remarked, "Before the liberation, there were hardly any working people here. They didn't even earn enough to buy food. How could they have money to pay for the park entrance ticket?"

The only place Tung-ping and I could find a moment of privacy was on the roof of the hostel. I hung out some washing on the clotheslines there almost every day. Sometimes Tung-ping and I would climb up there together in the evenings. It was nice and quiet, just the cobalt blue sky and twinkling stars above us. It seemed as if we were Adam and Eve in the Garden of Eden and could almost reach the stars.

"Tung-ping, can you get a star for me?" I asked jokingly.

"Well, maybe I'll be able to make a star for you some day. How's that?" He replied earnestly. (Did he already know that he was going to be involved in China's space program I often wondered.)

Every so often, the cadres in the hostel would ask us for suggestions about how to improve their work. The general response was, "We don't have any suggestions, other than we'd like to go to work as soon as possible."

However, one person in our group launched a specific complaint. "We once had very good jobs, but feeling very patriotic, we came back to China. How come, as soon as we came back, we were labeled returned students from 'capitalist' countries?"

Someone added, "We don't like to be called this. Why not call us 'patriotic returned students'? Or just plain 'returned students'?"

It was a brave suggestion, but it didn't get any reply. From then on, whenever we were solicited for suggestions, we generally kept mum.

Much later, during the 1990s, a lot of the Chinese students studying abroad did so with the intention of staying there. They took along with them the papers required by agencies such as the U.S. Immigration and Naturalization Service for applying for a green card. The few who did return to China were called *hai gui pai* (overseas returned students) by the government. Although these people had foreign residence permits or citizenship already, the word 'capitalist' was never mentioned anymore.

The officials would also ask us time and again how to attract more overseas scientists back to China. They even suggested that we write to our scientist friends and relatives abroad, to say that they were welcome to return. The cadres said we could tell the scientists that the government would meet all their requests. They told us that if more overseas scientists came back, the scientific and technical level of China would be accelerated by five to ten years.

I don't know whether any of us wrote to our friends abroad. But we were the last group of overseas students who returned. The reason was that people outside China had begun to hear about the Anti-Rightist Campaign. Starting in 1957, more than half a million people were branded as 'rightists' — most of them professors, writers, scientists and other professionals. They were sent to labor farms. Their only "crime" was to point out the mistakes and wrongs made by some Communist Party secretaries. Because of that, overseas Chinese stopped coming back and Yong-An Hostel had to be shut down.

In late 1957, Tung-ping got his work assignment: the Fifth Academy of the Defense Ministry. There were other *danwei* which would have liked to have retained him, such as the China Academy of Sciences, Qinghua University and the Institute of Iron and Steel. But Marshal Nie Rongzhen made the final decision to have Tung-ping assigned to the Fifth Academy. The Party leaders had already made plans to expand the Academy into a ministry for rockets, missiles and satellites (the Seventh Machine Building Ministry). But I didn't know anything about it at the time.

One day in December, Tung-ping invited me to go out. He said he had something important to tell me. I knew several *danwei* had been talking to him. I guessed he was going to tell me about his new job. I had on a padded jacket in Kelly green, a pair of black woolen slacks and black leather boots. Tung-ping had on the same navy jacket and gray trousers that he wore to the New Year's Eve dance, except that afternoon he also put on a dark navy coat he had brought back from West Germany.

We went to the Dong'an Bazaar. It was a nice place on Wangfujing Street, right across the street from Beijing Department Store. (There was only one department store in Beijing then.) There were many shops inside Dong'an Bazaar: clothing stores, hat and shoe stores, bookstores, arts and crafts shops, antique shops, and several popular restaurants, some of them hundreds of years old.

In the far corner of the second floor was the Peace Restaurant which served Western food. It was well known for its coffee and pastry. Chinese people didn't go much for Western food. There were only a few people inside the Peace Restaurant, seated behind the backs of high booths. This was exactly what we wanted.

Tung-ping and I each ordered a coffee. He asked my permission to smoke, then lit a cigarette. I knew immediately that he was going to say something important.

Tung-ping told me that he fell in love with me when he first met me. He said he was attracted by my vividness and outgoing way. Now that he had secured a post, his *danwei* would assign him an apartment. He said, even if I didn't have a job yet, he would be able to provide a home for me. Would I marry him?

Would I marry him! Of course I would! I fell in love with him when I first set my eyes on him at the dance. Oh! How happy I was! I was in heaven! Wait a minute, what was he saying now?

Tung-ping mentioned that he'd have to send an application to the Communist Party to get permission to marry. In my ecstatic state, I wasn't catching everything he was saying. Something about permission? From his mother, right?

"I need permission from the Party," Tung-ping said.

"Party? What Party?"

"The Chinese Communist Party," he replied in a steady voice.

"Are you a Communist?" I asked, incredulous.

"Yes."

"Omigosh."

My, this was something! I was aware of the American political parties, Democrats and Republicans, but had never paid much attention to them, let alone to the Chinese Communist Party.

My image of a Communist was like that of anyone living in the U.S. in the late 1940s or 1950s. A big, mustachioed Russian, "cold and stiff" — Josef Stalin. That was a Communist. Frankly, I hadn't thought much about Chinese Communists.

Now here was this handsome, vigorous, intelligent man, the

man who wanted to marry me, telling me he was a Communist. I thought someone who was a member of the Chinese Communist Party must be someone who talked about politics and ideology all day long, like the cadres at the Yong-An Hostel. I didn't know they were also people who could sing and dance. In an instant, Tung-ping had humanized the Communist Party member for me.

Tung-ping put his cigarette out in the ashtray and continued, "Chieh-ching, I must warn you of something!"

"Yes? Yes?" I was very tense.

I thought to myself: "Here comes the confession. He will tell me that he has a European girlfriend or something." I was all ears.

He said, "Since I am a member of the Communist Party, the Party's cause always comes first!" He looked straight into my eyes and added, "Even before you."

"Is that all?" I was immensely relieved. Just so long as it was not another woman, I would put up with it.

I said quickly, "It's OK. It's OK!"

"Not so fast, dear. There's one more thing. I am not allowed to tell you about my job. I can't disclose anything connected with my work."

"Tung-ping darling, even if you do tell me about your work, I don't think I'll be able to understand it. I never liked math, or physics or chemistry. I only love you. I don't care about your work."

Tung-ping was very happy and relieved at my words. He said it's an occasion for celebration, so he ordered some red wine. We clicked our glasses, his smiling eyes met with my smiling ones. And we toasted, *"Yong yuan xiang ai!"* (Forever in love!)

永遠相愛

17

3

The Man Born in the "Year of the Dog"

————————— ⟋⟍ —————————

For days, I was walking on clouds. I couldn't think of anything else but the love of Tung-ping. The words *"Yong yuan xiang ai"* kept echoing into my ears. Tung-ping and his love kept me awake at night. I could foresee the happy and sweet life ahead of us: me and the man born in the "Year of the Dog," Tung-ping.

According to the Chinese lunar calendar, there are twelve animal years. In customary order, they are the Years of the Dragon, the Snake, the Horse, the Goat, the Monkey, the Rooster, the Dog, the Pig, the Rat, the Ox, the Tiger, and the Rabbit.

In 1922, the "Year of the Dog," a second son was born to the Yao family in Huangtutang. This is a small village not far from Wuxi, an industrial city near Shanghai.

Father Yao owned a little shop. His eldest son Hong-ping helped him run the shop after graduating from primary school. A daughter had never been to school; she helped Mother Yao with the household chores.

Father Yao was very happy to have a second son. He named him Tung-ping. When the boy reached school age, Father Yao sent him to primary school. Tung-ping did exceptionally well in his studies, graduating at the top of his class. Now Father Yao thought, it was time for his second son to give him a hand in the shop. When the school principal heard about this however, he went to Father Yao saying Tung-ping was the best pupil he had ever had. He was sure Tung-ping would have a bright future if he continued with his education. After several visits, the principal persuaded Father Yao to send Tung-ping to a middle school in Wuxi.

Tung-ping was the first pupil from the village to go to middle school. The year was 1934. The principal of his new school, a graduate from St. John's University in Shanghai, was also his English teacher. He was strict and required his pupils to recite their texts. Tung-ping was one of his favorite pupils because he could always recite the texts fluently.

Tung-ping (at right) with two middle school classmates, all wearing the old-style costume. The description on the back of the photo refers to their close friendship.

19

Three years later, Japan swept south and occupied Wuxi. Chinese pupils now had to study Japanese and Japanese history. Every school was ordered to raise a Japanese flag. The Japanese forced the Chinese teachers and pupils to bow to the flag and stand in attention for the day's orders. Tung-ping also saw some Japanese invaders beating and killing people in that city. It was this kind of humiliation that steeled Tung-ping's resolve (and that of countless others) to work for his motherland and turned him fervently patriotic.

By 1939, young Tung-ping could not endure life in enemy-occupied area anymore. He and three of his schoolmates crossed the Japanese blockade and escaped inland. Tung-ping caught typhoid fever along the way. He had to stay at a farmer's house, taking Chinese herb medicine and staying in bed for several weeks. But as soon as he recovered he continued on with his journey. In early 1940 Tung-ping reached Jiangxi province.

Japan now occupied most of China, and the Kuomintang government had retreated to Chongqing (formerly known as Chunking). The Minister of Education Chen Lifu put out an order to set up national middle schools for students whose homes were in enemy-occupied provinces. Altogether there were 19 such schools. The students didn't have to pay tuition, room or board. The government also provided the textbooks free of charge.

Because of these efforts, Tung-ping entered No. 13 National Middle School. Situated atop a hill amongst tall trees, this school was well known for its high academic standards and rigid training. Tung-ping studied there for three semesters. When he took the mandatory city-wide graduation exam, he came out number one in all of Jiangxi province. He then took a nationwide college-entrance exam and was admitted by five universities. Tung-ping chose Jiaotong University. This was in 1941, when Japan occupied the coastal provinces of China and most of China's universities were driven inland.

Jiaotong relocated to Pingyue in Guizhou province.

Guizhou was noted for its harsh climate and poverty. There was even a saying about Guizhou: the climate is so bad, one can never find three sunny days in a row; there are so many mountains, one can never find three miles of flat and straight road; and the people are so poor, nobody ever had three ounces of silver to hold.

Pingyue (today known as Fuquan) was a very small town. There were no buses, no electricity, and no running water. Each student had a small tung-oil lamp lit by a dried stem. (At that time, kerosene had to be imported and was thus called "foreign oil" by the Chinese.) Although the tung-oil lamp was dim, Tung-ping was always the last one to put his light out at night.

During the war, university students received a government grant for tuition, room and board. Tung-ping had to earn his own spending money because he left home without telling his father. (His elder brother had given him some traveling money, but when Father Yao found out, he became furious at both boys — even threatening to break Tung-ping's legs when he returned home.) So Tung-ping worked in a lab and coached a middle-school student in physics an hour a day after school.

Tung-ping grabbed every other available moment for study. One of his favorite places to study was in some woods behind the library. It was out of the way and perfectly quiet. So much so that lovers would sometimes pick the place as a rendezvous. When lovebirds spotted Tung-ping reading there, they didn't mind. They knew Tung-ping was concentrating so hard on his books that he wouldn't pay any attention to whatever they were doing.

When I heard about this, I kidded Tung-ping. "I know why you were concentrating so hard on books and nothing else. You were waiting for me, right?" Tung-ping just smiled and touched me gently.

Although Tung-ping had a tight schedule, he always found

time to explain things meticulously to classmates who had questions. Even Professor Wang, the head of the Metallurgy Department, would often pause to ask Tung-ping when dealing with a new topic, "What do you think of it, Mr. Yao?"

With the Japanese on the move again, his school had to relocate to Chongqing, the wartime capital of China. Tung-ping and some friends walked all the way there from Guizhou. It took them weeks. Jiaotong University couldn't find any place for their classes, so the school had to move into a temple for a while — a temple for Confucius at that.

Tung-ping graduated from Jiaotong University in 1945 at the top of his class. The war ended a few months later, and he secured a job in a research institute in Chongqing. Later on he transferred to a job in Beijing. The following year, Tung-ping took a nationwide exam to compete for scholarships abroad. He was one of three winners in the field of metallurgy. Tung-ping applied to study in England. The government offered cultural immersion classes for students going abroad, so Tung-ping went to Nanjing for six months to prepare.

At that time, I was a middle-school girl in Nanjing. I asked Tung-ping if we had met, would he have fallen in love with me? He said probably not. I was too young to have a boyfriend.

Before going abroad, Tung-ping went home for a visit. His father had saved some money and bought a two-story house. He was happy to see that Tung-ping had done so well and gained face for the Yao family. All past threatening of "breaking his legs" was forgotten.

In August 1947, Tung-ping sailed for Europe via the Red Sea. He arrived at Birmingham University and studied under Professor Voya Kondic. The professor soon viewed Tung-ping as "one of his best students." Two years later, the Communists took over China. This interrupted the flow of subsidies from the Kuomintang (KMT) government. Tung-ping had to severely cut back his already frugal lifestyle. He lived in a small room in the attic and cooked for himself, spending most of his time in the lab and library.

Tung-ping and Scottish farmers at Bankfoot Farm, Scotland

Tung-ping received his Ph.D. in metallurgy in 1951. The following year, he earned a D.I.C. (Diploma of the Imperial College) from the Imperial College of Science and Technology in London. Tung-ping then worked in this school's research lab, publishing several articles by himself and with his advisors Professor M.S. Fisher and Professor C.W. Dannatt.

The breaking news from China thrilled Tung-ping and some fellow Chinese students in England. The idea of a "New China," the promise of land reforms and a more equitable government — all filled them with pride. China, for generations the target of imperialists, was rid of foreign influence at last. No more opium addicts, no more prostitution, no more poverty. And the end of foreign concessions with their own laws and signs such as "Chinese and dogs are not allowed" at the entrance to a park in Shanghai.

Tung-ping and his colleagues sent messages of congratulations to the motherland and received replies from top officials of the new government. He and his friends then took things a step further. They helped form the "Association of Chinese Workers, England Branch" and edited a student publication called simply *The Periodical.* Through these efforts he publicized the "New China," telling other overseas Chinese about developments "back home."

Tung-ping with three Scottish lads at Bankfoot Farm

Tung-ping even toured the continent, showing slides about China. His speeches had no flowery words, only facts, but they were still quite moving. Of course, his activities did not sit well with everyone. There were those in some audiences who challenged his version of events and questioned the legitimacy of a Communist government. According to some who heard him, Tung-ping handled provocative questioners with aplomb, resolutely sticking to reasoned argument.

Agents of the KMT government, which had fled to Taiwan, kept an eye on the activities of Tung-ping and others like him. So did Scotland Yard. The British government, entering into a cold war with communist Eastern European countries (at the same time United Nations troops were fighting China-backed North Korea), eventually made Tung-ping's life difficult in Great Britain.

Costume dancing party at Aachen Institute with the Frohbergs, 1957

A world-renowned materials scientist, Professor E. Pivowarski, heard of Tung-ping's situation and invited him to continue his metallurgical research work at Aachen University of Technology in West Germany. Tung-Ping agreed. To improve his German, he spent three months at the University of Munich, and then he reported for work as an assistant professor at Aachen in February 1954.

Tung-ping found that a great way to make new friends and learn everyday expressions in this university town was to go drink beer, and he had warm feelings toward his German friends. During this period he wrote and published several articles in German.

Tung-ping studying in his bedroom, Aachen

On the other side of the world, China and the United States were holding long and difficult talks concerning the fate of prisoners taken during the Korean War. One outcome which the reporters overlooked was the return to China of scores of scientists who had been educated in the West. China was doing all it could to hasten its progress in scientific fields, especially rockets, missiles, atomic bombs and satellites. Tung-ping's expertise in metallurgy was just what China, a scientifically isolated nation, was looking for. It was only a matter of time before Tung-ping returned to his homeland. It was easy to understand why Marshal Nie back in Beijing wanted Tung-ping so badly. It was his combination of brilliance, patriotism, and spirit.

And so this was the cascade of events shaping the first 35 years for the boy born in the "Year of the Dog." When I heard all this from Tung-ping and his younger brother Yong-ping (who often visited us at the hostel), I realized what a man this Tung-ping was! I also realized that we had both spent a major part of our youths traveling and studying across China during the War, and then studying and working abroad. In fact, we had crossed paths twice before without meeting. What would I tell him about the girl born in the "Year of the Horse?"

4

Marry First, Fall in Love Afterwards

THE FIRST TIME my father saw my mother's face was in the wedding chamber on their wedding night.

A well-known matchmaker had told my father about this pretty girl of seventeen years. Her father had died the year before and the family didn't want to have a marriage until a year had passed. It was a custom they didn't want to break.

The matchmaker urged my father to act fast. According to this woman, my mother was slim and fair skinned. In addition, the matchmaker said, "The Fang girl is well mannered, gentle, a good cook, and can do exquisite embroidery." My father was impressed by all that he heard.

My father found himself still single at age thirty, which was unusual at that time. Several matchmakers had approached him, but my father wanted to wait until he was sure he could provide a comfortable home for his family.

As a young orphan, he had to work as an apprentice in a tea-making shop. He learned how to read and write by himself and became an expert at the abacus. For doing all kinds of household chores — including looking after the proprietor's little son, he received no pay, just three meager meals a day and a place to sleep in a corner of the kitchen. But my father kept his eyes and ears open. He learned how to make good tea leaves and after five years time, my father was promoted to head of all the salesmen.

A few years later, Father amassed enough money to buy his own tea shop. It was a small one that also sold rice. Father devoted all his time to it and business flourished.

The matchmaker also visited my mother's home. My grandfather had died a year before and left behind a grocery store to my grandmother, my mother and my uncle. The matchmaker noted, "Since Mr. Peng has no parents, your daughter would run the house as soon as she crossed the threshold; she wouldn't have to wait on a mother-in-law." According to her sweet words, even the age gap was an advantage: "Such a man would treat his young wife nice and would not take a concubine or have wild flowers." (In China a wife is looked upon as the husband's garden flower and outside women are called wild flowers.)

My grandmother agreed to the marriage but said she would like to meet my father before making the final decision. My mother after all was her only daughter.

A few days later my father came to pay respects to my grandmother, accompanied by the matchmaker. His arms were full of presents. The meeting took place in the living room. My mother had to stay in her room. At that time, a good and refined young lady should not be seen by her future husband.

On their wedding day, my mother was carried on a sedan chair draped in red satin from the Fang house to the Peng residence. As my mother stepped out, the Peng household set off firecrackers to welcome the bride. They believed firecrackers would drive the evil spirits away.

My mother was dressed in a red satin jacket with a high collar and butterfly buttons on the right side. She had on a pleated skirt of the same material, showing only her tiny red satin shoes. As was the custom, my mother had embroidered her outfit with small silk-woven flowers. Mother's head was covered by a thin red veil. This silk veil was only supposed to be removed by the bridegroom. Therefore my mother had to have two women accompany her to the wedding ceremony.

Father wore a long Chinese robe with a red satin sash slung over his shoulder. Red has always been regarded as the happy and lucky color in China while white was the mourning color. Even now when young people do their wedding the Western way, the bride will change into something red immediately after the wedding ceremony for good luck.

When the wedding ceremony began, my father and my mother had to kneel down to the tablets of Heaven and Earth. Then they kowtowed to my grandmother. After that, they kowtowed to each other to end the ceremony. My father then went to the wedding banquet in the big living room and my mother was led to the wedding chamber. She had to sit on their new bed with the veil on, as etiquette demanded.

After all the guests had gone and the two accompanying ladies left the wedding chamber, my father lifted the veil gently. He saw a pretty young face glowing in the red candlelight. That was the first time my parents saw each other.

Although my parents' marriage was arranged by a matchmaker, they loved and respected each other. Some people say these kinds of old-fashioned marriages are "marry first, fall in love afterwards." Indeed this was true in my parents' case.

My father bought a silk and yard-goods store soon after he married and let my mother run the house while he took care of his two stores.

My mother had her first child when she was barely nineteen. My eldest sister was named Lotus because she was born in the summer. A couple of years later, my mother gave birth to a son, Ho-ching. After two more girls who died in their infancy, my second brother was born. My parents named him Hai-ching. Ching is our generation name.

The offspring in any generation of a Chinese family have one word common to all their names. From that word, you can tell to which generation a person belongs. (This way when you visit your Family temple, you can figure out who sat next to your great-great grandfather at the dinner table.) But in some families, only sons have the privilege of having the generation name. Hence, a few years later when my second sister was born, she was simply named Chrysanthemum — a signal to all that she was born in the fall.

For more than ten years, my mother didn't have any more children. Then in the "Year of the Horse" she turned forty and had me. My father was over fifty at the time. Both of them said that's enough. They named me *Manman*, meaning "all filled up." All my siblings called me *Manman*, but I had to address them as First Brother (or Brother Ho-ching), First Sister (or Sister Lotus). In China, only older siblings can call the younger ones by their given names.

As the baby of the family, I was doted upon. All the more so, since I had trouble holding my head up. My parents were very worried but there was nothing they could do. The herbs from the medicine shop on main street didn't help much. Instead, my parents decided to increase my nourishment and let nature take its course. I had soybean milk every day — cow's milk was not available. (The first glass of milk I had in my life was in 1946, while attending middle school in Nanjing. It was Klim powdered milk donated by the Red Cross to Chinese students.)

When I became older, Mother made sure I had either fish balls or chopped lean meat daily — without hot peppers. The rest of the family had rice, vegetables, and tofu, all heavily spiced.

Sometimes there was fish and twice a month they ate meat. There is an old saying to describe this in China: "One's teeth get feasted on the first and fifteenth day of the month."

Our hometown, Chenglingji, was on Dongting Lake, the second largest lake in China. It is this lake that gave Hunan province its name. For in Chinese, *hu* means 'lake' and *nan* means 'south.' Chenglingji is so small, most maps don't show it. But I can still remember the cobble-stone main street that went along the big blue lake. There was a Chinese herb shop, a silk shop and two tea shops. And a restaurant with a mud floor. Although it had four unpainted tables with wooden benches, to my young heart it was a grand cafe. Even today, no place I know serves freshwater shrimp on top of noodles as delicious as my hometown.

Hunan is known all over the world for its delicious cuisine, heavily seasoned and spicy. The chefs usually put hot pepper in every dish and serve food in huge bowls or on large plates. Even the chopsticks are half an inch longer than those of other places.

Besides being good chefs, Hunan men are noted for their bravery. Traditionally, many were army men. During the Qing dynasty (1645-1911) there was a Xiang Army of Hunan men led by one of its native sons, Zeng Guofan. In modern times, many top Communist leaders have come from Hunan. Among them: Mao Zedong, Liu Shaoqi, Peng Dehuai (one of the ten marshals of China), Su Yu (a former Minister of Defense) and many generals.

Hunan women are well known for their embroidery. (Xiang embroidery, as it is called, is some of the finest in China.) And the women along the Peach Blossom River there are noted for their exquisite figures... as well as rosy cheeks, blue-black hair and lustrous complexion. People say that bathing in that river makes women as pretty as flowers. There was even a popular old song: "Peach Blossom River is the Home of Great Beauties."

Alas! I am neither a great beauty nor skilled at embroidery.

In our hometown, when a child is one year old, the family would hold a birthday party with relatives invited. Each guest would bring a gift for the child — perhaps a book, a Chinese writing brush, a ball of yarn, a toy or some candy. Something that a one-year-old child could hold onto. The parents then add more things. The presents are spread out on the table and the child has its choice. Whichever object the child picks up is believed to point to the child's profession or symbolize its future.

At my first birthday party, my mother held me in her arms and walked around the table. She stopped a second at the spot where they had placed some candy. She was hoping that I would grasp it so I'd have a sweet life ahead. But I took a fancy to something on the edge of the table — my brother's textbook. From then on, my father insisted that I would be the scholar of the family. Mother wondered, "Could a girl be a scholar?"

My mother had to do the cooking for the whole family as well as for the three sales clerks who lived with us. The adults all sat at a big round table. I sat at a small table by myself. The fact that Father let the women sit with the men at the dining table was considered quite open-minded for those days.

My father might have been open-minded because he often traveled to buy merchandise for his two stores. He met a lot of people and found out what life was like outside Chenglingji. So sons and daughters were treated alike in our home. Still, I was my father's favorite. I was his *"zhang shang ming zhu"* (bright pearl in his palm).

Once my father had some business in Yueyang and took me

along. He tucked me in between his knees on the rickshaw seat. On the way, I spotted a pagoda. When we reached it, the rickshaw man asked my father if we could take a rest at the bamboo tea stand there. Naturally my father said yes, saying he too would like to drink some tea and have a smoke. We got down and I tried hard to crane my head upward. Father asked me, "Do you want to try counting it?" So I did: "*yi - er - san - si - wu - liu - qi* (1-2-3-4-5-6-7). *Baba*, it's a seven-layer pagoda."

Father then whispered into my ear, "It's a shame your mother is at home; I am sure she would like to donate some money to building a pagoda. That is even better than burning incense twice a day inside our house."

My father had a routine at home. Two smokes a day — one after lunch, one after dinner. He puffed on a long-stemmed pipe. Father usually had some rice wine before dinner. As cold wine was not good for the stomach, Mother would warm the wine in a small pot on the fire, then wrap the pot in a quilted cloth. She served the wine with roasted peanuts or smoked pig's tongue, sliced paper-thin. Sometimes she would cut a salted duck egg into four pieces length-wise and serve it in a small dish. I could see the red-gold yolk shining on top of the egg white. It was very tempting.

Father would put me on his lap, pour some wine into a moon-white cup and start our pre-dinner ritual. He would dip a bamboo chopstick into the gold-colored wine and let me have a taste. But I always reached for the appetizers instead. While having his wine, father would recite a poem from the Tang dynasty as if he were singing a song — with eyes half-closed, head swimming. And every time it would be "The Pure Brightness Day" by Du Mu (803–852):

It drizzles thick on the Pure Brightness Day;
I travel with my heart lost in dismay.

"Is there a pub somewhere, little boy?"

The boy points at the Apricot Bloom Inn far away.

I guess Father only knew that one by heart. After a few times, when father started: "It drizzles thick…," I'd recite the poem with him. I'd chime in with my eyes half closed and big head swimming. Hearing our chorus, Mother would come out from the kitchen and shake her head saying, "Like father, like daughter!" Father would give me a kiss and say to my mother, "Didn't I tell you, I knew our *Manman* would be a smart girl. Remember how she grasped the book at her one-year-old birthday party?"

My mother was a very devoted Buddhist. She believed that all lives were created by Buddha — human beings as well as animals. I remember there was a swallow's nest on the ceiling of our living room. Two swallows came in every spring to make their home there. Whenever we did house cleaning, Mother would always tell my sisters to watch out for the nest. She said the swallows only chose a happy and prosperous home to raise their little ones. She was also kind to all people. A beggar would always leave our kitchen door with his bowl filled.

On the night before the "Spring Festival" (as Chinese New Year is called), my mother would prepare a ten-course dinner. Fish and green vegetables were always two of the ten dishes. Mother told me fish meant "to have plenty" and green vegetables symbolized a safe and peaceful new year. The last course would be soup. Mother always put ten ingredients into the soup, such as chicken, pork, mushrooms, golden needle leaves, bok choy and rice noodles. She told us ten meant complete and perfect. So each of us would have our "complete perfect soup" before we left the table.

On Chinese New Year's Day, mother would dress me up in a

red cotton-padded jacket, blue trousers, and a new pair of cotton-padded shoes. She would then gather the center of my hair and tie it up with red yarn. My siblings would tease me, saying I had a red pepper planted on the top of my head!

Father would take me out to visit our relatives and friends. Instead of shaking hands, people would move their own clasped hands up and down and say *"gong xi fa cai"* — to wish each other success in making more money. My father would always ask me to bow to the elderly and wish them a prosperous New Year. Often they would give me something wrapped up in red paper. (It was money inside.)

When summer came, I remember going to watch the dragon-shaped boats racing on the 5th day of the 5th moon. Mother would make me new clothes and my brother Hai-ching would give me a ride on his shoulders. Everyone in the crowd cheered loudly. My brother would buy me some "inch-gold candy" covered with roasted sesame seeds, and we always had a good time.

When I became older, I learned that this kind of boat racing originally wasn't part of any festival. Two thousand years ago there was a great poet and statesman named Qu Yuan (339 B.C.–278 B.C.). He was kind to the people and never accepted any bribery. Qu wrote beautiful poems that shed light on the suffering of the poor. Qu's popularity among the people however eventually brought on his downfall. Other officials in the court became jealous and made false charges against him. The emperor believed them and had Qu exiled to remote regions. On his way, Qu drowned himself in the Milo River. People tried to row their boats out to save him but failed. From then on, people across the country would stage boat races on the 5th day of the 5th moon, the day Qu Yuan drowned, in memory of him.

Those days in my hometown were happy ones. I remember looking out across the blue expanse of Dongting Lake, thinking we were the only people on the earth. I also remember Dongting Lake flooding every year. When that happened, our whole family had to move upstairs. Little boats came and went in the streets selling daily necessities. We would put money in a basket, tie it with a string, and lower it. The boat people would then put the vegetables or fish we wanted inside and we would haul it back up.

Because of these yearly floods and the worldwide economic Depression, Father eventually had to close the silk and yard-goods store. But he continued on with the successful tea shop.

5

Candles in the Wind

———————— 🌊 ————————

In 1936 my mother suddenly became ill with typhoid fever. My eldest brother Ho-ching, a senior at a university in Nanjing, returned home to be with her. On her deathbed, Mother looked at me and told him, "I can't close my eyes until I know you will take care of your *xiao mei mei* (youngest sister)." Ho-ching pledged to do so. My mother soon succumbed.

Sadly my other brother Hai-ching could not come back home for the funeral. He couldn't get permission from his military academy. So my eldest brother was the only mourning son at our mother's funeral. He put on a robe made of white cloth, a white headband, and white cloth shoes — as Chinese tradition required. I was crying so hard that somebody in the procession had to carry me.

Even today, I still miss Mother. I don't have a picture of her since there was no photo shop in our tiny hometown. But I can still see her: a slim and fair lady doing cooking, washing or other household chores. And I can still remember her cuddling me in her warm bosom.

🌊

There would be plenty of sadness across China in the 1930s. As the decade wore on, China faced a creeping threat. On September 18, 1931, the Japanese government launched a full-scale invasion of three provinces of northeast China the size of France and Germany combined (known to some Westerners as Manchuria). Japan proclaimed this area an independent country and installed a puppet emperor, Pu Yi.

Japan wasn't satisfied with taking these three provinces. On July 7, 1937 Japanese troops, using the pretext of a missing soldier, fired the first shot at Lugou Bridge (20 miles to the southwest of Beijing) and started a major aggression against China. By 1939, the Japanese occupied much of China. They controlled from Beijing down to Shanghai and the fighting was now pushing inland.

Because of the war, Father had to close the tea shop. He didn't think it was safe for my sister Chrysanthemum and me to stay in Chenglingji, but he himself didn't want to leave his hometown. Fortunately, my eldest brother Ho-ching had graduated from university by now and was working as a journalist in Changsha, the capital of Hunan province. I was just nine years old when Father sent me and Chrysanthemum off to join Ho-ching. (Hai-ching had graduated from the military academy but was heading off to the battlefield to fight the Japanese.)

So my sister Chrysanthemum packed a wicker suitcase for us and we got on a sailboat filled with people. I watched the shore recede and saw my father become smaller and smaller. Finally, he disappeared from sight. It suddenly dawned on me that I would probably not see Father again. I screamed, "I don't want to go" and tried to get off the boat. My sister held me tight, saying that we would see Father again as soon as our soldiers kicked the Japanese aggressors away.

All the passengers on the boat slept next to one another. When mealtime came, we came out from under the cover made of split bamboo. Everyone got a big bowl of rice and some vegetables. There was only one toilet for all of us, at the back of the boat.

Our boat sailed along the Dongting Lake shore and up the Xiang Jiang River to Changsha, where my brother was waiting for us. The Japanese were approaching quickly.

My brother, a reporter for the Central News Agency, met us but soon learned that he was about to be dispatched to the Burmese front. My sister Chrysanthemum then decided to leave for Liuzhou in Guangxi province to attend a nursing school. I had to move further inland. Before leaving for Burma, my brother asked a friend to look after me. This friend found me a seat on a truck leaving Changsha.

We rattled down the road with thousands of others, fleeing the approaching Japanese. The truck driver was a kind man. He gave me the two essentials of life during wartime: transportation and protection. On our way, we stayed in little roadside inns overnight. The truck driver usually reserved a room for me, and he would stay in the room next door. He told me to bolt the door. I would push the table against the door, put a stool on the table and then place a basin filled with water on top of the stool. If someone tried to break in, I figured the noise would wake me and the driver up.

After weeks of traveling, we arrived at a small town called Yuanling, in the mountains of western Hunan. There I enrolled in a Catholic boarding school run by Franciscan Sisters. Still, the war was always nearby. Everyday, air raid sirens went off — one siren meant to get into the air-raid shelters, two sirens meant bombers were approaching. We would then hear bombs landing in the town. The Sisters had spread out an American flag on the roof of our school, hoping it could be seen from the air and would discourage an attack. (This was two years before the Japanese attacked Pearl Harbor.)

We couldn't have classes in the school buildings because of

the bombing. Every morning after breakfast, we would pack up our books, hike into the mountains and hold classes in the woods. The school's cooks carried food for lunch. Then we'd hike back, have a cold shower, a warm dinner, and retire to our dormitory where we slept in bunk beds, twenty to a room. The teacher had a hard time waking us up in the morning. Sometimes she would slide a cold hand under the covers onto our backs to get us up.

Life was hard, yet there were some beautiful moments that I shall always remember. One Christmas Eve, I went to bed at the usual hour. Suddenly I woke up and saw several girls from other classes coming to our dorm. They had white robes on and each one was holding a candle. As they were approaching, they sang "Silent night, Holy night, All is calm, All is bright…" softly. Their young faces and sweet voices made me think they were angels from Heaven.

I stayed in Yuanling for several years. Eventually, I moved on to the middle school in town, run by Christian missionaries. When I was thirteen years old, two friends, Lily and Rose, and I snuck away from the group as the others headed into the mountains for class. We went back to the school. When lunchtime came, Lily led us into the house of our English teachers, Miss March and Miss Bennet, and we followed. We went to the kitchen and helped ourselves to bread and jam — something we'd never had before. I found the jam tasted like orange peels. I thought, "Americans eat stuff like this?" In that kitchen, I also saw knives and forks for the first time. I remember reading somewhere that barbarians ate with knives. How come the Americans are doing the same? We didn't know how to use them, so we ate everything with our hands, in real barbarian style.

Playing hooky — a first for me — lost its appeal after a

couple of hours. Lily and Rose decided they would wash their clothes over by the well on the other side of the campus. I declined and went back to my bunk to read.

I was reading in my bed when the one-signal air-raid siren went off. I wanted to find my friends and hide with them, but they were on the far side of the campus. I had just put on my shoes and was slithering under my bed when I heard the two-signal siren, and then the planes themselves. An explosion shattered the air, a frightening sound. I covered my ears, squeezed my eyes shut and prayed to God. I stayed under the bed, as we had been taught. (Even after the war, when I heard a plane flying overhead, I would unconsciously look for a place to hide.)

After a while, the noise faded. I wondered where my friends had hidden. I looked around the dormitory. I was afraid to go out. Not long after that, the teachers and other girls came back from the woods. The teachers wanted to know what had happened. They didn't scold me for cutting classes. They just asked anxiously:

"Where are Lily and Rose?"

"They had gone to wash clothes," I replied.

We all headed outside. I was appalled to see the school auditorium in ruins. The well had collapsed and was covered in rubble. There was no sign of the girls.

Their bodies were recovered by midnight. All of us were numb with shock and grief as we gathered and sang in tribute, "God Be With Us Till We Meet Again." Some of us were holding candles. Most of us were crying so hard that we could neither sing nor hold the candles. The sight of Lily and Rose covered with white sheets made me cry out loud. Weren't they with me only hours ago, eating bread and jam, laughing and joking with one another?

I was too frightened to stay in Yuanling so I wrote to my

brother Ho-ching. He suggested I go to a town named Tongren, in Guizhou province. He said it was deep in the mountains, where the Japanese could not bomb. He said there was a national middle school for girls there.

The school was in a mountainous region so remote no buses could get there. I had to take a reclining chair made of split bamboo. It was carried by two men with long bamboo poles on their shoulders. When the mountain path climbed steeply, the front man would lower the poles to his waist and the back man held them high to keep me balanced. And when we went downhill, the front man held his arms straight up and the back man lowered the poles. Even so, I was completely exhausted when I finally arrived at the school. I was glad to walk into the dormitory and find a lower bunk to sink into.

Among the girls in the dormitory was a tall, older girl who had short hair and for reasons I didn't understand, dressed like a boy. One day, when I thought I was alone in the dormitory, she tried to molest me. I resisted and ran out; I was quite shaken. I didn't tell anyone about this, but arranged to leave as soon as possible. I packed my small wicker case and took a reclining bamboo chair to a small railway station. Luckily, I found a seat on the next train and headed south, toward Guangxi province. My sister Chrysanthemum had graduated from nursing school, gotten married, and was living there with her husband in Liuzhou. I managed to find them.

It was now 1944 and I was due to enter senior middle school (high school). I was admitted by Liuzhou Middle School. There were forty students in my class — only seven of them girls. Many girls in China traditionally stopped their education short of primary school. Their parents reasoned the girls would be married eventually and would become members of other families. Why waste money on their education?

Liuzhou was a lovely town. The streets were narrow and

lined with shops. Second-story balconies overhung the streets, protecting pedestrians from the tropical sun and showers. The place was humid and green year-round. Liuzhou had the best grapefruits. Even now, I can still see the white blossoms on the grapefruit trees and smell their lemony fragrance.

The climate was mild. We slept with the windows open and mosquito netting on our bunks. It was hardly a restful place though with reports of Japanese troops nearing Guilin, the capital of Guangxi province. The word came one day: Guilin was occupied. Our town was emptying. My sister Chrysanthemum and her husband had been transferred elsewhere a few months before. So, I packed up my things and headed for the train station. I couldn't get a ticket and I didn't know where I was going. All I wanted to do was to run away from the Japanese.

A train was getting ready to pull out. Everybody was pushing everybody else in order to get aboard. All the cars were crowded. There were people on the roof of the train. The toilets were filled with people. Some people even put boards under the train and lay on them. I tried hard to squeeze ahead but still couldn't get aboard the train. Just then, a Kuomintang (KMT) soldier came out from nowhere, he pushed people aside and told me to follow him. So I climbed aboard the train after him and sat on my tiny wicker suitcase next to him, between two cars.

The train lurched into motion. It moved slowly, stopping unpredictably. Occasionally, a Japanese plane would fly overhead and send me into a panic. When night came, the KMT soldier tried to fondle me in that small crowded area between the rail cars. I was paralyzed with fear — he was after all a soldier, not someone I could challenge. I kept standing up and sitting down, hoping to attract the attention of others. They noticed me eventually, but when they saw the KMT soldier, they turned around without saying anything. The next time the train stopped, I scrambled off with some people, disappeared into the crowd, and re-boarded between two other cars.

Two days later I arrived in Dushan, a small town in Guizhou province. I met a girlfriend I knew from Liuzhou, who stunned me with the incredible news: my father was in Dushan selling boiled water at the train station. For the next several days I went to the station again and again, searching for him — but in vain. Later, my brother Ho-ching told me that our father had indeed escaped from the Japanese and had tried to find him. Father went as far as Dushan, but died there, due to illness as well as starvation. My brother and I traveled there once, looking for his grave, but without any success.

I stayed a week with my girlfriend. She was only sixteen but had married a truck driver. I was surprised about that. She told me her father had died from a Japanese bombing a few months before. Her mother was illiterate and had no work. On top of that, she had a younger brother who was a primary-school pupil. She said the truck driver was willing to support her mother and her brother.

My friend confided to me that although her husband was older, he had never been married before and was extremely nice to her. "What's more," she continued, "Didn't our elders always tell us *'jia ji sui ji, jia gou sui gou'*? (When married to a rooster, obey the rooster. When married to a dog, obey the dog.) Now I am married to a truck driver. I'll be a good wife to him."

She mentioned her husband was driving to Chongqing in Sichuan province and I could go with him for free. She told him to let me sit up front, for safety's sake. I thanked her and grabbed the chance to go to the wartime capital, because I figured I might be able to track down my brother Ho-ching at the Central News Agency. I got on the truck and off we went.

Chongqing is a hilly and impressive city where the Yangzi and Jialing Rivers meet. (Years later when I visited Pittsburgh, it reminded me of Chongqing, with its hills and rivers.) I went to the Central News Agency and learned that my brother was still near the Burmese border. But a friend of his told me of a school that I could attend in a nearby town, Changshou. I got on a steamboat that took me down the river. It was early 1945.

The school I was heading for was No. 12 National Middle School. The classrooms and dorms were all in a former Buddhist temple which was on a hilltop.

I stayed there for about one semester. I distinctly remember getting the news of President Franklin Roosevelt's death because our school uniforms — navy cotton cloth — were called "Roosevelt Clothes." They had been donated by the Americans. Since he was dead, a classmate figured we'd get no more "Roosevelt Clothes."

We were required to take Chinese, geometry, physics, history, geography and English. The teachers would give us a lot of homework. We had to do the assignments in the evening, under tung-oil lamps. The schedule was heavy. It made us feel hungry all the time, since we only got rice porridge and salted turnips for breakfast. And we usually had rice and vegetables for lunch and supper. So the students decided to manage the kitchen, especially the purchasing. We took turns going shopping with the cooks. The closest market was six miles away. It did trading three times a month. The cooks had to buy rice and other provisions on these days.

When it was my turn to go to the market, it started to rain. The dried palm-leaf raincoat couldn't protect me from the heavy downpour, so I carried a large umbrella made of tung-oil painted canvas. And I had to put on straw sandals over my shoes because it was hard to pull my feet out from the sticky mud. Thus, the cooks and I struggled along on the "sheep-intestine trails" (narrow paths winding around the hills). When we got to the market, the cooks and I did the bargaining and I counted out the money.

When we got back to school we were all soaked through. We changed into dry clothes and shoes immediately. The kitchen staff boiled us some ginger tea with dark brown sugar. This kind of drink made us sweat and kept us from getting a cold. After the students started to manage the kitchen, we had enough rice and vegetables and we got meat three times a month!

On August 15, 1945, we heard the sound of firecrackers. Some schoolmates were running to each classroom, shouting *"gui zi tou xiang le!"* (The Japanese devils have surrendered!) All of us came out of our classrooms. Everybody was embracing everybody else. I saw some women teachers crying. These were tears of joy.

Almost all of our hometowns had been taken by the Japanese aggressors. Most of us had relatives, friends or even family members killed by the Japanese. Now the war was over. We could go back home. We could have classes in a school instead of a temple. Most important of all, we wouldn't have to be in constant fear of Japanese bombing.

I heard the Americans had dropped an atomic bomb on Hiroshima and another on Nagasaki. These bombings forced the Japanese surrender. Many Japanese died from the atomic bombs. It was sad. Yet, I couldn't help but think of the Chinese civilians the Japanese soldiers had massacred. I couldn't help but think of my girlfriends Lily and Rose who were buried alive in a well during a Japanese bombing. And I couldn't help but think of my poor father who had to flee from the Japanese and who died alone in Dushan. Now, the atomic bombs stopped the Japanese from killing more Chinese and other Asian people.

And the bombings prevented more American soldiers from being killed in the battlefields.

Years later, I was told that 25,000,000 Chinese were killed during the Japanese aggression of China, from 1937 to 1945.

I think it is the survivor's duty to record the facts.

Soon after the war ended, a letter arrived from my brother Ho-ching. He'd been transferred to Nanjing. This was the capital of China now. My other brother Hai-ching, who had been in the army and thankfully had survived the war, had also come to Nanjing. So I sailed down the Yangzi River in the spring of 1946 and a few days later Ho-ching was there on the docks to meet me.

I enrolled in a Christian boarding school for girls with high academic standards — with Ho-ching paying the tuition. Many of my schoolmates were daughters of top KMT officials. I remember private cars arriving to pick up the rich kids on weekends.

Author, at left, with a classmate at Xuanwu Lake in Nanjing in 1946

Life was getting better. As I neared graduation, a classmate told us that her cousin, a priest, was in charge of issuing scholarships for students interested in going to college in America.

America! Our friend during the war. Our source of powdered milk via the Red Cross and "Roosevelt Clothes." College in America? The idea interested me greatly.

A priest selected the candidates and then consulted with the teachers. After an interview, I was fortunate enough to be chosen, along with three other Chinese girls. Our English teacher, an American, was so happy about this, she invited us to her home. She lived in a house with a maid. I surmised from this arrangement that all Americans were rich. She also served us a drink that was very cold and sweet. She called it Coca-Cola. We drank it with a straw. I didn't like it. It tasted like Chinese medicine. Although Coke was available in some restaurants, this was the first time I had ever tasted a Coke or used a straw.

The Chinese priest who awarded the scholarships told us that we were expected to study hard so that China would not lose face. And we were expected to return to China after college. That was precisely what I intended: to learn something new, then come back and help my homeland.

I packed my suitcases and headed for Shanghai with my friends. Our English names were Susan, Beatrice, Cindy and Penny. We boarded the ocean liner *President Cleveland* and headed out into the Pacific. It was 1947. We traveled third class on a $171 ticket. It seemed most of the passengers were college graduates; we were the youngest. The ship had a theater, and the four of us, who had done so well in our English classes, confidently went to see "The Postman Always Rings Twice." Lana Turner was the leading actress. She was beautiful but we couldn't understand a word she said.

The ship stopped in Honolulu, Hawaii. When we climbed up the narrow stairway and went up to the deck, the four of us were all struck by the beauty of Honolulu. The tall palm trees, the colorful tropical flowers, the bright blue sky, the spectacular white sand beaches and the heavenly music! Honolulu was indeed like a paradise to us who had just been through a cruel war. Musicians were playing guitars at the dock. Passengers were greeted with leis by friends. We knew nobody, so we bought leis for ourselves and said "aloha" to one another. On our tour of Honolulu, I remember seeing my first juke box and liking the music that came out of it… and eating my first hamburger which I didn't like.

We sailed on to San Francisco where another Chinese priest met us. He found us a place to stay and after a couple of days, put us on a train bound for the East. Susan and Beatrice went to a Catholic school in Pittsburgh. Cindy left for another Catholic women's college in New York and I went to Joliet, Illinois.

I was a little frightened. It was a big new country filled with people who looked different and talked differently too!

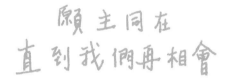

6

Chop Suey? What's That?

———————— 🍥 ————————

I SHALL ALWAYS remember arriving at the train station in Joliet, Illinois the last week of August 1947 and seeing a girl waiting to meet me. Since I was the first Chinese girl who had ever attended college there, a reporter was on hand too. Our picture was in the next day's paper! I was surprised to see how small I looked next to the American girl. At 5'3", I was considered tall in China.

I was enrolled in the College of St. Francis. It was a small school for women run by the Franciscan Sisters. The school wouldn't open till early September, so the Sisters of the college had arranged for me to stay at Shirley's home. She was a junior at the school.

Shirley's parents greeted me warmly at the door of their house and were very kind to me. As I unpacked, Shirley told me that her mother was getting hold of a recipe to make some Chop Suey especially for me.

"Chop Suey? What's that?"

"Isn't that what you have in China, Penny? We have Chop Suey in every Chinese restaurant here."

"Really? But this is the first time I've ever heard of the word 'Chop Suey'."

"Penny, what do you have at home then?"

"Oh, we have rice, all kinds of vegetables, and tofu. We have fish often and meat sometimes. But if you don't mind, I'd rather have American food." So we had mixed green salad, vegetable soup, roast beef, mashed potatoes, green peas and home-baked apple pie. It tasted delicious.

When Sunday came, Shirley asked me if I would like to go to Mass with them. I told her I'd love to. I put on my Sunday best, a traditional Chinese silk *qi pao*, a straight dress with high collar and slits on both sides. It was an egg-white silk with small yellow flowers. Shirley lent me a veil and told me to follow her. I remember several parishioners smiling at me warmly. It was probably the first time they had ever seen a Chinese girl in their church.

Shirley told me we were required to wear black dresses for classes. I didn't have any, so she took me downtown to do some shopping. As my scholarship covered only tuition, room and board, I had to save every penny. I had about one-hundred dollars and I didn't know when my brother would be able to send me money. When I told Shirley about this, she took me to some low-priced store. I bought a tailored black dress with detachable white collar and white cuffs for five dollars and a pair of black pumps, for which I paid a little more than the dress. When I put everything on, Shirley told me that I looked like any other St. Francis girl. That made me very happy. I so wanted to fit into the new environment.

The college campus was fourteen acres big. Trees and flowers everywhere. I especially liked the green grass and the little squirrels. We didn't have much grass in China and I hadn't seen any squirrels before.

I liked the school and I had a warm feeling towards the Sisters. Their habits looked exactly the same as those of the American Sisters at my primary school in Yuanling, Hunan. Now that I had come to America, I realized how much those Sisters had given up in order to set up a school in a tiny town in Hunan province. There was no electricity, no running water, no heating in the winter and no fans in the summer — well, no electric fans. I respect and admire the Sisters who dedicated their lives to our Lord.

I moved onto campus after staying at Shirley's home for about a week. I was assigned to a single room on the third floor. I had to share the bathroom with two other girls. That was fine with me.

In my room, there was a single bed with a mattress! Another first for me. I'd been used to a hardwood bunk. There was also a dresser with a mirror, a desk with a chair, and a rocking chair by the bed. The school also provided me with linens, blankets, a pale green bed spread and window drapes of the same color. I found a closet behind the door. It seemed too spacious for me at first, but by the time I became a senior, my closet was completely full.

Our classes began soon afterwards. Going to class in the U.S. was a new experience for me. In China, each class stayed in one classroom. The teachers of the various subjects came round to give lessons. Here, I found it was the other way around. We students had to go to this room for math, that one for literature, a third for biology. The rooms were on different floors and sometimes in different buildings. We had to carry our books and run from one classroom to another. I figured that since the United States is on the other side of the earth from China, the Americans would naturally do things the upside-down way.

I kept noticing more cases of this. For instance, Americans serve soup as the first course of the meal, whereas in China, soup comes last. Chinese put their family name before their given name(s), such as Peng Penny, Miss while Americans do it just the opposite way: Miss Penny Peng. Writing an address seemed upside down too, literally. In China the address on an envelope appears like this:

U. S. A.
Illinois, Joliet
College of St. Francis
Wilcox and Taylor Street
Peng Penny, Miss

I am sure that the mailman reads the envelope in this order. In the American way, he'd have to read the envelope from bottom to top.

There was another thing which seemed unreasonable to me. I was told that I had to take two years of a foreign language.

"Isn't Chinese a foreign language?" I asked at the school office.

The registrar, Sister Mildred, said, "But Penny, that's your mother tongue."

"How about English?"

"Penny, how can English be a foreign language?"

"It's a foreign language to me, Sister."

I couldn't convince Sister Mildred, so I ended up choosing French. But I got so mixed up trying to learn English and French at the same time that I had to put if off until my junior year.

While in her office, I told Sister Mildred that I would like to major in journalism. Sister said there was no journalism major at St. Francis College, so I majored in sociology instead.

One day in my freshman world-history class, Sister Borgia was talking to us about the Soviet Union. She mentioned a word I couldn't quite catch. I raised my hand and asked her to write it on the blackboard. She wrote "TOTALITARIAN-ISM." (For years afterwards I tried to pronounce it, but couldn't.) I asked her the meaning. She said it was when the government takes care of everything. No matter how she explained it, the other girls and I thought it sounded just like any other form of government.

It wasn't just long words — I could never get the names of the kings, dukes and generals straight. Or the dates of the wars: The War of the Roses, the Hundred Years War and so many others. It seemed to me so much of world history was a history of wars.

Besides world history, I had to take biology, math and two English courses my freshman year. One was American literature. Although Sister Mary of the Angels was a good teacher, it was difficult for me to enjoy the writings of O. Henry, Longfellow and Whitman. Somehow I preferred Edgar Allen Poe. I was especially moved by the love he felt for his wife in the poem "Annabel Lee."

The other English class was with freshmen from foreign countries. Its main purpose was to improve our English. There were four girls from Colombia, two from Mexico, plus one from Bolivia, Cuba, Puerto Rico, and me from China.

The girls from Colombia were all pretty. Mary Virginia was a stunning South American beauty. Amy was cute, yet she was always on a diet of carrots. Amy fell in and out of love so often but finally was "engaged" to an American boy. Her parents disapproved, so when she went home during summer vacation, she never returned. Jenny looked just like an American girl. She was the only one besides me who eventually graduated from our school. She later married a doctor.

We called the girl from Puerto Rico "Tita." She had a chubby face and curly black hair and was the best dancer among us. Tita worked in an ice-cream parlor part time. Whenever I went there, she would serve me a huge portion of ice cream. I protested, "Tita, do you want me to get fat?" "You are too skinny, Penny, a few more pounds won't hurt you." Martha was from Havana. She was tall and dignified. The girl from Bolivia was the only blonde Latin girl. I had a lot of pictures with the girls, but I had to burn them all during the Cultural Revolution. Now, I could kick myself for having done that.

All these girls spoke Spanish. I was the only Chinese speaker. And I was the one who always asked questions in our English class. Perhaps this was because I was brought up using a different script. One based on pictographs that have little to do with pronunciation. One has to memorize each character individually. Fortunately, Chinese grammar is simple. Unlike English, Chinese verbs stay the same in different tenses. Tenses tend to be expressed instead by adding an adverbial of time. For instance:

Every day I <u>study</u> English.
Yesterday, I <u>study</u> English for two hours.
Tomorrow, I <u>study</u> English with my friends.

Life at St. Francis was pretty strict. We were required to wear black dresses for class and had to change into different dresses for dinner. Breakfast and lunch were in the cafeteria, but dinner was always served in the dining room. About once a month our dinner partners changed. This way, we had a chance to get acquainted with girls from other classes. I must say I learned a lot of American ways at the dining table, including the right table manners for a young lady.

After the first semester, I got a weekend job at St. Joseph's Hospital in Joliet. My work was to develop x-ray films in the dark room. I was paid a dollar an hour plus a free lunch in the hospital cafeteria. Pretty soon, I learned how to take simple x-rays, such as that for a fractured arm. I loved doing the work and I liked the atmosphere of a hospital. Spotlessly clean everywhere, everything in the right place and everybody busy working.

There was a specialist, Dr. Raymond, who came to the hospital twice a week to view certain x-ray films. One day he told me that he had been to China years before for his honeymoon. He recalled, "There wasn't much scenery in China." I didn't like to hear that. I told Dr. Raymond he probably didn't go to the right places. "A country with five thousand years of civilization had nothing to see?" After Dr. Raymond had left, the nurses said to me, "Penny, you were right. You tell him, just tell him." I guess they were surprised to find that a Chinese girl would speak her mind.

In America, people had the wrong impressions about us Chinese. They thought all the Chinese were like Charlie Chan in the movies, speaking broken English and overly polite. In a way, I don't blame the Americans for having this kind of stereotype about the Chinese. We had wrong impressions of the Americans too: chewing gum all the time, always putting their feet on the desks, etc. We usually got these impressions from the movies we saw. Once, I was to meet an Italian professor. She told me she was easy to spot: "I look just like a typical Italian." When I walked into the lobby of the International House on campus, I kept looking for someone like Sophia Loren. It turned out that the professor was very slender, with no curves in her front or back. When I told Tung-ping about this years later in China, he couldn't hold back his chuckles.

With the money I earned, I could afford to buy my very first watch, a Bulova, some new clothes, and tickets to the movies with the girls. We would watch our idols on the screen. The ones we adored most were Gary Cooper, Gregory Peck, Cary Grant, and Humphrey Bogart.

It was new for me to know that the primary purpose for some girls going to college was to catch a good husband. This was especially true for a girl named Laura. All she ever talked about was her dates and how the boys kissed her. Laura was a blonde, with blue eyes and a baby face. She would do the "craziest" things. One day, Laura proposed that we raid the kitchen at night. Her roommates seconded her motion. I left their room without saying anything. I thought they were just bluffing. How wrong I was! That night someone knocked at my door. When I opened it, there stood Laura along with her roommates.

She whispered to me, "Penny, Let's go."

"No thanks. I am not going. I want to go back to sleep." I said drowsily.

"Come on now, Penny. You'll find it's a lot of fun," they all urged.

So we stole our way downstairs, then tiptoed down the hallway leading to the kitchen. Once we got there, the girls started taking some cookies, cold meat slices, bread, butter and soda. Then, it was Laura who discovered a door leading to another room. When we opened the heavy door, we saw rows of meat on racks. As the girls walked in, I started to follow them. But before I got into the room, a cold wave forced me stop. I said, "It's too cold here; I am not going in." It was a good thing we turned around; that was a refrigerated room, and the door probably couldn't have been opened from the inside.

Although we took a lot of food, none of us ate much. It was nearly midnight and we all felt sleepy. And it was no fun eating without talking, but it was a daring thing to do. As time went by, I found out that American young people would always try to do something new and daring.

The days at St. Francis were happy ones. But I left there after three-and-a-half years. By going to summer school, I graduated half a year ahead of my classmates. Then I went on to New York University for my graduate studies.

In New York City, I lived in a building for women students at Washington Mews in Greenwich Village. Still, the Sisters of St. Francis were concerned about their Chinese girl. They thought I might have a hard time adjusting to life in a big city. They wrote to the chaplain of NYU, asking him to look after me. And they kept sending me home-made brownies. I was very much touched by their kindness.

Soon after I moved to New York, the Korean War broke out and mainland Chinese students in the U.S. were able to receive a stipend of a hundred-and-six dollars a month from the U.N. as displaced persons. With my tuition free, this stipend was more than enough for me.

After I started to work in New York and Chicago, I noticed there was some discrimination against the Chinese. Once when a Chinese girlfriend, her brother and I drove to Florida to have a vacation, we stopped at some roadside towns in the South for meals and gas. I noticed that the streetcars were segregated. We also spotted two entrances to the railway stations. (I wondered if I had to buy a ticket, which entrance should I use?) And people there kept staring at us. It made us extremely uncomfortable. I remember bringing this subject up one day at St. Francis and one of the Sisters replied, "Well, Penny, Rome wasn't built in one day, and we are still trying to improve things."

I always liked my American friends. But I never felt America was my home. It was like staying at a rich relative's house — although nice, one doesn't feel as comfortable as in one's own home. And I had a marriage failure which made me very depressed and lonely. I craved a change of scenery.

Just about that time, there were some revealing books on China. Several British people had visited China, including

Clement Richard Attlee, who had been the Prime Minister from 1945 to 1951. They were impressed by what the Communists had done for China. A book titled *There Is No Fly in China* gave the readers such a rosy picture of the "New China" that my heart filled with pride for my country. Furthermore, I thought I could do something for China. So after more than ten years in the United States, I decided to return to my homeland.

I wrote to my brother Ho-ching (who was now in Taiwan) about my decision. He asked me not to return to the mainland. And he wrote me again pleading, "In the name of our dearest deceased mother, please stay in America until I can come over." (He was starting his M.A. in journalism at Northwestern University that fall.) Yet I knew that if I met with him, my heart would become soft and I might not leave. So I left him $2,000 of my savings — which was needed for some foreign students as a condition of entering the U.S. at that time — and hopped on a train for the west coast a week before he arrived. I boarded the ocean liner *President Wilson* in San Francisco.

7

Chasing Sparrows on the Rooftop

I HAD WORKED at a title and trust company in Chicago, but with nobody owning private property in the People's Republic, my expertise wasn't of much use. I felt out of place. I didn't think I could fit into this society.

But God was merciful to me. I had the good fortune to meet Tung-ping and fall in love with him. After hearing how I felt out of place in Beijing, Tung-ping encouraged me, "This is our country. I know you can adjust to a different kind of life easily. Don't worry, my dear girl, you'll get used to it."

Finally the news that we had been waiting for came: Tung-ping and I were granted permission to get married. Tung-ping had made his application to his *danwei*, and when they checked up on me — a non-Party member who had lived in America for ten years — evidently there was nothing to upset any Party officials. However, they did suggest to Tung-ping that he concentrate on improving my ideological awareness. They thought a title and trust company was a bank and that I'd been tainted by capitalist surroundings. They said Tung-ping should try to help me embrace Mao Zedong Thought, so I could fit into our socialist society.

The next day we took a bus to the Fengtai district office and filled out the necessary papers. A district official examined our papers closely. He granted us his approval and we were married by him. There was no wedding ceremony since we wanted to do our wedding like other Chinese. (However, since China opened her doors in the 1980s, many people are now doing their weddings in a much more lavish way with white satin gowns and wedding banquets with ten or more courses on each table.)

Tung-ping wanted to buy me a wedding band. I noticed none of the other Chinese women wore one. So I thanked him and told him not to. We bought a lot of candy and spread it around to colleagues and friends like other newlywed Chinese couples did, because candy symbolizes a sweet life. We had our wedding photo taken in a store on Wangfujing Street, the main street in Beijing. Both of us were in our Sunday best. Tung-ping had on a gray suit and I had on a navy dress, a white silk scarf with small red polka dots, and a pair of pearl earrings.

On our wedding night, we did something in a Western way. Tung-ping carried me into our bedroom. I whispered the marriage vow in English which we couldn't say at the district office, "…for better for worse, for richer for poorer." Tung-ping joined in, "to love and to cherish, in sickness and in health…" Then I added something of my own, "Darling, we'll live happily ever after; on this earth and in heaven. We'll be together forever in heaven. We'll be in the Ninth Heaven."

Tung-ping's *danwei* provided us with living quarters. We had a furnished three-bedroom apartment in a compound next to the Navy Hospital. Later on, the State Guest House compound, Diaoyutai — where President Nixon would stay when he first visited China — was built a couple of blocks away.

When you walked into our apartment in Building 8, you

entered a foyer with a full-length mirror. Beyond that, there was a living room facing south. In it were two large sofas in navy corduroy and a walnut coffee table. There was also a square dining table known as a *baxian* table, so-called because it was big enough to seat eight persons, or literally "eight fairies." To add some brightness to the room, I put white-lace curtains on the windows and tied them up with red silk ribbons.

To the west end of the apartment, there was a small study. The master bedroom was on the east end, connected to a second bedroom by a door. I am a light sleeper so that extra bedroom adjoining usually stayed unoccupied. The third bedroom was small and faced north as well.

Since the master bedroom had only a double bed and a three-drawer table, I asked Tung-ping if we should buy some more furniture for our bedroom. He joyfully agreed. We went out and I picked out a walnut chest of drawers. This was the only piece of furniture we owned. I treasured it so much that I still keep this old-fashioned chest of drawers today.

We were provided with a telephone. At that time, and for decades to come, very few people in China had a telephone. However, there was one public phone in every neighborhood. In each such location, there was a person in charge of the phone, whose duty was to relay messages and collect fees.

I was delighted to see a tub in our bathroom, another rarity. People used public bathhouses then. But in recent years, people in big cities have begun to have showers with gas heaters.

These living conditions were considered luxurious. And the rent, including electricity and water, consumed only about five percent of Tung-ping's salary. In addition, we enjoyed free medical care. There was also a clinic in the compound, which was very convenient for me since I was in delicate health.

However, I was still not working. I told the cadres again and again, "I'm accustomed to working. I don't know what to do at home by myself." Tung-ping's place of work was quite distant, and he was away for long stretches of time.

"I've never been unemployed before," I added.

An official explained to me, "We've already arranged work for your husband. So you should wait patiently. You are not unemployed. You are just waiting to be assigned. There's no unemployment in a socialist country like ours."

So I stayed at home. But being a homemaker in China was no easy matter for me. Every neighborhood had a Neighborhood Residents' Committee under a Communist Party Branch which looked after those who did not work. I explained to them that I was just at home temporarily, awaiting assignment. But they replied that I must participate in the approved activities, especially political study.

One day while I was cleaning the bedroom of our new home, I heard some heavy footsteps on the stairway. Then someone opened the door and walked right in. It was our group leader, Lao Wang, a tall, heavy-set, mannish woman in her early fifties. She had wide shoulders, short hair and coarse skin. She apparently was of peasant stock from Shaanxi province in northern China; Lao Wang spoke with a heavy Shaanxi accent that I had trouble understanding. She told me to report for the next morning's political study.

Every Neighborhood Residents' Committee had a group leader like Lao Wang whose job was to relay the Communist Party's instructions and to carry out the Party's orders. She also organized our work details: sweep the compound, pull weeds. There was not much grass in Beijing to begin with, but that did not matter. (We were told that getting rid of weeds would help eliminate mosquitoes.) So we pulled up all the weeds in our neighborhood leaving barren earth. When it rained, the roads became so muddy everyone had to wear rubber boots.

I went about my tasks dutifully. But I detested the way Lao Wang would burst into our apartment without knocking to order me to do this or that. She became angry when I locked my door. Apparently it never occurred to her that people might like some privacy. (If Lao Wang is still in Beijing, I wonder what she would think of the iron security door that almost every family has installed, with a small glass cat-eye on the inner door.)

Once, as she was leaving, I started to close the door quickly behind her when suddenly she turned around. We were face to face, inches apart. I stepped back. "Oh, Comrade Peng," she said brusquely. "After you get the residence registration, go get the food and oil booklet. Then apply for a supplementary booklet. You will need that for your monthly portion of tofu, soap, matches and other items."

The more she told me, the more confused I became. When Tung-ping came home that evening, I told him I was so confused by everything that I didn't know where to start. He told me he was sorry that he wouldn't be able to help me. His *danwei* had arranged for him and some other engineers to leave very soon on a tour of factories across the country.

"You are going away? How long?" I asked anxiously. "You are going to leave me here all by myself? You know I am a stranger in Beijing. What am I going to do?"

"I can't help it," he said. "My *danwei* has arranged for me to go. I must go. I'll be back in two or three weeks. I'll write to you every day. How's that? My girl."

So, I was all alone. The apartment felt empty without Tung-ping.

But thanks to Lao Wang, I was kept busy. She would always

have us housewives doing something. One day, she told us that the cadres of the Neighborhood Residents' Committee, possibly including the district leader, would be coming to see whether we were keeping our houses and neighborhood clean. "Let them come," I said. "I clean my apartment every day anyway."

When I got home, I started cleaning: windows, walls, floors. I was warned that these people would pay particular attention to places that were normally overlooked, such as underneath tables, the top shelf of a bookcase, and so on. I cleaned room by room, each piece of furniture in turn, inside and outside, top to bottom.

Tung-ping had kept his promise and wrote every day. When I got tired of cleaning, I stopped and took out his letters. He told me of the different places he'd been to, the great achievements of new China and the wonderful sights in our country. He told me that he missed me, he knew I was lonely, and he would be back soon.

Soon the leaders of the district and Neighborhood Residents' Committee came to check up on our house. I opened all the doors inside our apartment. They looked everywhere, moved chairs, pulled out drawers, looked in the bathroom and peaked inside the kitchen cabinets. They couldn't find a speck of dust. "Clean, very clean," said one inspector, smiling. They left a little red flag on the door of our apartment which read, "*wei sheng zhi jia*" (a very clean home).

When Tung-ping came home three weeks later, the first thing he saw was the red flag. He came through the door, smiling ear to ear.

"How's my girl? You must have been working day and night, cleaning all the rooms by yourself. And I couldn't help you at all. Thank you."

His words made me much happier than the red flag award.

"Will you be coming home every day now?" I asked, hopefully.

"I'm afraid not," he said. "Too many things to do." My heart sank. "But we usually have movies on Wednesday and Saturday nights. I'll skip the movies to come home on Wednesdays also." Then he cheered me up further: "We'll move as soon as the new residence buildings are completed near my office."

One day, in the summer of 1958, Lao Wang read us a statement from the government. She said that the Party had called on the people to wipe out the "four pests" across the country. The "four pests" were: flies, mosquitoes, rats and sparrows. I could understand the first three. But why sparrows? Before I could check myself, the words slipped out from my mouth: "Comrade Lao Wang, how come the sparrows are considered pests? What harm are they to us?"

"Hmm… It seems that Comrade Peng has never been to the countryside," she responded condescendingly. "Sparrows eat grain. Naturally they are pests, everyone knows that."

I had walked right into that one.

"Pardon me for asking such a question," I said, trying to summon an apologetic tone. "But I've never heard that sparrows are pests before."

"Chairman Mao says sparrows are pests. Isn't that reason enough?" Lao Wang told me impatiently. But I didn't believe Chairman Mao said something like that. Even if he did, how could Lao Wang know? After all, she was only a group leader. However, I decided to keep my mouth shut in spite of my doubt.

Lao Wang proceeded to tell us what to do. Even though we had been diligently pulling up weeds, there were still a lot of mosquitoes. So we were now asked to burn 666 powder, a poison, to kill them. Someone else — not me this time — asked an obvious question. "Lao Wang, wouldn't 666 contaminate food?"

"Cover up your food, close all the windows and doors, light

the 666 powder and leave the house," she answered curtly.

Another woman said she'd read somewhere that 666 powder was harmful to humans.

"Then open all the windows as soon as you return to your home," was her quick reply. That was that.

In a way, I don't blame Lao Wang for losing her patience. She had a long list of things on the agenda and she didn't expect that we would dare ask questions regarding Chairman Mao's dictates.

She announced that we should all have fly swatters to kill the flies. A neighbor sitting next to me whispered that her primary-school son was supposed to hand in a fixed number of flies to his teacher every day. With screen windows and screen doors, there were simply no flies in her house. Therefore, her son had to go outside, even to the public lavatory, to find flies to kill.

Another woman spoke up saying she had to do the killings for her son, because she didn't want her son to touch the flies. She would swat the flies and put them in a bag so that the boy could hand them in to the teacher. "Believe me, that's quite a job," she added, "because I have my own quota of flies to meet too."

Everybody was now talking at the same time. Lao Wang had to shout to be heard.

"Hey, comrades, stop talking and listen to me. This is an important meeting. We must carry out the Party's orders. We must wipe out the 'four pests.' This is a patriotic act." Then she announced that she would distribute rat poison to each family to kill rats.

"Are we required to hand in the dead rats too?" someone asked.

"That won't be necessary. Their tails will do." She snapped.

She looked around the room. "Any more questions? No? Good, let's get on with our work."

Nothing could top the way Lao Wang organized us to wage

war against the sparrows. Each person was told to get a wash basin, frying pan or anything else that could be used to make loud noises. I had to carry a long bamboo pole with a piece of red cloth tied to one end. And then I was assigned to climb up onto the roof of our three-story building through a sky-window. The roof was sloped on both sides, with a narrow flat cement top. I had to walk back and forth on it, waving the pole constantly to keep the sparrows from landing. People down below kept up a racket with those pots, pans and other noisemakers to frighten the sparrows and prevent them from landing. The theory was that the sparrows would die of exhaustion.

So I climbed up on top of the roof of our building, Building 8, just as I was told and started waving the pole. Every rooftop had a person doing the same thing. I suddenly thought of that American pop song, "Sparrows on the Tree Tops." The song was about how the sparrows were flying in the sky, and chirping merrily on treetops. It seemed only yesterday that I was listening to Doris Day singing it while I was in Chicago. Wait a minute — or was it Rosemary Clooney? I pondered this.

"Comrade Peng," came a shout from below, "Why are you standing there, doing nothing?" Oh my goodness! I had stopped doing my job. I began to walk back and forth on the rooftop again, waving the pole as vigorously as I could.

I couldn't help thinking: only in China could this happen. In a less populous country, I'd bet all the tea in our country that the people would die from exhaustion long before the sparrows.

But it worked. The war against the sparrows was a great success. The sparrow population plummeted. But in reality, it was hard to tell which side won. We may have won this battle, but Mother Nature would win the war. A few years later, people began to notice there were many more worms and insects than before, doing great damage to crops. It dawned on them — a little too late — that the sparrows eat more worms and insects than crops. Quietly, bedbugs replaced sparrows on the list of the "four pests."

Our war on sparrows went on for three days, with just a short time down on the ground for lunch. I was sick and tired of it, physically as well as psychologically. So when Tung-ping returned home on Saturday evening, I complained.

"Isn't that funny? Men declaring war against sparrows? Are we living in the 18th century or something? I felt stupid walking on the roof and waving that damn pole. I got scared stiff up that high, you know, and I felt dizzy after a while."

Tung-ping was concerned. He suggested that I talk to the Party Branch Secretary of the Neighborhood Residents' Committee the next day. Especially since I was pregnant.

"Oh, no," I protested, "I am not going to talk to any Party Branch Secretaries. I don't know how to carry on a conversation with a person like that. Even Lao Wang gets on my nerves. Remember when we first moved in, I threw half an unfinished *mantou* (steamed roll) into the garbage can? And Lao Wang fished it out and asked if it was me who had thrown it away?"

Fortunately, Tung-ping had been able to calm her down, telling her I was in delicate health, carrying a baby. He pointed out that if I'd finished the sour *mantou*, I might have gotten sick and spent some money on medicine. And since we had state medical care, Tung-ping reasoned with her, we probably would have had to spend more of the state's money. But he kept agreeing with her that I had been wrong to throw it away. And he went on and on thanking her for helping me.

"No wonder Lao Wang says you are a very nice comrade," I said peevishly. "You know what, Tung-ping? Your friend Lao Wang recently asked me how many years older I am than you. She did it on purpose — she knows my age from our residence registration, and..."

"Do you intend to go on like this all night?" Tung-ping interrupted.

"Yes," I said, "I am sick and tired of being by myself. I can see you only on Sundays. Just think, one day out of seven. No — less than that. You are always out of town on business. And a lot of times, you would not even tell me where you are going. "

I was getting worked up. Tung-ping didn't say anything. He just held me in his arms. His embrace quieted me. I looked up into his face and asked, hopefully, "I know I am not politically qualified to work in your *danwei*. But can't you ask them to get a job for me?"

"I'll ask them Monday," he said. "I think you'll adjust to the life here more rapidly when you have work. How's that, my girl?" I answered him with a tender kiss.

8

Catch Up With the Yankees

————————⟨⟩————————

Not long after that in 1958, I finally got news about my job: I was assigned to teach English at the Chinese Science and Technology University. It had been founded only a few months before and was administered by the Chinese Academy of Sciences. (The Director of that Academy, Guo Moruo, also served as president of the school.) Most teachers and lecturers there were distinguished scientists.

I found my way to the school one morning in early summer. It was located in northwestern Beijing, not far from *Babaoshan* (Eight Treasure Hill) Cemetery. As I walked through the main gate, red banners with large Chinese characters came into my eyes. They said: "Education must be combined with production and labor" and "Education must serve the proletarian politics."

Those were the words of Mao Zedong.

I reported to the Department of Foreign Languages. At that time, Russian was the main foreign language followed by English, German and Japanese. The man in charge of the English group, Comrade Chi, was a young Communist who had recently been promoted. As we usually say in Chinese: "When a new official takes up his post, he raises three torches." This young man was no exception: he aimed to do something extraordinary to attract attention.

He decided to require us to stay in our office after classes. We couldn't go to our bedrooms to do our work or relax. All the teachers were dissatisfied with this. We talked among ourselves.

"Who ever heard of university teachers having to remain in their office all the time?"

"Yeah, he just wants to show off."

"In the office, people keep coming and going. It's not half as quiet as in the dormitory."

Although we aired our complaints among ourselves, none of us dared to tell the group leader. Not only was he the English group leader, he was the Party Secretary of our group as well.

Everyone still remembered the crackdown of the previous year. In the spring of 1957, *People's Daily* had carried an article, "Let A Hundred Flowers Bloom, A Hundred Schools of Thought Contend." The article called on people, especially the intellectuals, to make suggestions to help the Communists improve their work. Many intellectuals were invited to voice their opinions. After some hesitation, intellectuals responded vigorously. Too vigorously, it turned out. The "Hundred Flowers Bloom Movement" was followed by the "Anti-Rightist Campaign." Those who dared to voice disagreement with the Party were labeled "bourgeois reactionary rightists." More than 550,000 people, most of them intellectuals, were branded as rightists and sent to work on labor farms to "learn from the peasants."

So we had no choice but sheepishly stayed in our office after class as ordered.

One late morning, as I was preparing to leave the office, I mentioned to a middle-aged teacher that Americans work eight hours a day, five days a week. She countered immediately, "It's the same here. We work five days a week too. We have no classes on Wednesday and Saturday afternoons."

A young teacher named Jade pointed out, "That isn't so — we have political study on Wednesday and Saturday afternoons. So actually we're working six days a week." (China only started to have a five-day work schedule in the mid-1990s.)

"Jade, what are you talking about?" the other teacher said, "Political study is a must. It's not work. You're lucky to be educated in the new society. You were assigned a good job right after graduation. In the old society, college graduation meant unemployment because the graduates had to look for work themselves and lots of the time they couldn't find a job. I'm sure you've heard about this."

She made this little lecture with a solemn face.

Not wanting to prolong the discussion, I quickly said, "Gee, I didn't know it was so bad in the old society. I guess I didn't know too much about the old society, being away from China for such a long time…"

Before I finished speaking, the teacher cut in sharply, "Teacher Peng, what do you mean by not knowing too much about the old society? Didn't you just come from America recently? Isn't America an old society? A capitalist society can never be a new society."

Now I was getting angry, but I tried hard not to show it. I didn't want to antagonize her.

"I beg your pardon," I said. "I guess I don't have as high a political consciousness as some comrades."

Throwing those words at her, I walked away. Jade followed right behind. She was furious. "What's the matter with her? Does she want to join the Communist Party or something? Listen to the way she talks! You'd think she is Marx himself."

"Oh, Jade," I said, "it really didn't bother me that much. Her words went in one ear and out the other. I wouldn't be bothered by it."

"What makes me mad," Jade said, "is that she doesn't work harder than any of us."

"Let's forget about her, OK? Please forget about the female Marx and talk about something pleasant. We're going to have our lunch now. Don't let her ruin our appetite."

Jade was a very pretty Shanghai girl, petite, with skin as smooth as ivory. She had hair like black satin and was an excellent singer and dancer. Jade married her college sweetheart who had been born and raised in Indonesia. A few years later, during the great famine in 1960, she received a telegram from her mother-in-law who was seriously ill. Jade and her husband got permission to visit his ailing mother in Indonesia, and they never returned.

When in school, there were other unhappy incidents like this. Once, our group leader read a document saying that Mao Zedong intended to retire as Chairman of the State, and just be the Chairman of the Party, so he'd have more time to concentrate on studying Marxism-Leninism. As head of state, he had to spend a lot of time meeting foreign dignitaries and performing other duties.

After reading the document, group leader Chi announced, "Now, comrades, this document hasn't been published in the newspapers yet, so please don't tell anyone about it, especially not foreigners."

A colleague said, "We don't know any foreigners, how could we tell foreigners?"

Chi glanced at me for less than a second. But it got everyone's attention. They knew right away what he meant. It meant they didn't trust me. They didn't think I was one of them.

While I was getting used to my new work environment and my role as a mother, Tung-ping himself was deeply involved in the start-up (if not the fathering itself) of a new entity. It was a top-secret institute devoted to the development of high-tech materials for rockets, missiles and satellites. But I didn't know the exact nature of his work until years later when I came across some papers written by the Red Guards.

One night, back in our apartment, Tung-ping came home and asked me to sew two shoulder pads under his Mao uniform. I asked him why. He replied, "I have to go to the Ming Tombs next week to help build a reservoir. I haven't done any heavy labor before. Maybe some pads will help keep my shoulders from getting sore. We'll probably carry heavy loads."

The reservoir project was some thirty miles north of Beijing, near the tombs of the Ming dynasty (1368–1644) emperors. At that time, Mao called on the whole country to build reservoirs. PLA soldiers, government staff, workers, and students — all of the people — had to go there to dig for at least two weeks, often longer.

Two weeks later, Tung-ping returned from the site. He had become darker and thinner. Seeing this, a pain came into my heart. I asked, "How was the hard labor? It must have been tiring."

"Well, for the first couple of days, it was really something. But later on, I got used to it. I was moved by the enthusiasm of the people. We worked three shifts. The lights were on all night. And all of us slept in tents."

"A lady comrade from your institute came by to see me a few days ago," I said. "She had gone there for two weeks and said you were working very hard. You were dressed like everybody else, working like everybody else; nobody guessed that you had just come back from abroad."

Tung-ping said, "Even Chairman Mao, Premier Zhou and other government leaders went there to participate in the labor. So, for me, it was really nothing."

After returning from his digging duty at the Ming Tombs Reservoir, Tung-ping immersed himself again in work at the institute. But now the focus was on a metallurgical pursuit that was far less high-tech: "backyard steel furnaces."

Mao had taken a trip to the Soviet Union in 1957 and was much impressed by Nikita Khrushchev's claim that the Soviet Union would surpass the United States within fifteen years. On November 17 of that year, Mao gave a speech to the Chinese students studying in the Soviet Union. In the speech, he said, "The east wind surpasses the west wind." Mao declared — and *People's Daily* duly repeated — that China would "*chao ying gan mei*" (surpass Great Britain and catch up with the United States) in iron and steel production within ten and fifteen years respectively.

Mao ordered steel output doubled in one year — from 5.35 million tons in 1957 to 10.7 million tons in 1958. In order to achieve this goal, Mao turned to the masses. Soon every *danwei* — whether school, factory, or military unit — and even peasant families in the countryside were building backyard smelters. Jobs were put on hold as everyone looked for iron ore or coal. No coal? Then cut down trees for fuel. 90 million people were trying to make steel in their backyards, courtyards and alleyways, day and night.

Since very few people had ever seen a real steel furnace, most people didn't know where to start. And so they asked Tung-ping, doctor of metallurgy, for help. He was needed on the front lines of the "backyard steel furnace movement," which had become priority number one for the nation.

It seemed to me that he was gone all the time — days, nights, and weekends. Late one night, I felt myself starting to go into labor. The baby was arriving early. Tung-ping was not home, and I didn't have his office phone number. I had asked for it, but he said that he was not allowed to reveal his office phone number.

Now I was going to have the baby. What was I to do? I woke up our neighbor. They offered to accompany me to the hospital. I thanked them but just asked them to help me get an ambulance. They told me they'd try to notify Tung-ping. When I entered the emergency room of the Union Hospital alone, I felt the eyes of the staff on me; no doubt it crossed their minds that my husband and I weren't getting along. But I knew Tung-ping loved me deeply, but he felt devoted to helping his country as well.

At dawn the next day, I gave birth to a baby girl. When I woke up from a drowsy sleep, the first person I saw was a smiling Tung-ping with a bouquet of flowers. My, this was impressive, because the entire capital city of Beijing had just one florist. Everyone used paper flowers for decorations, even at banquets. (Now there are florists in many business centers in Beijing.)

"Did you see the baby? She looks just like you — the spitting image."

"Is that right?" he said. "How nice! I hear if a daughter looks like her father, that means she'll have a happy life." His eyes were red, apparently he hadn't slept much. But I saw twinkling in his eyes and an enormous smile on his face.

Then he asked, "How about naming our baby Chao-ying?"

I groaned inwardly. The name meant "Overtake Great Britain." Such names were all the rage at the time. I put a stop to that in a hurry.

"Oh, no," I said. "I know several parents have named their children 'Chao-ying' already." I'd also heard, 'Gan-mei' — that meant "Catch up with the Yankees."

"Why don't we name her something different?" I suggested.

Tung-ping thought for a moment. Then he asked, "How about naming her Weiming since she was born at 5 a.m., at dawn."

Weiming (dawn). "That's a terrific name." I agreed wholeheartedly.

My mind and mouth were racing.

"Since we have named the baby, let's get the hospital to prepare her birth certificate so we can notify the police station and get her a residence registration," I said. "That way, we can start getting the grain and cooking oil that she's due. After you get the residence registration, grain and oil coupons, please order some milk for her. I hear that now you can only get a half-pound of milk a day for an infant under seven months. And she can get two catty (a catty is about 1.1 pound) of dry rice powder a month…"

"Hey, stop!" Tung-ping held up his hand to signal a time-out, like a basketball referee. "You're giving too many orders, you're talking too fast, my dear girl."

I calmed down. It was a difficult time, especially for parents, because food was becoming scarce. Food was always on our minds, and now we had another mouth to feed. Fortunately, babies were entitled to their own rations of grain and oil, with the amount increasing as they grew.

I stayed in the hospital for a week. Women were allowed fifty-six days of maternity leave with pay. Because the baby arrived unexpectedly early, I hadn't used any of it. Our *ayi* (nanny of sorts) had gone to her hometown in the south and wasn't back yet. It was just the baby and I in our quiet home, with Tung-ping home at night.

Did I say quiet? Weiming cried all the time. She woke up every night, and woke us up too. Tung-ping was afraid I wasn't getting enough rest. He would pick the baby up, pat her lightly, and walk her back and forth, singing her to sleep with lullabies he made up himself.

"Tung-ping what are you humming?"

"Shh… don't talk, our baby is sleeping."

I always told my children how lucky they were to have such a wonderful father.

9

A Month's Pay for One Chicken

Now at home on maternity leave, it wasn't steel I was concerned about, it was food. I watched food become increasingly scarce. We rarely saw meat, chicken or eggs in the supply stores. Even noodles, tofu and bok choy were rationed. In Beijing, each person was entitled to 5 ounces of cooking oil per month. But now it was reduced to 2 ounces per month and our grain rations were cut to 16 catty a month.

I kept thinking of my girl friends in America, always counting their calories but still gaining weight. I realized a Beijing diet would guarantee them a weight loss. No more exercising, no more diet pills.

At that time, articles in *People's Daily* talked of huge improvements in yields: "The field will yield as much as people dared." One day, a picture appeared showing four kids standing on top of wheat stalks in a field, illustrating the benefits of dense planting. We all believed that. We thought we would soon have a bumper harvest. But in a few months there was a shortage of grain.

Years later, we found out that the diversion of tens of thousands of commune members to steel-making contributed to the grain shortages. A lot of wheat went unharvested. We also found out that the articles heralding an immense improvement in yields were not true. Even the picture of four children on top of the wheat had been faked. They took the wheat from other fields and bundled it into one field. Then they hid a bench among the wheat and the kids were actually standing on the bench.

But at that time, we did not doubt such things. After all, this photo had appeared in *People's Daily*, the paper of the Communist Party.

The newspapers continued to carry articles about "the Great Leap Forward" saying that communism was paradise, and the people's commune was a bridge to that paradise. The radio also let us believe that communism was imminent. We attended political study groups regularly. Nobody voiced any doubts.

"I didn't know communism could come so soon," enthused one colleague.

"If communism is here, and everybody lives so freely and happily," wondered another, "what are we going to do with our time?"

"We can take vacations, and have all kinds of recreation," answered the third.

While we in Beijing were increasingly feeling hardship, the rest of the country was already in serious straits. This became clear to me when, to help with the newborn, I hired a new *ayi* from Anhui province. She happened to arrive around New Year's Eve when we were serving rice and pork — a rare treat. She announced that she couldn't remember the last time she had a decent meal and promptly devoured three big bowls of rice and pork. I'd never seen anyone eat that much in one meal. Fifty years old! And a woman too!

I was literally frightened — because she didn't have a Beijing residence registration, she couldn't have Beijing ration coupons. She saw my reaction and explained that she had not had rice in a long time. Her village had been ravaged by famine and many had died. She told me many commune members had tried to leave the village, but only those who could secure official permits were allowed to buy train tickets. She said she was lucky to have a cousin in the commune office who helped her to get a train ticket.

I was sympathetic, but I had to let her go. I had no choice. We couldn't afford to keep her. I gave her some money to get home and some food coupons, which were necessary even to eat at restaurants.

When my maternity leave was over, I went back to the Chinese Science and Technology University. But nobody was in class. They were all out making steel or digging the Ming Tombs Reservoir! Due to lack of proper nutrition, I was getting weaker and weaker; steel smelting or digging at the reservoir was out of the question for me. And besides, I was going to have another baby. A baby we didn't really expect. How on earth could we afford to feed another mouth? But my second daughter Jibin arrived in 1960... in the midst of the great famine.

A few months after her birth, a truck pulled up to our apartment near the Navy Hospital. We were finally going to move. With the help of some young engineers from 703, we loaded up the truck. All of our stuff plus father, mother and two children fit inside. We drove for half an hour over paved roads and then came to some bumpy roads past cornfields in the southern suburbs of Beijing. We drove into a compound and saw a lot of new buildings. The driver took us past a nice courtyard, turned the corner and stopped in front of a building marked #35.

I was thrilled. Our new home would be only 20 minutes away by bicycle from Tung-ping's office. At the same time, I realized it would be much farther away from my university job. I could not possibly return home every day. So I applied to stay at home, asking the officials to keep my job open without pay.

Back from a bicycle ride with our first daughter, Weiming

I ended up staying home for four years. But it wasn't much of a rest. All day long, all my thoughts, all my actions were aimed at one goal: feeding my husband and our two daughters. Once while visiting a neighbor, I watched her use a scale to weigh rice. She put the portions in individual bowls, steaming them separately.

"What are you doing?" I was curious.

She said with a bitter smile, "I have two sons who are going to middle school. If we don't divide the food, they will eat the family's entire ration."

I didn't say anything.

"As a wife and a mother, to have to do this, I feel awful," she continued. "But what else can I do?"

She moved closer and spoke in a low voice.

"In Beijing, we are lucky. I hear that outside Beijing, people are eating grass and leaves, anything they can find. A few days ago, a relative of mine came from Henan province. She told me many people were starving to death there."

One day, a neighbor came to me with a plan to get some nourishment. She said we might be able to get some chickens or eggs directly from commune members in the far suburbs. These people didn't want to sell their goods to the state stores at the set price. So my friend and I set out on foot. For hours we walked, visiting the homes of commune members. We were in no mood to enjoy the sunshine, the gentle breeze, or the stretches of green fields. We didn't even talk much. Both of us were thinking about the same thing: how to get food for our families.

At house after house, we got the same answer: sorry, nothing to sell. We were about to give up when we found a commune member willing to sell us a chicken.

The catch: it would cost 30 *yuan*. This was outrageous!

"Can you lower the price a little? Do you know a college graduate's pay is only 46 *yuan* a month? And a lot of the people get only 28 *yuan* a month? "

"No bargain, comrades," he responded. "You can take it or leave it, as you please. To tell you the truth, these are the last few hens I have left. If you think the price is too high, others will be glad to buy them. I'm positive."

This was a comrade with a firm grasp on the concept of supply and demand. But we imagined what those chickens would taste like. Our salivary glands won out. We paid the 30 *yuan*. We walked back home, each with a live chicken flopping in a sack.

After I got home, I asked someone to kill the chicken for me. I then plucked it, washed it and made a big stew in a wok. Normally I would have used a little cooking wine and some ginger and green onion. We had none of these. Even so, the children were thrilled. "Smells nice! *Mama*, is it ready yet?"

I told them to wait until their father came home. We watched for Tung-ping's approach. As soon as he opened the door, the kids ran to him. "*Baba*! There's something nice for dinner! We have chicken!"

Tung-ping, looking dubious, lifted the lid off the wok and turned to me. "Where did you get the chicken?"

"I bought it from a commune member."

He was not pleased.

"You know, Chieh-ching, there are regulations. We're not allowed to buy anything from private sources. And I'm a Party member. I should abide by this rule."

I became sarcastic. "I already bought it, had it killed and made the soup. Maybe I should carry the wok with the chicken in it back to the commune member?"

He didn't argue with me but went on calmly, "I'm sure this food shortage is only temporary," he said. "The Party will do its best to overcome it." And he continued, "Please don't buy anything from the commune members again." Then he was silent. We knew that meant it was OK for us to eat the meal.

We sat down. The kids and I dug right in. The kids had helping after helping. I had intended to save some for the next day, but I couldn't bear to stop them. Although they were just toddlers, they finished off the entire stew!

Tung-ping didn't eat a morsel of chicken or a drop of broth.

With no chickens in the state-run groceries, and Tung-ping forbiddng me to buy from the commune members privately, there was just one solution: raise chickens myself.

I bought quite a few books on chicken raising, and soon could name all the famous breeds by memory. There was the Canadian Gray, the Australian Black, the Leghorn, and various Chinese breeds. The breed I settled on was the Leghorn, for two reasons. It was originally raised in Italy (a place known for its good food) and more important, the books said it laid eggs every day, all year round.

We lived on the first floor at the time, so we carefully built a small chicken coop on our back porch. We filled it with baby chicks.

Tung-ping teased me because I followed the advice in the books step by step, word by word. One day when colleagues from my university were visiting our apartment, the conversation soon turned to food. In fact, whenever people gathered and talked among themselves, the subject was invariably food.

"Chieh-ching does a wonderful job tending the chickens," Tung-ping told them. "She does it the Western way too — giving them water before feeding them." My colleagues burst into laughter. It was a little East-West humor: Westerners always have soup at the beginning of the meal, while Chinese serve it at the end. I chuckled along with my friends, but I said to myself, "Making fun of me in front of my friends! You just wait till they are gone. You'll hear no end from me, Tung-ping my boy."

The books said when the face of a hen turns red, it will soon lay eggs. One day the children called out: "*Mama*, come quick! The faces of the hens are red now!" I hurried to see, and sure enough, several of the little hens had red faces. How lovely! We all clapped our hands with expectation.

We waited. For days, we waited. Finally, we found an egg under a hen. We carried it around proudly, sure that this was the start of daily egg dishes: hard-boiled eggs, fried eggs, scrambled eggs, steamed egg mix… Too bad, it didn't happen. The Leghorns did not give us eggs every day, for one simple reason: no chicken will lay eggs unless it is adequately fed. In those days we didn't have much food left over after our meals. Whatever was left, I ate myself. So there was little to feed the chickens.

Then someone suggested rabbits. I liked that idea, because rabbits reproduce quickly and eat grass for the most part. And wild grass could be found easily. I started learning how to cook rabbits. There was just one catch: getting the fur off the rabbits. I didn't know how to do it, so we had to give up on this idea.

So much for chickens and rabbits. But there was a patch of ground behind our building. Tung-ping had the idea to grow some corn there. Again, we did some research, learning that two strains, the Golden Queen and the White Horse Teeth gave the highest yields. But a southern Chinese strain of sticky corn was much more tasty. The kids shouted in concert, "We want the tasty one." That settled the issue.

But a garden needs fertilizer, and in China, fertilizer doesn't come in bags from the hardware store. It comes from pigs or — from us. Every household planted some food, so pig droppings became very precious. The compound's canteen had pigpens which scarcely needed cleaning because the pig manure was snatched up by neighbors to be used as fertilizer. So we had our neighbors show us how to compost the children's night soil over the winter for use as fertilizer the following spring.

We planted the corn. The plants were growing nicely because we spent a lot of time working in our little plot. But before we harvested the corn, we left for vacation to Qingdao. By the time we returned home, all the corn was stolen. I was so mad that I wanted to go out and shout: "Who stole our corn?" Tung-ping stopped me. He said it was no use doing that. I wouldn't get back the stolen corn anyway. Whoever stole the corn probably had eaten it days ago.

養雞養兔種玉米

86

10

Our Second Wedding Chamber

———————————— 🎵 ————————————

THAT AUTUMN OF 1960 Tung-ping's younger brother Yong-ping was getting married. He was now an editor in a publishing house in Beijing. Tung-ping invited his mother to stay with us for the wedding because we had a spacious apartment. Since Tung-ping was fully occupied with work, it would be my duty to entertain her.

The first time I met Tung-ping's mother was as a new bride, soon after we were married. Tung-ping had asked me to journey down to Huangtutang, his hometown, to meet her and other family members. I knew this was proper, but I had always been shy with strangers. I didn't really want to go.

I had another reason for not going. Tung-ping had told me that when he was growing up, the whole family had to bathe in the winter time in a huge wok with a low fire underneath. The bather sat on a piece of board while bathing. The family bathed in the following order: father, sons, mother and daughters — without changing water!! That was why I didn't want to go to Huangtutang. But Tung-ping assured me that they had stopped that practice long ago. Now, each family member had clean water. But still I was reluctant to go to see my new in-laws.

"Why don't you go by yourself?" I pleaded. "I'm nervous. I'm not used to meeting people, and I don't know how to greet your mother and relatives."

"That's easy," he assured me. "Just follow my lead. Call my relatives what I call them."

"Do you think your mother will like me? I lost my mother early in my childhood. I don't know how to deal with the elderly."

"As the saying goes," Tung-ping said, "'An ugly daughter-in-law has to face her in-laws eventually.' In your case, it's a pretty daughter-in-law facing her mother-in-law. Besides, my mother loves me so she will love you too. Don't be nervous, my dear girl."

Tung-ping later told me that his mother was just as nervous about my visit. As a result, Tung-ping's elder brother even wrote him to ask about my likes and dislikes, my favorite dishes, and so on. Tung-ping wrote back, "Chieh-ching is not at all particular about anything. She likes to eat whatever I like. Please don't prepare anything special."

Tung-ping was aware that I was not conversational with strangers. So he told his elder brother that I didn't understand Huangtutang dialect and hoped that all their relatives would make allowances. In China, people in some neighboring provinces, and sometimes even in neighboring towns, speak different dialects. Some of these local dialects are so different that they sound like foreign languages. Tung-ping's family accepted his explanation.

It took us fourteen hours to reach Wuxi by train from Beijing. Wuxi is known as "*yu mi zhi xiang*" (a place bountiful with fish and rice), but it is also famous for its its tea, silk and broad-leafed mulberry trees. These leaves are fed to the silk worms which grow in abundance there. Not surprisingly, Wuxi's main industry is textile factories.

After we disembarked at the railway station of Wuxi, we had to take a wooden boat with a motor to get to Huangtutang. The boat passed under a lot of lovely stone bridges with traditional moon-shaped arches. Some of them were hundreds of years old. There were many willow trees along the river banks. I could also see a lot of bamboo groves as well as peach, plum and apricot blossoms. The scene was idyllic, the air fragrant with the scent of the blossoms. Some women were doing their laundry by the river beating the clothes on smooth stones. They were laughing and talking to one another boisterously.

When we finally arrived "home," Tung-ping opened the front door and there stood my mother-in-law. She was tall for a lady of her age and had her hair combed back into a bun. She looked just like Tung-ping, so I immediately felt warm toward her. I called her "*Mama*" as Tung-ping did. She smiled

Yao family home near Wuxi. Our second wedding chamber was on the second floor.

and said something that I couldn't understand. Tung-ping acted as our interpreter. She seemed to be pleased with me. So I got a high score in this test.

I found my mother-in-law had made many preparations for our visit. She had furnished a "wedding chamber" especially for us: a big four-poster bed with a stepping block before it. On either side of it was a tiny night stand. There were even several drawers on the bedstead. A white mosquito net hung over the bed. Behind the bed there was a night stool painted crimson!

"Tung-ping! Come over here, quick! See how many accessories there are to the bed! And a night stool! A brand-new one. Can you smell the new paint?"

"Shh…" Tung-ping put a finger to his mouth. "Not so loud! The furniture here is Wuxi's latest style. Mother ordered it from the city. Don't forget to thank her."

At the same time Tung-ping's elder sister was also hurrying to Huangtutang from nearby Jiangyin to enjoy the family reunion. She walked in and was overjoyed to see him. "Oh, Tung-ping, you haven't changed a bit in ten years. And you still have that maroon vest I knitted for you before you left China."

Tung-ping flashed a big smile and said, "Thank you, elder sister, every time I wear this, I always think of you." I was moved by their endearment and I said to myself, "I'll learn how to knit and make a sweater for him one day."

He introduced us and I noticed she brought along a lot of freshwater crabs. At dinner, she placed the best part of the crab, the eggs, in my bowl.

"Elder sister!" Tung-ping said. "Thanks, but Chieh-ching is allergic to crabs."

"What a pity!" said the sister. "Our crabs at Yangcheng Lake are famous throughout the country."

His aunt then poured everyone some rice wine into handle-less cups of moon-colored china. The first cup was for Father Yao, her brother-in-law, who had died while Tung-ping was abroad. I never met him, but as I sat there looking at his cup I recalled what Tung-ping had told me about him. He said his father was the absolute ruler in his house. Only the male members — his father and his two brothers — could have meals at the dining table. His mother and his two sisters had to eat whatever was left in the kitchen, after the men were through. Tung-ping and his two brothers objected to this strongly. Their father finally gave in. He allowed their mother to have meals with them, but the two girls had to remain eating in the kitchen.

In the big bed that night, under the high-hung mosquito net, Tung-ping put his mouth close to my ear. "Darling, are you still nervous?" I turned to face him, caressing his hair, without saying anything.

Now that Tung-ping's mother was coming to Beijing, I wanted to repay her kindness and hospitality. I decided I would take my mother-in-law on a sightseeing tour of the city. But our range was limited. She was unable to walk far because her feet had been bound as a little girl. Besides, she said she was more interested in watching her granddaughters play than visiting parks. I was able to buy some pound cakes for her — a special treat in those days — but she would not take them herself. She gave them to her granddaughters.

One evening during her visit Tung-ping and I were reminiscing about the New Year's Eve dance. His mother suddenly asked: "Tung-ping, I haven't seen anybody dance before. Can you two do a dance for me?"

"Sure, *Mama*. Chieh-ching and I will be glad to put on a show for you."

Then Tung-ping said to me in a low voice, "Do you mind dressing up a little for the show?"

On our back porch with Tung-ping's mother, younger sister and brother in 1960

I went into our bedroom and put on a white blouse and the same navy blue skirt I wore when I first met Tung-ping at the dance. Tung-ping moved some furniture out of the way. There was no doubt what record Tung-ping would put on the phonograph. The familiar strains of "The Blue Danube" filled our apartment.

As I walked into the living room, Tung-ping bowed to me in a knightly fashion, and asked, "May I have the honor, Madame?"

I smiled sweetly and curtsied, "With pleasure, Sir."

We joyously spun around the room. We kept the proper distance and danced in the traditional way. From the corner of my eye, I could see my mother-in-law's eyes and mouth were wide open.

That night, in bed, Tung-ping repeatedly thanked me for the kindness I had shown to his mother. "Darling, you are such a nice person," he whispered. "You know, Tung-ping, I love you so much that I feel close to your mother. I only feel sorry for not having good food to entertain her. It is so hard to get any food now."

"Mother surely appreciates the reunion with her son and

daughter-in-law and her grandchildren, even more than ginseng, seabird's nest, or shark-fin soup."

Tung-ping's mother wasn't used to the northern climate. She went back to Huangtutang after a month. There she lived with a widowed sister after Tung-ping's father passed away. Tung-ping sent money to them every month, enough for the two elderly ladies and his nephew, who was living with them.

We had to eat rice and bok choy day in and day out. Even then we were the lucky ones. Tung-ping's younger brother came every Sunday not only to see us, but because Tung-ping would invite him to stay for lunch and supper.

One day I said to Tung-ping, "What about going into town and dining out at a restaurant to have some better dishes? And we can bring something back for the children too." He agreed cheerfully.

There were no privately-run restaurants in China at that time and few state-run ones. We decided to go to a Western-style restaurant where we had dined shortly after our return to China. I remembered the place fondly: its quiet location, the snowy white tablecloths, white lace curtains with a bamboo design. I also remembered how the waiters in uniform had waited on us attentively.

Now, four years later, everything had changed. For a moment we thought we'd come to the wrong place. No tablecloths, no menus. Every table was crowded with people. Others were hovering right behind them, waiting for a seat.

"Funny," I said. "All of a sudden people are taking a fancy to Western-style meals."

A man who was in line next to me spoke up: "You know, comrade, this is the only kind of restaurant that serves meat now. All of us here have not had meat for months. As long as there is meat, nobody cares if it is cooked Chinese style or Western style."

I felt most awkward standing behind someone dining, waiting for their seat. Tung-ping convinced me that since we were there, we'd might as well take it easy. So we waited patiently.

No sooner had we sat down at the table then we were shadowed by other people standing behind us. I glanced about and noticed each diner was having the same dish. I couldn't help chuckling. It was funny, in a way. I told Tung-ping, "That's what I call equality. Everyone has the same food." Tung-ping replied, "I like it that way. Usually it takes quite a while for you to order, and sometimes you change your mind and I would take the blame from the waiter."

Instead of a menu, there was a small blackboard on which was written: Curried beef rice, 10 *yuan* a dish. So, curried beef it was: four dishes, two for us, two to take home to the children.

It was five in the afternoon when we got home. As we entered, one of the children burst out, "*Mama*, what goodies did you bring home?" Her sister lectured her: "All you think about is goodies. You should have told *Mama* that there is a notice for a parcel."

The parcel was just what I had been hoping for: my relatives in Hong Kong had sent a package of milk powder and other food. In Beijing, babies older than six months weren't entitled to milk rations. After age two, not even dry rice powder was available. Now, with this package, I'd be able to give the kids powdered milk.

Tung-ping served the curried-beef dishes to the children, and boy did they love it. He then beckoned me to the bedroom and asked me to sit down. "Chieh-ching," he said, "Do you mind if we don't claim the parcel?"

"Why not? That was sent by my relatives of their own accord. I didn't ask them to."

"We appreciate their kindness," he said. "But you know if we accept food from abroad, there could be rumors to our disadvantage, saying that we Chinese are starving."

This made no sense to me. "Aren't we starving?" I asked. "Why can't we speak about it?" Still, I held my tongue. I was sure Tung-ping had some reasons for his suggestion. It wasn't until the Cultural Revolution that I realized accepting food would reflect poorly on our family. A well-known scientist's family in need of food? What would the imperialists say about that? Tung-ping knew this. Upon returning to China, he had watched his step in all such matters. He even made a special point of cutting off correspondence with his friends abroad. (Every year his colleagues back in Aachen sent a Christmas card and birthday card via his younger brother. Even though Tung-ping knew it was impolite, he never answered.)

I ended up refusing to accept the parcel at the customs office. My relatives in Hong Kong never wrote to me again.

One day in midsummer, a neighbor hurried over with some big news: there were popsicles at the grocery store! I grabbed my purse and joined the stream of people converging on the store. Nobody was lining up; it was just a crush of customers. I managed to squeeze in and bought some for the kids. I knew they would love to have something like that.

When I got home, I froze: my purse was gone! I began to panic. Inside my purse was not just money, but that month's ration coupons for grain, cooking oil and other food items. The money hardly mattered at this point — we literally couldn't live without the coupons.

I ran back to the grocery store. The popsicles were sold out, the counter was empty and two sales ladies stood there chatting. Nearly out of breath, I asked them if anyone had picked up my purse.

"No," they replied.

"We are in hard times," one said. "Anyone who picked up food coupons would consider them valuables. Why would they have handed them to us?"

The other shrugged. "A person with 'three hands' (a pickpocket) probably stole your purse during all the pushing and shoving."

I searched every inch of the store, every stretch of ground on the way home, hoping against hope that my purse would suddenly jump into view. No such luck. At home, I ransacked all the drawers, irrationally thinking I'd somehow left it there. Then the kids reminded me: "*Mama*, didn't you take out the money from the purse when you paid for the popsicles?"

When Tung-ping got home, he found the house turned inside out and me still sweating and searching. I told him what had happened. He realized the seriousness and started helping me look.

In my heart of hearts I knew my purse had been stolen, but I was obsessed with the idea that it would somehow miraculously appear.

"Tung-ping, what am I to do? Please help me."

"I'm afraid it's hopeless," he said.

He thought for a while.

"Chieh-ching," he finally said, "you'd better write a self-criticism. I'll hand it to the leadership to see if anything can be done about the lost grain and oil coupons."

"Why should I write a self-criticism? It's no fault of mine."

"Well, after all, the theft occurred because of your carelessness, right? If you don't make a self-criticism, how can I bring it up with the leadership?"

The anxiety I felt churned my stomach; I couldn't eat. Finally, I resolved to see Tung-ping's boss, Comrade Chang. He lived in a two-story house not far away. When I arrived, they were just finishing supper. Chang showed me into the living room. I started right away telling the story of the coupons. He asked me to calm down, to take a seat and have some tea. I couldn't.

"That Tung-ping is incorrigible," I began. "The other day I bought a chicken from a commune member so the children could have some meat. He wouldn't take a bite, and he lectured me. My relatives in Hong Kong sent milk powder to me, and he forced me to return it. Today my grain and oil coupons were stolen. He told me to write a self-criticism. Why should I criticize myself? I didn't do anything wrong."

Comrade Chang grinned at my outpouring. He tried to soothe me. "Comrade Tung-ping is right in being strict with himself and the family, on political matters. I am well aware of your anxiety over the loss of the coupons. We'll talk it over among the leadership and see what we can do about it. Please don't worry."

The next evening when Tung-ping returned home he tried to put on a sober face, but there was glinting in his eyes.

"Hey, Chieh-ching, you are really something! You went to Comrade Chang's house to register a complaint against me, hmmm…, I guess I'll have to watch my steps from now on." Then he pulled out some coupons, warning me over and over to keep them in a safe place in the house.

"Don't take them with you unless it's absolutely necessary. If you lose them next time, the leadership won't give us any more."

During the years from 1959 to 1961, Tung-ping's *danwei*, the Seventh Ministry, took it upon itself to find food for the whole group. The ministry sent people to Inner Mongolia to hunt for antelopes and to Shandong province to buy vegetables and green onions. All was shared among the staff.

I didn't like the meat of antelopes. It had a distasteful odor, so I refused to eat any. Tung-ping got real mad. He ordered me: "Don't be so picky, eat it." Seeing his face turning red, I dared not argue. I ate the antelope meat obediently.

Malnutrition was universal. All government institutions initiated a practice of going to bed early to reduce the consumption of energy. My situation was different: insomnia kept me awake most of the night. One evening, as usual, Tung-ping went back to his office to work. I sang the children to sleep. I was doing some kitchen work when suddenly a wave of dizziness swept over me. I fell to the floor. When I came to, I was lying in Tung-ping's arms.

"Feeling better now?" He asked anxiously. "I've phoned the clinic. They told me that they will send a doctor here soon. I'm sorry, darling, I haven't taken good care of you. I'm so sorry."

Grasping his hand, I said, "Tung-ping darling, it's exactly because you are so busy that I should have taken better care of you. Look how thin you are!"

The doctor arrived and examined me. My liver was distended, he said, and I should get my blood tested in a hospital. He noticed that my ankles were swollen, something he was seeing a lot of lately. It was a sign of malnutrition and edema. He prescribed rest and better nutrition. I couldn't even get enough food to eat, how on earth could I get "better nutrition"?

As the famine worsened, the government did its best to keep its rocket and missile program on track, starting with proper nutrition for its scientists. Tung-ping was given extra food: half a pound of milk a day (about one glass), two pounds of meat, two pounds of eggs, four pounds of soy beans and two pounds of sugar every month. And there were even two cartons of cigarettes.

Tung-ping let the kids share the milk and the whole family share the soy beans, meat, and eggs. (He asked me if it was OK to send half our sugar allowance to his sister in Chengdu.

Of course, I agreed.) I tried to reserve the eggs for Tung-ping but he wouldn't take them. With such hard work, he needed more nourishment. So, I tried another tack. I boiled the soy-beans with a little salt and served them at breakfast. I counted forty out and served them to Tung-ping every morning. I tried to make him eat his due, but he always left some on the plate, saying he was full. When the kids came to the breakfast table a little later each morning, I let each have twenty.

After the famine was over, Tung-ping told me that he had estimated that if he ate forty soy beans a day, there wouldn't be any for me. So, he had left some for me purposely. That was just like him — always thinking of my well-being.

But our suffering wasn't as bad as that of the people in the countryside. We city dwellers had guaranteed grain rations however small. Commune members had to rely solely on themselves. With the men ordered to work at "backyard steel production," some crops rotted in the fields.

During the period of "*da yue jin*" (the Great Leap Forward) from 1959 to 1961, it is now calculated that about 21,580,000 people died "unnatural deaths."

11

A Most Famous Seaside Resort

———————————— *∕P*. ————————————

Each day Tung-ping went off to work at a place called Institute 703. This was China's research center devoted to the development and manufacture of high-tech materials needed for rocketry, missiles and satellites. When Tung-ping began work there after the New Year holiday in 1958, the workplace was a rundown barrack from the Qing dynasty (1644–1911). It was located in the Fengtai district, far to the south of downtown Beijing.

The institute was in its embryonic form, with only a dozen college graduates and a single microscope. China in the 1950s could not even produce low-alloyed steel, let alone make aeronautical materials. For the creation of rocket materials and components, Tung-ping and his colleagues literally had to start working empty handed.

They poured all their time and energy into nurturing this institute. By 1960, Institute 703 already had about eight hundred people. It was now a galaxy full of Ph.D.s and holders of Master degrees. Tung-ping had become the Institute's director, in charge of technological aspects of all operations. He had a thorough knowledge of the properties of different materials. Under him, there were two deputy directors. One assisted him with technological matters, the other dealt mainly with administrative affairs.

In China, every place had someone from the Communist Party watching over things, to make sure everyone's political orientation stayed true to the Party. Institute 703 was assigned such a person. Commissar Li was an able administrator and an intelligent man. Although only a middle-school graduate, he attended night schools to advance himself and showed a strong interest in learning material sciences. But he was transferred to another *danwei* a couple of years later.

Commissar Li's replacement, Huang, was also a middle-school graduate, but he was an entirely different kind of person. He didn't know any science or technology and wouldn't learn any. He thought he was the Communist Party himself. Commissar Huang came to work at Institute 703 in 1960 but didn't perform so well. As a result, some higher ranking cadres told him he should work harder and learn from the technical people. Huang would nod his head respectfully at this advice, but then turn his back and mutter, "That comrade reminds me of the old saying: a crow standing on a black pig's back. It only sees the black hair of the pig, but not the black feathers of itself."

Commissar Huang felt he had to keep a close eye on these intellectuals. "We should put class struggle above everything else," he declared. Now Tung-ping had a lot of experience in the scientific sphere, but when it came to "class struggle" he was at a loss. He was preoccupied with research and overseeing hundreds of special projects. He only wished he had more time for his work. He had no time to play politics.

Making a rocket was more than just good design. Other crucial aspects included materials and electronic equipment. At that time, China was rather backward in industry. It couldn't manufacture good-quality steel for consumers. So it was a great challenge for the people of 703 to develop space-qualified materials. This was a huge undertaking, for a rocket has many systems and subsystems. And each subsystem has hundreds of components and devices. In fact, in a single rocket there are more than 100,000 components and devices.

The quality of each component or device directly influences the reliability of the whole system and is one of the most important factors for the success or failure of the rocket launching. Hence, a rocket needs thousands of kinds of materials: metal, non-metal, composite materials, different kinds of alloys, organic materials, inorganic materials, etc. If a single piece of wire, single component or device at some key position was unreliable in quality, the whole launching might end in failure and might even bring about unimaginable consequences.

It is a well-known fact that the failure of several launches in various countries was a result of the failure of components. And these in turn were mostly the result of deficiencies in the materials.

When a new material or technology is being developed, that's just the beginning. There are a whole series of ground tests required, such as: normal, dynamic, static, environmental, transportation, adaptability, simulation, complete-system and life tests. Then comes testing under the extreme conditions required by rockets: (ultra) high temperatures for blast-off, (ultra) low temperatures for space, high pressures, high vacuum, vibration, air tightness, erosion, ablation, aging, fatigue, etc. The temperature of a rocket engine can get as high as 3,000 C or more and as low as −250 C or so.

In addition to a wide-ranging exposure to science at Jiaotong University, Tung-ping's years abroad — in England and West Germany — helped prepare him for this research. While abroad, his primary research focus was on the viscosity of metals. He devoted every spare moment to soaking up the latest technical know-how. When he returned to China, he kept collecting related papers. Whether at home or abroad, Tung-ping made it a point of visiting bookstores and libraries. As for me, whenever I would go to the bookstore with him, I would buy a novel — one written by one of the Bront' sisters, for example. Something to read before going to bed.

At home, Tung-ping was always reading and taking notes. Since his university days, Tung-ping had been a constant note-taker when reading. When his right hand got tired, he'd support his wrist with his left hand and continue.

"Darling, you know what? You should have married a woman engineer," I told him once. "At least she would know how to help you with clerical work. I'm utterly ignorant about your field. I can't help you in any way."

"Oh, no, my girl, you are the one for me," he responded. "I like you in every way. When you are home, your chatting and your giggling enliven the whole family."

Everyday, Tung-ping plunged whole-heartedly into his work. He wanted the institute to produce not just R&D space materials, but a new generation of scientists upon whom the motherland could rely in the future. The staff included a lot of young scientists with university training, some with Ph.D.s from the Soviet Union, but few with practical laboratory experience. Tung-ping was determined to train them properly. He lectured, he tutored, he demonstrated, he invited experts from other *danwei* to give lectures. His work was virtually nonstop — if he wasn't discussing a design problem, he was working out a manufacturing process with engineers or double-checking technical reports for errors.

Amid the constant work and endless political struggle, Tung-ping managed to keep his sense of humor. Whenever there was a party at the institute, he'd be there. Some knew he liked to dance. At one Spring Festival party, some young men pushed him to the front as the music for a rural folk dance began. First, Tung-ping asked an old worker to lend him his sheepskin coat. Then he turned it inside out and put it on, with a white towel around his head in a northwestern rural style. Tung-ping grabbed a pointer from a blackboard to use as a whip, and sang with gusto the folk song "The Girl from *Daban Cheng*":

The girl from Daban Cheng has long braids.
How beautiful your eyes are!
If you have a mind to get married,
    just marry me and not any other.
Bring along your dowry, together with your younger
    sister, come to me in your cart.

Then shouting "Hey!", Tung-ping cracked his whip and sang the refrain again:

Bring along your dowry, together with your younger
    sister, come to me in your cart!

After an initial moment of stunned silence, hearing this outburst from the taciturn, hardworking scientist who corrected their research reports brought rolling waves of laughter and applause. Tung-ping had brought down the house.

In 1961 the Seventh Machine Building Ministry arranged a summer vacation for Tung-ping to Beidaihe, one of the most famous seaside resorts in China. And best of all, family included!

Beidaihe was a former fishing village on the Bohai Gulf, 190 miles from Beijing. It was transformed into a vacation area after being "discovered" by British railway engineers in the 1890s. By the turn of the century, foreigners, diplomats and rich Chinese living in Beijing and Tianjin retreated to this place to escape the stifling heat of northern Chinese summers. After 1949, Beidaihe became the choice spot for high-ranking Communist Party leaders. The resort is well-known for its white sandy beach that extends over several miles. A gentle sea breeze blows in each morning and evening.

Our lodging was in a huge walled compound, known as Eagle Corner. There were numerous red-brick bungalows, set amongst evergreens which stood out against the blue sky and white clouds.

We were assigned a bungalow all by ourselves. From our doorstep, a gravel path led directly to the beach. I spent every day at the beach with our daughters, swimming and playing in the sand. Some East Europeans even let their children run around naked, which we thought was a fine idea. So we let our little kids, Weiming and Jibin, take off their bathing suits (which I had made out of colorful towels) and play with the foreign children.

Tung-ping loved picture-taking. He snapped many pictures, including some of our naked children. There were pictures of us too, with me in a one-piece aqua bathing suit that I had brought back from America and Tung-ping in navy trunks. Sadly, these precious pictures of happy times are now just memories. We had to burn them during the Cultural Revolution, because we were afraid they would be declared "pornographic" by the Red Guards.

It was a struggle to keep Tung-ping on the beach. He had toted along a case of books and wanted to take advantage of this distraction-free zone to catch up on his reading.

The resort was dotted with prominent personalities. Tung-ping ran into Mao Yisheng, a great bridge-builder (with a Ph.D. from Cornell) who had been his professor at Jiaotong University. I was glad they ran into each other; their chat kept Tung-ping on the beach with us, instead of in the house reading. Still, I was mad at Tung-ping. I'd tell this to people I knew. "You know what? Tung-ping brought a whole case of books with him. Isn't that something?" Tung-ping pleaded, "Chieh-ching, I just couldn't find that big piece of time to read while I was in Beijing. I have to prepare for research projects and do some editing work for a translated article too. Why don't you go out with the kids? I can see people are very fond of them." So, I went out with Weiming and Jibin.

The setting was beautiful and soothing. We took our meals at a cafeteria, sitting on the veranda where it was cool. We could see the blue ocean with seagulls flying low above the beach.

Every day there was a fully dressed elderly lady sitting under a parasol, watching her grandson play. I noticed that she had on a wristwatch, so I would politely ask her for the time. When we got back to our bungalow one day, Tung-ping berated me. "Chieh-ching, why do you keep bothering Mrs. Lu?"

"What are you talking about? How could I bother Mrs. Lu? I don't even know her."

"I just don't know what to say. You have been asking this lady for the time for the past few days."

Lu Xun was a great Chinese writer and social critic of the 1920s and 1930s. He was known as the Gorky of China.

"So I have! Why didn't you let me know her identity? You could have told me who she was the first time I talked to her."

Tung-ping had to stop me, "All right. It's my fault. OK?"

After that, I never asked Mrs. Lu for the time anymore. It turned out that the little boy was indeed her grandson. Years later, when he went to Japan to study, he met a girl from Taiwan, they fell in love and got married. It was the first time someone from the mainland married a girl from Taiwan. Their wedding made front-page news abroad. The young couple settled down in Taiwan.

Also at Beidaihe that summer was Dr. Qian Xuesen. He was considered the father of China's space program. Qian had gone to the United States in 1935. He had studied and worked at MIT and CalTech. He studied under Theodore Von Karman, a world famous aerodynamicist at CalTech. Qian helped to lay down the foundations of the Jet Propulsion Lab. His work in the field of fluid dynamics helped make possible America's entry into the space age. But during the years of McCarthyism, Qian was accused of being a Communist. Although Qian denied it vehemently, he was locked in a cell for two weeks and then placed under house arrest for five years. Qian was deported in 1955.

After Qian returned to China, he was received by Chairman Mao, Premier Zhou Enlai and other high officials. Qian helped build up China's space program. He joined the Communist Party in 1959.

Qian had come to the beach with his wife Jiang Ying and their two children, a boy and a girl. Both kids were Young Pioneers and thus wore red scarves around their necks. Jiang Ying was about forty. She was teaching at the Central Conservatory of Music in Beijing.

One day we were on a stroll with Dr. Qian and his family, enjoying the bright blue sky and rippling sea, white sails visible in the distance. Suddenly Dr. Qian burst into poetry. It was "Beidaihe," a poem by none other than Chairman Mao.

BEI DAI HE

The northern land is battled in a torrential rain,
White breakers leap to the sky.
No fishing boats off the Emperor's Isle,
Are seen on the boundless main.
Where are they floating?

Nearly two thousand years ago,
Wielding his whip, the Emperor Wu of Wei
Rode eastward to Mount Stone; His poems still remain.
Today the autumn wind is blowing as bleak as then,
But the world has changed its reign.

The recitation finished. Qian praised Mao Zedong high to the sky, saying Mao was a great leader and calling his poetry graceful and profound.

On our way back, Tung-ping asked Qian if he was planning to go to the Yu Opera that evening. "Sure we're going. How can one miss such a nice opera. How about you?" I broke in before Tung-ping had time to reply, "I can't go because I have to take care of the children. And Tung-ping brought a case full of books with him. I wonder if he has the time…" Tung-ping was afraid I would start nagging about his books. He quickly said, "I'll go."

That evening, Tung-ping and the Qians watched Yu opera, a style of opera from Henan province. When Tung-ping came back, he was in a joyous mood. He told me how beautifully the actress sang. He said she gave a superb performance.

To please Tung-ping, I started to develop an interest in Chinese operas. Being so used to Hollywood movies with their handsome gentlemen and beautiful ladies, I couldn't take didactic Chinese films and operas when I first returned to China. But Tung-ping's enthusiasm for operas helped bring me around. Nowadays, even foreign students are learning how to sing Beijing opera. Well, the world is definitely round!

12

A Crouching Tiger
Blocking the Way

————————— ⌇ —————————

IN THE SPRING OF 1962, Guangzhou was all dressed in green: green grass and trees pushing out green leaves. Magnolia, jasmine, plum and almond blossoms scented the air. One could tell spring had come to this city, once known as Canton, by these captivating fragrances. The atmosphere seemed serene.

Tung-ping had gone down to Guangzhou for the National Science and Technology Conference. Presiding over the conference was Marshal Nie Rongzhen. (This was the man who had chosen Tung-ping for 703.) The Marshal met with the scientists and listened to their complaints. As intellectuals, they were uncertain about their status in the shifting political climate of the country.

Nie rose to address the gathering, saying: "Someone asked me how to comprehend the word 'bourgeoisie' since whenever intellectuals are mentioned, they… are called bourgeois intellectuals. Even their descendants are discriminated against. I have never heard anyone consider them as proletarian intellectuals. This is a problem we need to tackle."

Nie said he had gone straight to the top and asked for clarification from Premier Zhou Enlai. He relayed the Premier's response: "Intellectuals are intellectuals. They're people's intellectuals." That was just what the delegates wanted to know. Tung-ping and other scientists were greatly cheered, and vowed then and there to redouble their efforts.

Premier Zhou turned out to be the headline speaker at the conference. His topic: "On the Intellectuals Issue." Tung-ping listened attentively as the Premier addressed the very issue bothering him back at Institute 703: non-professionals leading the professionals in the technical sphere.

"There should be limits to non-professionals leading professionals," Zhou said. "We used to say non-professionals could lead professionals, in the sense of exercising leadership. We mean leadership in politics, in ideology and in organization." Premier Zhou's words were like a spring shower to intellectuals across the country who felt their lifelong pursuits drying up under political heat.

There was more encouragement from Vice Premier Chen Yi, talking about plays and operas. He said calling intellectuals "bourgeois" after twelve years of ideological remolding was "not in accordance with reality." He went on to say that the country should "take the cap of bourgeoisie off the intellectuals and crown them with the cap of working people. And so today, I am taking the cap of bourgeoisie off of you." His words were greeted with a long and loud round of clapping.

But some top leaders didn't agree with their message. One of these people was Mao's wife Jiang Qing. Several years later during the Cultural Revolution, she labeled this meeting a "black conference," accusing Zhou and Chen of having kowtowed to bourgeois intellectuals when calling for the removal of their "bourgeois caps."

Nonetheless, Tung-ping was encouraged by the speeches. When he returned to Beijing, he threw himself into his work. He was determined to train his inexperienced staff in the rigors of science. The result was a long article, "Methodology in Doing Research Work," which outlined the scientific procedures he had absorbed in his years overseas. These included: identifying the specific purpose of the research, data gathering, data analysis, failure analysis, investigation, and the correct way of writing a technical paper. This article was highly praised by Dr. Qian Xuesen who asked Tung-ping to submit this article for publication in the internal magazine of the Fifth Academy.

But Tung-ping's work was hardly carried out in an atmosphere that was conducive to research. Good science normally requires not only an inquisitive mind, but also a setting where hypotheses can be tested with experiments. Other points of view and previous research by scientists in other countries are indispensable. Commissar Huang of Institute 703 however was of the precise opposite view: question nothing, follow blindly, and ignore anything from capitalist countries. He criticized "Methodology in Doing Research Work" and branded it a poisonous weed.

Sir Isaac Newton once remarked that the reason he could see new ideas was because he was standing on the shoulders of giants — those scientists who had preceded him. Tung-ping agreed with this, saying that the knowledge passed down through the ages is the common wealth of all humankind, no matter what country it originated in.

Tung-ping required all technical personnel to master a foreign language. He said foreign languages were essential to understanding developments in the scientific world. Many already knew Russian, having studied in the USSR. But Tung-ping stressed that English was the language to learn, since any scientific development of importance would be published in it. He arranged to have English classes at Institute 703 and even gave the first lesson. It seems a common thing now, but this was in the early 1960s, when China and the U.S. were in a cold war and China regarded the U.S. as an imperialist country, the number one potential enemy. It was a risky decision for Tung-ping to make.

Tung-ping was nothing if not methodical. "Do you know what research is?" he once asked. "In English, the root of that word is 'search', meaning to seek, while the prefix 're' means repetition. So research means repeatedly seeking... Only by mastering all the aspects of a difficult problem can we get at its principal contradiction and thus solve it... We must be meticulous in every detail."

Being strict wasn't just good science; it was also safer and prevented costly mistakes. One winter Saturday in 1961, Tung-ping went to the office after dinner as was his custom. When he walked past a lab, he found a newcomer there. He asked the young man if he had gotten used to the harsh Beijing winter yet. While talking, Tung-ping looked around the lab and was appalled to find it a mess. "This doesn't look like a lab at all!" he said. "Tomorrow is Sunday. Let's come and give it a good cleaning. How's that?"

The young man didn't dare ignore Tung-ping's "invitation." He got up early and was in the lab around six, but only to find someone had come in earlier; Tung-ping was already there cleaning up. Both of them pitched in on the windows and floors. Tung-ping then told the young engineer where to place each piece of equipment. "This is not only about looking nice and neat," he told the young man. "Putting certain equipment in the right place might prevent accidents from happening. And with better organization," Tung-ping continued, "you'll save time." By the time they had finished moving the heavy equipment and putting hundreds of pounds of metal ingots in order, their clothing was soaked through with sweat.

Tung-ping insisted that every experiment or test have a detailed formal report. Huang dismissed this as "bourgeois stuff," but Tung-ping insisted on this system. He read each report personally and added his comments. If there were some mistakes, he would ask the engineer to redo it. If there were still errors, he would work together with the engineer and coach him step by step until the report met the standards. A senior engineer remembers how "Director Yao was so particular, he would correct not only technical mistakes but wrongly written Chinese characters and punctuation as well. I still keep one of my reports by him."

Sometimes, this kind of guidance wasn't enough. Once somebody was using a hand fan while measuring something on the $\frac{1}{100,000}$ of a gram scale. Another time, an engineer mistakenly burned a pile of research papers when moving to a different lab. His colleagues chided him, "One match burned up our research record of two years."

In order to raise the performance level of the technical personnel more quickly, in early 1962 Tung-ping organized "a work-style display" for the main conference room at Institute 703. More than 770 charts, data and reports were put together to illustrate how important one's working style was to the quality of research. Most of these were exemplary models that summarized good research techniques. However, what caught everyone's attention was a display of the 50 most common mistakes

Tung-ping addressing the staff members at Institute 703 in 1963

113

side-by-side with their corrected versions.

Another senior engineer told me that his graph was on display because he hadn't done the curves right. I asked, "Didn't you blame Comrade Tung-ping for making you lose face?"

"As far as I know, none of us felt this was a loss of face. We all knew Director Yao did this to help us. In my case, he not only pointed out my mistakes, but also taught me the correct way to do it. The two graphs were put side by side, so people would avoid making the same mistakes again. Besides, my name wasn't on it. Only the model ones showed the engineer's name."

The work-style display was a great success. A lot of people from other research institutes came to visit it.

As if Chinese politics and the Institute's own internal politics were not enough to worry about, Tung-ping's work was profoundly affected by the split between China and the Soviet Union in 1960. That year Nikita Khrushchev tore up the joint contracts and called home the Soviet scientists and engineers. This rift was a severe setback. After all, the USSR had already put a satellite, Sputnik, in orbit in 1958 and was beginning its manned space program. Furthermore, the development of the rocket materials in China had started under a licensed copy production of the Soviets' P-2 missile. (This kind of missile was in fact Germany's V-2 missile which had been copied and improved by the Soviets.) Hence, the loss of the Soviet scientists — along with their formulas and blueprints — was devastating.

Tung-ping's group realized that they now had to make one crucial material that was no longer available. The Soviet Union used a special material, a high-temperature brazing alloy, to make different types of metals stick together in the rocket's combustion chamber. It was essential because the temperature in the engine could be as high as 3,000 C or more, making welding out of the question. (Also, the complicated structure of a combustion engine makes it impossible to position a welding gun.)★

In 1958, the Soviet Union had signed a contract to help China with brazing. Even at that time, the Soviets kept the manufacturing method a secret. They told the engineers at Institute 703 that they could buy it through the Soviet Embassy. In other words, the Soviet Union preferred not to do a technology transfer. But when the Soviet Union broke her technical contracts, the Chinese couldn't buy this kind of alloy anymore. Tung-ping looked at the situation as a challenge to his country. He personally directed the effort to produce a high-temperature brazing alloy in China.

They had nothing to go on, except some commercial marks on the shipping boxes. Everyone viewed this challenge as a *"lan lu hu"* (crouching tiger blocking the way). But this didn't discourage Tung-ping. He and his colleagues spent months analyzing the material's contents, with repeated tests. Finally, they discovered the contents of the alloy! But that was just the beginning — how much of each ingredient was needed? And what was the precise temperature required?

Tung-ping quickly realized that Institute 703 by itself didn't have the resources to handle the high-temperature brazing alloy project. So with Marshal Nie's consent, he sent engineers to work with different research institutes and factories across the country. He followed every step of the process closely. He worked extremely hard, making prompt decisions, discarding one choice, accepting another, or beefing up a third.

Finally, the high-temperature brazing alloy was ready. The quality was excellent, it performed superbly. This achievement

---

★ During brazing, an alloy is placed between two metals. The melting point of the brazing alloy must be lower than that of the metals. The brazing alloy then fuses to the metals, and a complete structure is realized after cooling — much like making a grilled cheese sandwich.

was remarkable for a country that could not produce high-grade steel for consumer products.

But then the quality of the alloy began to suffer. Tung-ping suspected that there was something wrong with the purity of a certain ingredient. His suggestion was to buy some of the ingredient from overseas and make a comparison study. Quite logical, right? But the suggestion was rejected. Commissar Huang said it revealed Tung-ping's slavish attachment to all things foreign. Furthermore, the high-temperature brazing alloy project was singled out as a "typical bourgeois way of doing scientific research." So a technical problem of production now became a political one.

Tung-ping was persistent. He ignored the criticism and led a group to the factory in Shanghai where the alloy was being produced. They inspected the manufacturing process and soon discovered that the factory had far too many weak links to ensure purity of the substance. Tung-ping talked over the problem with the Shanghai metallurgists. They updated their facilities and carried out more than 700 brazing tests on simulated pieces, followed by explosives tests. Finally they succeeded. They also mastered the technique of vacuum brazing.

The tempest over his "bourgeois" methods, however, was a portent. While Tung-ping was in

Toasting a success of Institute 703

Shanghai, the criticism of him evolved from the "exposure" stage to determining the political nature of his mistakes. He was called back to Institute 703 by Commissar Huang for his "bourgeois way of doing research." Huang even asked the engineers involved with this project to make a clear break with Tung-ping on that basis. For Tung-ping, however, all that mattered was that the high-temperature brazing alloy had succeeded.

When I heard of this, I couldn't help but think of General Yue Fei (1103–1142) and his famous poem "The River All Red." The poem has been passed down from generation to generation and I had read it when I was in primary school.

During the Song dynasty (960–1279), the Jin people oc-cupied the north part of China and captured the Chinese emperor. A lot of officials escaped south to Hangzhou, includ-ing a royal family member who became the new emperor. A young man named Yue Fei decided to join the army. Shortly before his departure, Yue's mother tattooed "*jing zhong bao guo*" with a hot needle on his back. It meant to dedicate one's life to one's country whole-heartedly. Yue eventually rose to com-mander and his army won one victory after another. Even the Jin people praised Yue for his bravery, saying "it is easier to remove a mountain than to remove General Yue's army."

To reverse the situation, the Jins decided to bribe Prime Min-ister Qin Hui. On the verge of defeating the invaders, twelve times General Yue was ordered to retreat by the new emperor and his prime minister — who thought only of keeping his throne and what little piece of territory he could hold onto instead of the greater opportunity to dispose of the aggressors. Finally, Yue ordered his army back. Not long after Yue returned, he was put to death. (Years later, both the Jins in the north and the Chinese in the south were conquered by the Mongols who established the Yuan dynasty from 1280 to 1368.)

Eight hundred years later, while Tung-ping was winning the

battle in identifying the high-temperature brazing alloy, he was called back to Beijing from Shanghai by Commissar Huang to be criticized for his "bourgeois way" in doing scientific work. It seemed to me history was repeating itself.

In 1978 during the National Science and Technology Conference, Institute 703 and that Shanghai unit would be awarded "the outstanding development and achievement reward" for their work on this high-temperature brazing alloy.

When people informed me about it, a lump rose in my throat. When Tung-ping and his colleagues started their work, they had little to go on. Today this high-temperature brazing alloy and its technology are used in both medium-range and long-range missiles. And from this pioneering effort, China was able to develop a series of magnesium-based brazing alloys. (The making of these alloys is still regarded as top-secret by the Russians.) This is one of the reasons why people today regard Tung-ping as the pathfinder and founder of China's space materials technology.

13

Helsinki, Finland

———————————————

By 1963, food became more plentiful and I had regained my health. Our two daughters, Weiming and Jibin, were now five and three years old. I was still hoping to give Tung-ping a son, but it was time for me to go back to work. I didn't relish the idea of returning to the University of Science and Technology because I didn't like to teach technical English. Tung-ping helped me to land a position at a new institute, a branch school of the Institute of Foreign Affairs. But since it was also in the northwestern suburbs of Beijing, and our home was in the far south suburbs, it meant another long bus ride. Another job that would keep me away from my family for days at a time.

The first day I reported to work, I noticed a creek running in front of the institute. The water was so clear that you could see the small pebbles on the bottom. As I walked through the front gate, tall trees guided me toward the main building. It was a pleasant six-story red brick building. Here students took general courses in Chinese and political science. But they spent more time studying major foreign languages: English, Japanese, French, German, Spanish and Russian.

Each class had about fifteen students with one lecturer and one assistant, both of whom stayed with the class till graduation. My first class had four girls and eleven boys, all of whom came from one of the five "red" categories: workers, poor and lower-middle (class) peasants, revolutionary army men, revolutionary cadres and revolutionary martyrs. All of these groups were politically favored. And every one of these students was a member of the Communist Youth League.

Also on campus were the ideology coaches — Communist Party members assigned to keep the ideology of the students abiding by the Party's principles. The ideology coach of our class was Comrade Gu, a Cantonese from a poor peasant family. He had graduated from the People's University in Beijing. He kept tabs on the students' ideological outlook by reading their "thought reports," talking with them and counseling them. He was quite open and above-board, and most important for my sake, he didn't discriminate against us non-Party members.

The president of the institute was a veteran cadre from the northeast of China who wore a Mao cap all year round. He would have a private talk with each new teacher. He told me that the institute was run on the same principles as the *Kang-Da*, which was the academy in Yan'an for military and political leaders. Those principles, as set down by Mao himself, were: firm and correct political orientation, plain living and working style, and flexible strategy and tactics. I thought it was odd to run a foreign languages institute with *Kang-Da*'s principles. But I knew I'd better not tell him my opinion.

Everyone, from the president to the janitor, lived in one of the dorm buildings on campus. I lived in Building 6, which had forty rooms on each floor. Two of the rooms had been converted into kitchens, but many of us parked our small stoves in the hallway along with a pile of "beehive" coal cakes. (These were made of coal powder and mud in the shape of a beehive, with twelve holes in each.)

I lived in room 204 which faced west. People usually disliked rooms facing west because they were hot in summer and cold in winter. But I did not mind. There were only two stories on our wing, so nobody would disturb me from above. Well that was what I thought anyway. One morning at dawn, I was awakened by "cock-a-doodle-do, cock-a-doodle-do." I soon found out that some people were taking the blood from roosters and injecting it into themselves. Their reasoning? Since each rooster usually has ten or more hens, they figured roosters must be very strong. I thought this was ridiculous — and when I told Tung-ping, he agreed with me.

Being away from Tung-ping was unbearable for me. As is stated in the Bible, Eve was made from a rib of Adam. That's the way I felt too. It had been more than six years since we had married, but every time I saw him, I felt the same soul-stirring. I knew he loved me too. He was always a kind and thoughtful husband — and always a good Communist through and through. Many times he couldn't help but combine both of these drives in his actions.

One Spring Festival, he gave me a set of *Selected Works of Mao Zedong*. Many people would not think this a romantic gift. But I knew he was sincere in his desire to raise my political consciousness. He had once mentioned to me that we would be even closer if I could become a Party member. I did not respond because I only loved him, I did not care for politics. To please him, I began to read Mao's work in earnest.

Not long after I started at the school, I had to return home to get another quilt as the weather had become chilly. On the way back, I had to change buses several times. At one stop, I waited for half an hour while holding the quilt. When I got back to the school, I was completely exhausted and started to bleed. The school clinic doctor examined me and said it looked like I'd had a miscarriage. I was taken to a hospital. I was devastated. I'd known I was pregnant, probably about two months. Perhaps this had been the son I had longed to give to Tung-ping, though it was too early in the pregnancy to know. After a day in the hospital, I returned to our home. Tung-ping was not home; he'd gone to Finland for an I.I.W. (International Institute of Welding) conference.

One day during my recuperation in bed at home, I heard someone at the door with a key. "Who is it?" I called. A familiar voice answered, "Me!"

I jumped down from the bed and hurried to open the door in my bare feet.

"Oh! It is you! Why didn't you tell me beforehand? You wanted to surprise me? Ooo! I am so happy!" We sat down and I told him about the miscarriage.

"Darling, I am glad you are well. To me, that is the most important thing." He put his arms around me. "Don't worry about anything else," he said. Seeing Tung-ping again and hearing these words moved me so. I nestled my face into his chest, his body warming my heart.

Several days later, I was ready to resume my teaching. In order to be punctual at school at 8 a.m., I got up a little after 5 a.m. to brush my teeth, wash my face and eat breakfast before hurrying to the bus stop. As usual, Tung-ping got up at the same time to see me off to the bus stop. In the dawn light, I could see the black shadows around his eyes. "Don't walk with me to the bus stop, Tung-ping. You have just returned from a long trip and haven't yet readjusted to the time lag. Please go back home and rest."

He sighed. "I'm too busy with my work. There's so little time for us to be together. Let's cherish these hard-won bits of time!"

Tung-ping felt truly sorry for his frequent absences from home on business. To make up for them, he would sometimes buy *Fuliji* roasted chickens or *Tianjin* dumplings on his way home. One time he was in Shanghai for more than forty days on business. When he returned, he brought me a long woolen scarf with red and black stripes. Even though I could get the same kind of scarf in Beijing and didn't like red and black, I didn't tell him that. I just thanked him. He was in his study when I put the scarf on and called out, "Tung-ping, come here quick!" He came out and asked anxiously, "What's the matter, don't you feel well?"

"I am OK, but don't you think I look different today?" He shook his head and said, "I don't see any differences. Are you sure you are OK?" Then I pointed to the new scarf and asked him, "How do I look?" He seemed relieved and told me that I looked great in anything then hurried back to his study.

Tung-ping's trip to Finland had been interesting. He had headed the Chinese delegation to that symposium on welding, the first time since 1949 that a Chinese group had attended an international conference in this field. For Tung-ping, it had been a reunion of sorts. He saw many of his old friends from his days in England and Germany. They talked shop — welding fatigue was his big interest then — and relived old memories. He made new friends as well, impressing many with his command of English and German.

A former colleague was curious: "You worked so long in our country, why would you forsake such a good research environment and return to China?"

Tung-ping didn't hesitate a moment in his answer. "I'm Chinese," he said. "I studied abroad with the intention of serving my motherland. Though China is now relatively backward, I am sure it will be strong one day."

However there were some awkward moments, as might be

expected when a Chinese Communist was mingling with Westerners. At one point, Tung-ping asked for some conference documents. A member of the organizing committee made some smart-aleck comments, along the lines that Tung-ping probably wouldn't be able to understand them, and certainly a place like China could do nothing with them. Tung-ping remained calm.

Tung-ping and three other scientists at the I.I.W. conference in Helsinki

"Your comments," Tung-ping answered patiently and with much better English than this fellow had used, "might have been prompted by the propaganda about China in your news media. The China I know is quite different. I've seen it myself. Seeing is believing, right?" The man's demeanor softened, and he handed Tung-ping the papers with a smile.

On the flight home, Tung-ping told his colleagues, "Foreigners look down upon us out of historical prejudice. We must work with all our might to rebuff them, with facts."

Back in Beijing, Tung-ping was energized by the experience. In a written report, he proposed that Chinese scientists keep in contact with foreign scientists, and urged that they be allowed to attend other international conferences to broaden their views, to follow world trends. He didn't receive any reply. But fifteen years later China became a member of the I.I.W.

14

Our Little Buddha

I<small>N</small> 1964 I was about to give birth to our third child. How I longed for a son. I continually pestered Tung-ping — did he think the new baby would be a boy or a girl?

"Oh, you'll always get what you wish," he'd say.

I thought there might be something to what he said. After all, I had prayed to God for a husband after my heart. Didn't I get one?

The famine years were over. Food was plentiful, and I ate my fill. Then it came time to deliver. I knew the baby was big, but I was stunned to hear the weight: nine pounds, six ounces.

"It's a girl," the nurse told me. My face fell.

"Why aren't you happy?" the nurse said. "Your husband didn't want to have a baby girl?"

"No, it's me who wanted to have a son."

Tung-ping came in, smiling, his eyes danced with joy and his hands held a bouquet of roses.

"What rotten luck," I said lamely from the hospital bed. "Another daughter."

Tung-ping would have none of it. He was beaming. "Remember the saying, 'A daughter is worth one thousand pounds of gold!' Now we have three thousand pounds of gold in the family. And I've seen our newborn! She weighs more than any of the babies born here! Everyone was wondering, how could a mother with such a slim figure give birth to such a big baby?"

I didn't reply. Still smiling, Tung-ping boasted, "Whenever groups of foreign visitors come through, the nurse always holds our daughter up, to show how healthy Chinese babies are. So you see how lovely our darling baby is?"

He then asked me, "How about naming her Chenfang? She's as lovely as a morning flower."

"Lovely? bah!" I said. "It's only because she's as fat as a laughing Buddha that they show her to the visitors."

Tung-ping looked at me, then paused to consider.

"Well, why don't we nickname her Little Buddha?" From then on, Chenfang was known as Little Buddha.

When I was in the hospital, Tung-ping called up our friend Teacher Gao to tell her the good news.

"You have another baby? A boy or a girl?"

"A beautiful baby girl!" Tung-ping answered proudly.

"Another girl?" After the words came out she tried to amend what she had just said. "Girls are nice too. They are closer to their parents."

Tung-ping agreed with her a hundred percent.

We had talked it over beforehand. And Tung-ping had suggested that this baby be our last. I agreed. But now that another daughter was born, I wanted to change our decision. I longed for a son. A son like Tung-ping in every respect, someone who would remind me of him when he was away on trips.

But Tung-ping, noting how slowly I was recovering from the delivery, felt I was not strong enough for another pregnancy. We stuck to our decision; Tung-ping had a vasectomy. I thank God for letting me have such a loving and devoted husband. This was before China focused on population control, long before today's one-child-per-family policy. And not many men would volunteer to have a vasectomy.

Tung-ping didn't feel bound by Chinese feudal tradition which considered it a catastrophe if there were no sons to carry on the family name. Like other parents, he naturally wanted to have both sons and daughters. Besides thinking of my poor health, he felt another child would make claims on his time, which he needed to devote to his work.

"Since we already have three lovely daughters, we need no more children," he said.

After Little Buddha's birth, I took the fifty-six days of maternity leave allowed, then returned to my job at the branch school of the Institute of Foreign Affairs. I decided to bring the baby over with me and hired a second *ayi*. The *ayi* and the baby stayed in Room 205 across the hall.

We still had our other *ayi* at our home in the southern suburbs, looking after the older girls. And so our family broke into two. But it proved so inconvenient that, when Little Buddha reached six months of age, I brought her back to live with her father and sisters. I was able to return home only on weekends, and sometimes a few nights during the week as well, when movies were shown at the school.

One Sunday, which was our *ayi*'s day off, I placed Little Buddha in our double bed. Tung-ping was reading a newspaper in a chair by the window and answering my questions with "Yes," "No," "Really?" — strictly one word conversation.

It went on like this:

"Tung-ping, are you reading *People's Daily*?"

"Yes."

"Did you bring the *Reference News* with you?"

"No."

"Do you know the non-Party members are allowed to subscribe to the *Reference News* now?"

"Really?"

Tung-ping answered my questions without lifting his eyes from the papers. I said to myself: "I'll make him turn around and look at me."

Just about that time, I noticed that Little Buddha was "walking." She was sliding her little tummy up and down to move from one end of the bed to the other end.

"Tung-ping, come here, look at Little Buddha. She's only seven months old and she can 'walk' by sliding her little tummy already. Isn't she cute?"

Tung-ping put down the papers, walked over, his right arm around my waist. He stood together with me, watching Little Buddha "walking." A bright smile lit up his face. He said with a merry voice, "*Ah ya!* Many a mother thinks her daughter is the prettiest baby on earth! Well, now, how about us taking a picture of the baby and sending it to the papers?"

When Little Buddha was one year old she could really walk. But her head was big and she had a high forehead. One got the impression that her forehead would reach her destination before she would. Her sisters would tease her by saying that she didn't need an umbrella during a rainy day because her big forehead would prevent the rain from dropping on her face.

Little Buddha would come to me complaining, "*Mama*, Wei Ming and Jibin are making fun of my forehead."

"No, sweetie, they are just teasing you. All of us think our Little Buddha is the cutest little girl."

Whenever an engineer or a staff member of Institute 703 got married, they would invite Tung-ping to the wedding ceremony and ask him to preside. He always took Little Buddha along to these events. "Where are you going, Little Buddha?" her sisters asked. "I go wedding *Baba!*" she'd squeal proudly, and we'd all burst out laughing.

Each time I returned home, Little Buddha would ask me to go play with her outside. Hide-and-seek was her favorite game. Behind our building in the southern suburbs of Beijing was a cozy backyard with pine trees, cypresses, hibiscus plants and grapevines. Under the canopy of two large trees were parked a few stone tables with drum-shaped stools. It was a perfect place for kids to play.

The children of the family on the second floor often joined us in the backyard. Sometimes the parents also came down in the evenings. The father of the family, Comrade Yang, was a Long March cadre. This was the 6,000-mile journey on foot by Chinese Communist forces that began in October 1934 from their base in the south of China. They fought their way out of encirclement by Chiang Kai-shek's Kuomintang army, "marched" through eleven provinces, and finally arrived in northwest China in 1935. They settled into Yan'an, a busy town in a poor area of Shaanxi province where some Communists had already established a base.

From the sanctuary of the mountains around Yan'an, Mao led the Communist army fight against Chiang's army. Finally, the Communists had control of the mainland; they chased Chiang to Taiwan. On October 1, 1949, Mao proclaimed the founding of the People's Republic of China on the rostrum of Tiananmen Square.

Comrade Yang, our neighbor above, had come from a poor peasant family. He had tended pigs for a landlord when he was a little boy. When the Red Army was stationed in his village, he joined the Communist army and became part of the "Long March." Comrade Yang told us he learned how to read and write while he was in the army.

Mrs. Yang was a middle-aged woman, a bit on the plump

side. Her skin was still smooth, her eyes clear, and her hair thick and black. One could see that she was a beauty in her younger days. She doted on Little Buddha, saying she was a lovely child. "She was born in the new society into such a happy family. I'm sure luck will follow your darling baby all her life," my neighbor said.

I thanked her for the kind words and said a quiet prayer that our "*baobei luohan*" (Precious Little Buddha) would grow up as lovely as a morning flower and would never suffer, as so many had in the old society, or as I had during the war.

We Chinese people are like people everywhere: anything forbidden becomes all the more attractive. This certainly includes art. *People's Daily* frequently carried articles criticizing "questionable" novels, plays and movies. Many movies once considered good were now tagged as "poisonous weeds." One such movie was "Sisters on Stage." It depicted the lives of two actresses on and off stage. The movie was criticized for not making class struggle its central theme.

Our school had a projector and would show movies in its auditorium. During warm weather, people would bring their small folding stools outdoors to watch movies on the sportsground. The movies weren't intended as entertainment but as political enlightenment. Homework would be postponed, and criticism sessions would be held the next day to discuss how reactionary the movie was.

I myself would often skip the flicks and catch a bus for home to be with my husband and children. In the dark nobody would notice that I wasn't at the movies, I figured. I could fake my way through the criticism session the next day as the newspaper was full of articles about the film; I'd just parrot these. Little did we know then that that was the prelude

131

of "the Great Proletarian Cultural Revolution."

Once, it was my turn to hand out the movie tickets. I knocked on the dorm door of Teacher Wang of the English Department and told him what the movie was that night: "Early Spring in February." A sad love story.

"That's great!" he exclaimed, forgetting for a moment that the movie had been roundly criticized in the papers for its sympathetic portrayal of the bourgeois class.

"What?" I was surprised at his reaction. Wang realized it had been a slip of the tongue. He scrambled to cover his mistake.

"It's good," he stammered, "to be able to see movies for criticism, and read critical articles in newspapers, and thus raise one's political consciousness."

I handed Wang the ticket without saying a word. What I was thinking was this: "You don't have to be frightened, comrade. I would not for the world be an informer and tell the Party Secretary of your words."

While I sneaked back home as frequently as possible, sometimes Tung-ping found himself up in our school's neighborhood on business. He stopped by my room one day, when Little Buddha was with me. My neighbor down the hall, Teacher Han, saw him for the first time. She called to the others, "Teacher Peng's husband is here. Come and have a look at him! He's so young, so tall and so handsome!"

Teacher Han's clucking attracted more of my colleagues, who peeked in the door.

"They are coming to see the handsome husband of mine," I teased.

Tung-ping was at ease. He said we'd been married long enough that others' staring shouldn't bother us. "We'd better open our door wide and invite them in," he proposed. And so we did. My friends had a nice chat with my husband, and I admit I was quite proud to show off both my husband and my daughter.

Teacher Han lived in 208 with her daughter, a middle-school student. (Her husband was working in their hometown of Tianjin.) Teacher Han had graduated as a top student from the English Department of Furen University, a Catholic school, and was an orderly, logical teacher. One day she told us that one of her schoolmates at Furen was Wang Guangmei, who later became the wife of Liu Shaoqi, the Chairman of our government. Han had just started telling us what an elegant, graceful woman Wang Guangmei was when another teacher interrupted with big news: tofu was available at the grocery. "Let's hurry. It's the end of the month. I don't want to waste my tofu coupon!", someone else added.

Han knew the real reason for the interruption: nobody dared to talk about the wife of the Chairman of our country. At that time, none of us could foresee that Wang Guangmei and her husband would both become prisoners a year later.

Next door to me in Room 206 lived Teacher Woo. She would always stop by to drop off the newspaper we both subscribed to. She shared her room with her son and daughter. She was tall and fair-skinned and some people thought she looked quite Caucasian. (During those times, she of course was quick to deny she had any foreign blood.) Her husband also lived on the far side of town, and so she too took the bus to be with her spouse whenever she could.

On the other side of my room in 202 lived Teacher Lee. He was a portly ethnic Korean with narrow slant eyes and a round jovial face. Lee had been educated in American schools — primary, middle and college. Naturally his English was superb. Lee had a lively teaching style; we could often hear laughter burst out in his classroom.

Across the hall in Room 201, facing east, lived Teacher Ming and his wife. Mrs. Ming taught political science at a middle school. They were a quiet couple. We only saw them when they cooked outside of their room. When the Cultural Revolution started, Ming suddenly became very active. He wrote lots of big-character posters criticizing the Deputy Dean of the English Department. He wrote beautiful Chinese characters in flowery handwriting and had a knack for quoting Chairman Mao. Ming's big-character posters were a sensation — but only briefly. Somehow it came out that he was of bourgeois origin. Furthermore his brother had been branded a rightist in 1957.

It was not long before the students ransacked his room. One night, I heard a student striking Ming's desk and shouting at him, "You are a rogue full of indecent ideas yourself! How impudent you are to write posters against other people." I held my breath in my room. I wondered how Ming could be considered such a "rogue full of indecent ideas" when he was so obviously in love with his wife. I got the answer later: Ming had been an interpreter during the Korean War. He had to leave for the front not long after his wedding. Using that same flowery handwriting, he had written sentimental love letters to his bride.

The students who ransacked his room had gotten hold of these letters. They thought they were indecent. In one he had written: "The bright moon high up in the sky made me miss you, my dearest one, all the more. Are you doing the same helpless sighing at the moon too?"

That was too much for one student: "Damn it! How shameful you were! People go to the front with one conviction: to annihilate the enemy. But you thought of nothing but your blessed wife. What rubbish, lines like 'Would that my love could share this beautiful moonlight, though thousands of miles apart.'"

Another student said, "Let's not waste our time! Take all the letters away."

We teachers were afraid that the students might ransack our rooms as well. But they did not go on ransacking that night. I suspect that they went back to their dorms to read Ming's love letters.

Next door to the Mings was Teacher Yuan in Room 203. She was the best cook among us. She showed me some cooking secrets that never failed to impress Tung-ping, such as chicken with ginger and soybean sauce. A native of Taiwan, she was a petite woman with olive skin. I asked her one day how she could keep such a nice figure after giving birth to two children; my waist would expand an inch or two after each childbirth. Yuan told me that her mother-in-law was very strict. She made her bind her waist after each childbirth.

"What an odd practice. Where is she from?" I asked her.

"Japan."

"No wonder."

Teacher Yuan told me that her Japanese mother-in-law was a competent homemaker and she had learned a lot from her, including sewing and knitting. I asked Yuan to teach me how to knit, since I wanted to make a sweater for Tung-ping. I would knit all my love into that sweater, a gift for his 46th birthday.

15

A White-Beard Project

―――――――――――――――― ◈ ――――――――――――――――

Tung-ping spent his days like few other Chinese in the early 1960s. In ways that even I did not know. As the Director of a top-secret institute, his primary concern was not cooking, knitting, or movie tickets. There was much more important work to be done.

When Tung-ping first started at Institute 703, he had immediately seen the need for certain pieces of equipment available only from abroad. These purchases cost tens of thousands of U.S. dollars and were approved by the institute's original commissar. But when Commissar Huang came to work in 1960, he promptly criticized the purchases as extravagant. Moreover, he said, they evidenced a craving for foreign things. Surely the institute could make do with less sophisticated instruments. To illustrate his point, Huang would raise the cup in his hand and say, "I've used this old cup for years and it still serves me well. No need for a new cup."

As a result of the commissar's objections, some of the equipment Tung-ping had carefully ordered was sold off to other *danwei* at low prices. The rest was left outside, exposed to the elements, reduced to expensive junk.

Tung-ping kept plugging away. He stressed the value of extensive research before attempting to build anything. He pointed out that in the United States and the Soviet Union — where space programs were well on their way — research and development took longer than design and production. It was safer, better, and in the long run much less costly because it avoided expensive mistakes. But Huang called that approach a waste of time and money. He said it was a bourgeois approach to research. So Tung-ping's suggestions for researching certain space materials were brushed aside.

Soon after, the design of a new missile changed. Commissar Huang called a meeting of engineers. He took out a piece of paper from his pocket and read a list of materials that were now deemed necessary. The engineers listened, then looked at each other, stifling smiles. That man was reading a list of the very materials Tung-ping had wanted to concentrate on. One of them spoke up: "Aren't these the materials you told us not to make?"

"It was correct to cut them out then," came the reply, "and it is correct to reinstate them now."

Carrying out research takes time. One such case involved the hardware for getting the fuel propellant into the rocket engine. Because the propellant-injector mounting plate is under the action of high temperature gas in the combustion chamber, its surface temperature may reach 3,000 C or higher. At such extreme temperatures, the liquid hydrogen cooling it from behind will be vaporized right away, reducing its cooling effect significantly. This will produce huge thermal stress in the mounting plate, causing it to buckle, deform or be ablated. The end result is unstable combustion. Tung-ping was aware of this, so he set up a project to deal with the problem. But Huang called it a "white-beard project" — something that wouldn't yield results even when Tung-ping's beard grew white. The project was killed.

In spite of this, Tung-ping as the director of this research institute had to keep the project going "underground." Finally, a solution emerged: they adopted a processing method similar to human perspiration. The mounting plate was made porous so that a certain amount of liquid hydrogen might permeate it; this prevented the plate from overheating. (Much like when a person perspires, his or her temperature goes down.) From then on, there was no more burn-out or deformation of the plate. A major difficulty of the hydrogen-oxygen engine was solved.

A few years later, when China launched its first missile, that research proved its worth. It decreased the temperature from more than 3,000 C down to 200 C. At the same time, the specific thrust of the missile was raised and this increased its range. All it had cost was the salaries of several engineers, who made 62 *yuan* a month. Had the missile failed, however, it would have cost millions of *yuan* and set back the program for months or years.

Later, this project concerning porous perspiring materials — that had been dismissed as a "white-beard-project" — won a national award. And much later, an improved version of porous perspiring materials was used in Long March III, a rocket which successfully launched communication satellites.

Even though such breakthroughs proved Tung-ping was doing research the right way, Huang still persisted in his efforts to harass Tung-ping. During one period of political campaigns prior to the Cultural Revolution, he staged criticism meetings against Tung-ping. The leading Party members of Institute 703 were required to recite instances of Tung-ping's alleged bourgeois behavior. The meetings sometimes lasted more than ten hours.

Huang tried to elevate the matter further by having Tung-ping declared a "class alien," but a higher official rejected this, saying, "Who else is going to oversee the research work at the institute? Besides," the official added, "you and Comrade Tung-ping have differences in work matters only. Why do you want to elevate the issue into a political one?"

Having failed in declaring Tung-ping a "class alien," Huang went to lengths to pin something else on him. In 1962, a colleague asked Tung-ping to proofread his translation from English into Chinese of a book on high-temperature testing. It turned out to be more than a simple proofreading job; there were both technical and grammatical errors. I recall distinctly how mad I was at Tung-ping because he was working on this proofreading during our vacation. He explained that it was harder to edit somebody else's translation than to create the work.

The book was finally published in 1963 and Tung-ping, while expecting nothing, was paid 75 *yuan* for his months of proofreading. He hesitated at accepting the money, but it was officially approved and the others wouldn't take the money unless he did. So Tung-ping accepted it.

In the following years, whenever Huang wanted to make things difficult for Tung-ping, he trotted out this incident. He would bend the story, saying Tung-ping had ordered the translation so he could get paid to do the correction. Tung-ping never told me about this. I wondered if my hot temper had something to do with his silence. But that was probably a smart move. For if Huang had ever found out that Tung-ping had told me about such meetings, he would have used it as ammunition against Tung-ping. He would have accused Tung-ping of disclosing Party affairs to his wife who was not a Party member.

At the start of the Cultural Revolution, Huang brought up the subject of the translation again and told people to post big-character posters about this incident. Finally, Tung-ping had to write a letter to a deputy director at Institute 703 clarifying the matter. He also returned the money. Ironically, the very fact that Tung-ping did these things was convenient for Huang, it enabled him to say: "This shows that Yao Tung-ping admitted he has made a mistake. We didn't wrongly accuse him."

My husband reacted like any other Chinese intellectual (or like myself) during that era. Whenever we were criticized, we always thought it was because of our educational background and our previous life abroad.

If Tung-ping had been after fame and fortune as Huang had charged, he wouldn't have returned to China. He was already a well-known scientist in his field when he was abroad.★ And his salary in Europe was much higher than what he got in China where 75 *yuan* is less than 10 U.S. dollars.

It seemed Huang could always find reasons for whatever he wanted to do. It was like an old Chinese saying: "Where there is a will to condemn, there is always evidence."

欲加之罪 何患無辞

★ In a letter written in November 1991, Professor M.G. Frohberg of Berlin Technical University noted Tung-ping in the 1950s was "a well-known scientist on viscosity phenomena of metals and alloys… occupied in building up a narrow apparatus to measure metal viscosities (by crucible oscillation)."

16

Madame Mao — the Blue Apple

TUNG-PING AND I had been happily married for eight years when the year 1966 rolled around. Beijing enjoyed a beautiful spring that year — bright, sunny and warm. But the upper political atmosphere harbored cross winds that would soon reach all of us at street level.

On May 16, Mao Zedong presided over an enlarged session of the Political Bureau of the Central Committee of the Chinese Communist Party. A document called the "May 16 Circular" was passed at that session. "May 16" spoke of "bourgeois agents who have sneaked into the Communist Party, government, armed forces and circles of literature and art." It warned that they would "turn the proletarian dictatorship to bourgeois dictatorship." It said some were hiding, some were in high places, and some were like "Khrushchev sleeping next to us."

Neither Tung-ping nor I knew however that Liu Shaoqi, the Chairman of our country, was the person branded as "China's Khrushchev." During the entire period of the Cultural Revolution, in all the Chinese papers one would always find this term in place of the name Liu Shaoqi. Some historians have pointed out that when Liu became Chairman of the State, he tried to correct the damage caused by the "Great Leap Forward." Liu was for letting the peasants have a small plot of land near their houses. Mao looked upon this as taking the capitalist road.

When the "May 16 Circular" was made public, the Great Proletarian Cultural Revolution swept across the country like a prairie fire, starting with college students in Beijing. On May 25, 1966, seven teachers at Beijing University put up a big-character poster against the University's Party Committee. On June 2, *People's Daily* carried the poster on its front page. This made Beijing University the center of the Cultural Revolution for the entire nation overnight.

Beijing University has played a leading role in Chinese history in the past century. Mao once worked as a librarian there when he was a young man. At that time, Beijing University was located at Shatan, one bus stop away from the north entrance of the Forbidden City. The red brick building that used to be the library there is now preserved as a national historic site.

In 1952, Beijing University replaced Yanjing University, a Christian school, and the whole of Beijing University moved onto Yanjing's beautiful and quaint campus on the northwestern fringe of the city. There one finds traditional Chinese buildings nestled among pine and fir trees. Weeping willows line a lovely lake, the "No-Name Lake," where students like to sit and read or take walks. During the early 1960s, the air was thick with scholastic endeavor.

But all of that changed on June 2, 1966. On that day, *People's Daily* carried an article explicitly praising the poster written by those seven teachers from Beijing University who were opposing their University Party Committee. After reading this article in *People's Daily*, posters were pasted up all over campus, making charges against the Party Committee. When the walls were filled, bamboo frameworks were set up to handle even more posters.

Students from other universities followed suit, criticizing Party Committee members and teachers relentlessly. Chaos descended.

⁂

At our institute, as at every school, classes were suspended for the purpose of "making revolution." The Beijing Municipal Party Committee sent a "work team" of veteran cadres to our school. Even this group was met with disdain, as some students declared they would rather make revolution by themselves, on their terms.

On a Saturday evening in July, two groups of students debated the entire night whether to kick out the work team. I phoned Tung-ping that night, telling him I wouldn't be coming home because of the debate. Tung-ping didn't ask me anything over the phone but he was relieved to see me the next day. He thought I had been put into the "cowshed" by the students.

What were cowsheds? Well, on June 2, *People's Daily* also carried an editorial titled "Sweep Away All the Cows, Devils, Snakes and Demons." From then on, every *danwei* had a "cowshed" for people belonging to the five "black" categories: landlords (former land-owners), rich farmers, counter-revolutionaries, bad elements and rightists.

That was the only time I was able to make a phone call from my dormitory that summer. There was only one telephone in Building 6 where I lived. The phone was on the first floor; when it rang, the people who lived near the phone had to shout, "A phone call for so and so." They got tired of doing it, so they cut the phone line off. At that time, only people who had reached a certain social status could have a phone installed in their home, government paid.

One evening in late July, I was at Beijing University reading posters with some friends when word spread that Jiang Qing — Mao's wife — was there. She had called for a mass rally on the east sports field to criticize the "work teams." Madame Mao was a former movie star, whose stage name was Blue Apple. She was an irresistible combination of celebrity and political power. There was no way we'd miss this.

When Madame Mao stepped to the microphone, I saw a tall, slim woman. She had glasses on. Her skin was fair, her hair neat, short and black. She carried herself well and looked youthful, though she was over fifty. However, when I heard her shaky voice I thought, "This is the voice of a movie star?" She sounded like a sick old woman. Her speech was supposed to be about the "work teams" sent out to the schools and whether the students themselves should be leading the revolution instead. (The "work teams" were sent by order of Liu Shaoqi and Deng Xiaoping. Mao was in Hangzhou at the time.) But she drifted, and soon was talking about radioactive tests in the Physics Department which might cause cancer for the workers. "A case of covert persecution against the working class," she screamed. "I know how painful it is, because I have cancer myself." Then, veering off again, she screeched about a certain woman, "Zhang Wenjiu is a political cheat!"

I could scarcely make out what Madame Mao was driving at. She hollered something about "Zhang's ulterior motives" and "the Chairman's sick son." My friends filled me in on the background of Mao's two sons from his previous marriage. The eldest son had died during an American bomb attack at an early stage of the Korean War. The second one had slight mental problems at the time. They married two sisters from the same mother, Zhang Wenjiu. But still, I couldn't fathom why Madame Mao was airing her family's dirty laundry in front of ten thousand people, on such a solemn occasion as this. Maybe it was a spur-of-the-moment digression while under stress.

At last, Madame Mao got back to the topic at hand, and said she supported the students kicking out the "work teams." The students roared their approval: "Learn from Comrade Jiang Qing," they chanted and raised the Little Red Book *Quotations from Chairman Mao* — the book of aphorisms drawn from his speeches and writings that we had to bring along to every meeting we attended.

Back at Institute 703, where brilliant scientists and engineers were laboring to build rockets and missiles that would protect the country, the Cultural Revolution also reared its irrational head. Tung-ping was called in by Commissar Huang to read some posters. The posters were about Tung-ping himself.

As the Cultural Revolution started, Huang told his followers to write posters about Tung-ping, accusing him of various things: he was an individualist who did not put the Party's cause above his own; he took the "white expert" road not the "red way." (Anyone who spent more time on his particular field than on political study would be so labeled.) Huang walked into each room and urged people to write such posters. At one point, there were more than two hundred posters about Tung-ping. I was worried sick when I heard about this. But Tung-ping told me not to worry. He said he hadn't done anything wrong. There was nothing to be afraid of.

On August 1, Mao presided over a meeting that adopted a "Resolution on the Great Proletarian Cultural Revolution," which was termed "16 Articles" for short. It fully approved all that was going on by the masses, and said the goal of the Cultural Revolution should be "to expose and punish the capitalist-roaders" in the Party. "16 Articles" explicitly said Party members in authority taking the capitalist road were the object of the Cultural Revolution. As a result, Huang couldn't crush Tung-ping as he had wanted to.

That summer of 1966 also saw the birth of another new political force. In early June, several pupils from a middle school attached to Qinghua University wrote a letter to Mao. They called themselves "The Red Guards of Chairman Mao." And they adopted Mao's quotation that had been carried in *People's Daily*, "Rebellion is justified," as their motto. After that, "Red Guards" sprang up in middle schools and universities all over China.

On August 18, about a million Red Guards gathered in Tiananmen Square at midnight. Mao Zedong appeared on the Tiananmen rostrum in PLA (People's Liberation Army) uniform and a red-starred cap. As the sun rose in all its splendor, the military band struck up "The East Is Red" and the square seethed. The Red Guards waved their little books *Quotations from Chairman Mao* and shouted, "Long Live Chairman Mao." Mao was hailed as "the great teacher, the great leader, the grand commander, and the great helmsman."

There were eight such mammoth rallies between August and November 1966. The students wore army green uniform and red armbands with the words "Red Guard" on them. They took over the schools; they roamed from house to house, destroying anything they thought was connected with the old society.

After the mass rallies of 1966, any meeting of any kind began with a speaker waving the Little Red Book, shouting, "Long live our great teacher, our great leader, our great commander and our great helmsman, Chairman Mao!" The crowd would raise the Little Red Books and shout, "Long live Chairman Mao!" This was followed by "Eternal health to Chairman Mao's closest comrade-in-arms, Vice Chairman Lin Biao." And once again all those at the meeting would raise their red books and shout, "Eternal health! Eternal health!" At the end of a meeting, everyone would stand to sing "Sailing on the Seas Depends on the Helmsman":

Sailing on the seas depends on the helmsman,
And all the things rely on the sun for their growth,
Timely rain and dewdrops make young crops strong,
Making revolution depends on the Mao Zedong Thought...

Father's "bright pearl"

My father (who ran a tea shop and silk goods store in Hunan) wearing a half-melon skin cap

With my middle-school classmates at a missionary school in hills of Yuanling, during War with Japan (author back row, second from left)

交大唐院鑛民卅四級同學合影

Jiaotong University junior-year class photo, 1944 (school relocated inland to Pingyue in Guizhou Province during wartime)

Tung-ping at age 24, graduation photo from Jiaotong University

Dormitory at Jiaotong University in Guizhou

...g-ping (back row,
...nd from left)
... colleagues from
...search institute
...ront of the Temple
...Heaven, Beijing

Temple of Heaven, Beijing
(where Emperors came to
worship ancestors and
pray for good harvests). Its
design reflects the work-
ings of the universe: slabs
of Round Altar laid in
groups of 9 — considered
the most powerful digit; 4
central interior columns
symbolize the 4 seasons.

Tung-ping studying in room at Birmingham University

Tung-ping with fellow students and an English friend on graduation day 1952 at Imperial College, London.

Flashing a sunshine smile as an assistant professor in German

American plaid shirt and a Mao uniform, 1961

A father and daughter out for a walk in Beijing, 1962

Little Buddha with a big Mao badge

Feeding the chickens in our backyard, 1960

Author and Tung-ping (at right) with his mother and younger brother at front entrance of the Summer Palace

Mao Zedong viewing a crowd at the Gate of Heavenly Peace (Tiananmen), 1966

Reunion of Tung-ping's classmates from all over the world (America, Anhui, Brunei, Guizhou, Indonesia, Taiwan) and Author for the dedication of a memorial bust of Tung-ping at Jiaotung University (May 1996)

*thor at the home of
ng-ping's math professor
d his wife in Chengdu
ecember, 1995)*

Unveiling of Tung-ping's bust at Institute 703 in the summer of 2000

Author with her family in front of Dr. Yao's Golden Medal in the National Museum of China, 2001

Author making presentations to university students in Beijing & Tianjin, 2002

On August 18, a middle-school girl put a red armband on Mao's left arm. On the armband, were the three Chinese characters for "Red Guard" — *hong wei bing* — in Mao's handwriting.

Mao asked the girl's name. She replied, "Bing Bing."

"Does it mean gentle and refined?"

"Yes, Chairman," she replied respectfully.

Mao said to the girl, "Why not 'Yaowu'" (meaning "be militant").

The next day when *People's Daily* carried this piece of news, the girl's name had been changed from Bing Bing to Yaowu.

From that day on, all over China, young people started to change their names. They usually changed to Weidong (Guard Mao Zedong), Yonghong (Forever Red) and so on. And the main street in Beijing, Wangfujing Street became the People's Road. The Sino-Soviet Hospital became known as the Anti-Revisionist Hospital. When I went to the Union Hospital on August 19, I saw Red Guards changing its sign to Anti-Imperialist Hospital. (Ironically the Union Hospital was built with funds from the Rockefeller Foundation.)

I walked past a famous roast duck restaurant and saw a new sign "Beijing Roast Duck Restaurant" on the door; the broken old sign with the owner's name was still lying on the ground. I was about to go in for lunch when I saw a man in front of me get stopped by a waiter who roared, "What's your class origin?" The man just turned and left. I did the same.

Marshal Lin Biao, Mao's Vice-Chairman and heir apparent, called on the Red Guards to destroy the "four olds": old ideas, old culture, old customs and old habits. He called on the entire nation to support the "proletarian revolutionary spirit" of the Red Guards. From then on, Red Guards were posted on all the streets. Among the vital tasks they performed were making sure nobody wore pointed shoes, high heels, or narrow trousers. Some girls with long braids had their hair cut off. Dark blue and gray clothing soon dominated, except for the young people, who considered it a great honor to wear military green and of course considered themselves worthy of such an honor.

I soon realized that I should change my style of dress at the institute. I bought a pair of baggy blue cotton trousers and a pair of black cloth shoes from the Beijing Department Store. I was carrying them with me when I entered the school gate.

"Halt!" a girl yelled. It was one of my own students. "Why do you still wear narrow trousers and pointed shoes?"

I hurried to explain, "I've just bought cotton trousers and cloth shoes. I'll change into them in no time."

The girl could have easily pulled out a pair of scissors and cut open the bottom of my trouser legs. It was a common form of public rebuke. Instead, she pointed her finger directly at my nose. "Even if you put on cloth trousers and cloth shoes, you will not change your bourgeois air!" she shouted.

I did not respond and hurried away. Still, she got off a parting shot: "Even if she changes her clothes, look how she walks — just like an American."

The girl was one of the four girls in my class. She was petite, with a small face, small nose, small mouth and a pair of small eyes. She would have looked cute if she didn't talk like a male truck driver. After the Cultural Revolution, I meant to ask her just how an American walked, but never got the chance to meet her again.

The mass hysteria of the Red Guard rallies and the public humiliation of citizens found its way into people's homes. Squads of Red Guards went from house to house in a frenzied search for anything that suggested the "four olds." Any resistance would be treated as evidence of guilt.

On the evening of the day that my students challenged me at the gate, my neighbor Ming's home (Room 201) was ransacked. This was the night all the letters between him and his wife were confiscated. We all got the message. The next day was a Saturday; all the teachers who had apartments in the city hurried back to their homes in the afternoon, anxious not to have their letters made public. As soon as I finished lunch, I squeezed onto a bus for home.

17

You're Great, *Baba*!

───────────────── 〰 ─────────────────

W HEN I GOT HOME, I was hot and tired. Tung-ping told me to get some rest before we started our personal house cleaning for the "four olds." The next day was Sunday, the *ayi*'s day off. We would start then.

On Sunday morning, we began with the letters. There was so much to go through, but I kept getting distracted by all the memories. I'd pick up a letter and feel Tung-ping's love and his longing for me. I'd laugh again at his sly jokes. In some ways, my letters to him were even more interesting; sometimes my writing switched back and forth between English and Chinese. Tung-ping would always kid me, saying my letters were like Josephine's love letters to Napoleon.

I read our letters over and over. Each one reminded me of a time and a place. I couldn't bear to throw them away. This was our life together.

"Tung-ping, can we hide them somewhere?" I pleaded.

Tung-ping was adamant. "Let's burn them all! Do we have to let others read the endearments between us? There'll be plenty of days to come. I promise to write you one letter a day after the Cultural Revolution is over. How's that, my dear girl?"

So Tung-ping and I burned the letters. Then we moved on to photographs. At my school, the Red Guards had arranged a display of "indecent photos" taken from ransacked dormitory rooms. Actually they were nothing more than snapshots of a student and her friends, some of them more artistic than usual, but nothing remotely obscene.

Tung-ping loved photography. It matched perfectly his artistic and scientific urges. When he lived in Germany, he had bought a Leica camera, and quickly mastered photo taking as well as developing and printing.

Personally I wasn't terribly interested in photography, but when he would turn the bedroom into a darkroom and develop his films, I always joined him. I loved it — just the two of us in this tiny, closed world. I sat close to him, savoring his presence. I cherished these rare moments with him.

"I thought you didn't like photography," he'd say. "How come you're suddenly interested in developing film?"

"Well, I have my reasons," I'd reply, "but I'd rather not tell you." But I said to myself, "I am still not interested in developing film. I am only interested in being alone with you, my big boy."

We had a lot of pictures, a record of the happy days we shared since we had fallen in love. Here were shots of us at the beach in Beidaihe wearing our bathing suits. Here we were holding hands in Tiantan Park at the Echo Wall. Here were shots of Tung-ping and me under a willow tree by the West Lake. Many of the shots were the kind that might get us in trouble — our arms around each other's waist or Tung-ping's arm draped over my shoulder. Typical harmless affection, except in China (back then, anyway). The pose was more typically Western. Combine that with the "pornography" angle, and these pictures were asking for trouble.

The snapshots were priceless to me. Nevertheless, fearing the Red Guards might ransack our home and display them as

151

obscene objects, we burned them all. I would regret it for the rest of my life. Today in China people can hold hands and embrace in public. Nobody gives them a second glance. They are lucky indeed!

Next came the phonograph records. How we loved our music. I flipped through the records, hearing the tunes as I looked at the labels. I hated getting rid of all my popular stuff, like albums of Rogers and Hammerstein melodies, and the Broadway cast recording of "South Pacific." And my favorite, Harry Belafonte — I used to love that "Day-O" song. I'm sure my neighbors didn't know what to make of the calypso music coming from our apartment, and frankly I didn't care, until that day. Suddenly I had to worry what other people thought about one of our private joys, music. There was Mozart's 39th …and Chopin's mazurkas, Tung-ping's favorite. His beloved Beethoven, Bach and… here was "The Blue Danube" — how could we ever forget that one?

Why did we have to destroy it? According to the current thinking then, classical music belonged to an era of feudalism. Popular music was capitalism. I knew what had to be done. I picked up a record and threw it to the ground. It bounced. I did it again. It bounced again. I turned to Tung-ping for help. He tried, with the same result. The records remained intact.

We had very little luck breaking the phonograph records. The scene sounds funny now, but at the time I was actually a bit panicky. Finally, Tung-ping said, "Let's just put them aside until the Red Guards come and take them away."

On to the books. Before the Cultural Revolution, the demarcation line was 1949 — anything published before then was considered reactionary. Now the line had been moved up: anything published before 1966 was considered revisionist. It was as absurd as it sounded; this rule eradicated virtually everything except the *Selected Works of Mao Zedong*, *People's Daily*,

PLA News and *Red Flag*, the Communist Party magazine. Classical Chinese novels stood no chance in this campaign against the "four olds."

Our home — Tung-ping's study especially — was filled with books on all subjects, in several languages. There were far too many of them to burn, so we put them aside with the phonograph records.

I went through the closets. I'd brought some high-heeled shoes back from America but had never worn them. Now I didn't dare to keep them in my closet. So I asked Tung-ping to throw them away carefully.

"Ride on your bike as far as possible and drop them in different garbage cans," I added. "One at a time."

There were vases and a picture of the University of Aachen, Germany, where Tung-ping had worked. On the bookshelves were small iron figures, showing metal workers at various tasks. We left these alone. They were workers, after all.

Tung-ping rode off to throw away the high-heeled shoes. I stayed at home, burning nylon stockings. I felt bitter as the stockings turned to white ashes. They were bought abroad with hard-earned money. But who would listen to reason then! We were especially worried about my position. After all, I was not a member of the Communist Party. I had overseas relations — a brother in Taiwan, no less — and I was teaching English at a college. If anyone were a likely target, it would be me.

Tung-ping came back with some groceries and a portrait of Mao Zedong that he put on the most prominent wall in our living room. He said he had thrown away all my high-heeled shoes. He declared proudly that he did it without attracting anyone's attention.

Seeing how busy I was with the clean-up, Tung-ping volunteered to cook. His specialty was stir-fried pork with hot pickled mustard tuber, something he'd perfected during his student days. It was inexpensive but tasty. With it, he served cubed cucumber with a little salt, Chinese brown vinegar and sesame oil, scrambled eggs with tomatoes, and seaweed soup. It was quite inviting, laid out on our *baxian* dining table — the colors, the aromas, and especially the flavors!

We all sat at the *baxian* table. Once, while sitting at that table, I told Tung-ping that we should have three sons so that there would be eight persons sitting at this square table. Tung-ping replied that we already have three lovely daughters. That was just fine with him.

We placed the dishes in the center of the table. Each one helped himself to whichever dish he or she preferred. We didn't pass the food around the table like Westerners.

"*Baba*, you're great!" the kids said. "You cooked this up in no time and it's delicious."

Tung-ping smiled merrily and announced: "From now on, girls, I'm in charge of the kitchen when *ayi* is off."

That evening, as usual, Tung-ping boiled some water and filled his thermos to take to his office for his tea the next day. Before the Cultural Revolution, an attendant cleaned his office and got boiled water for him. Recently though, this man had declared to Tung-ping: "We are all equal. Why should I wait on you?"

"All right, comrade," Tung-ping replied. "How about switching our posts: you be the director and I get boiled water for you and clean the office?" The attendant glowered at Tung-ping but said nothing. After that, there was no more boiled water and no cleaning.

Such absurdities happened everywhere during that period of chaos. Nurses at hospitals demanded equal rights with doctors in diagnosing illnesses and prescribing medication while experienced doctors were sent to clean toilets. Workers and peasants were lecturing on classroom platforms while teachers were sent away to do hard labor.

The next day it finally happened, when Tung-ping was at work and I was at school across town. Some Red Guards burst into our home and ransacked the place. Flower pots were smashed to the floor. Rugs were rolled up and taken away — even though one had been provided by Tung-ping's *danwei* — as they were articles of a "bourgeois way of life."

They moved on to Tung-ping's books. None of them knew any foreign languages. The surest way to make sure the books wouldn't exert "bourgeois poison" was to tear them apart. They tore and tore until it wore out their patience. No doubt they left feeling victorious, leaving the mess behind. There were books everywhere on the floor. Tung-ping carefully put them back on the shelves. The small iron figures of workers were not touched.

Our neighbors assessed the situation. "This batch of Red Guards was rather civil. They didn't force you to kneel down and they didn't beat you." I learned all of this after it happened.

At my school, I was trying to rest when I heard a timid knock. "Come in, please," I said listlessly.

It was the daughter of Teacher Woo from Room 206. Woo and I shared newspaper subscriptions. After reading them, she would pass them to me and we'd have a chat for a few minutes. But today her daughter was dropping them off, which was unusual.

"The newspapers, Auntie Peng" she said. She wasn't smiling. I detected traces of tears.

"What's wrong?" I asked. "Is your *Mama* sick or something?" Lowering her head, the little girl whispered, "No."

I walked with her back to the next room. Opening the

door, I saw Woo sitting blankly in a long-sleeved shirt, with a scarf over her hair.

"Hello!" I asked. "Why are you wearing a scarf and long sleeves in such hot weather?"

She spoke in a low voice, "The Red Guards shaved off half of my hair. I don't want people to see it, so I'm covering my head."

Then she pushed up her sleeves. Her arms were covered with marks from a whipping. I was shocked.

"How could they beat you and shave off your hair? How could they treat you like this? You are neither a counter-revolutionary nor the wife of a landlord or capitalist." I was enraged.

Shaving off half the hair — named "*yin-yang tou*" in Chinese after the opposing forces in nature, *yin* and *yang*, that are often drawn in black and white — was an invention of the Red Guards. Whenever they decided that a person was a class enemy or a suspect, they would shave off half of the person's hair and cut the other half in a ragged way. I never thought Woo would be the first victim among our colleagues.

Woo told me that it happened at midnight Saturday. She was at her home in town with her husband and two young children. The girl was a primary-school pupil and the boy pre-school age. Red Guards broke in, with members of the Neighborhood Residents' Committee guiding them. All the family members were ordered to kneel down in the courtyard, including her mother-in-law. The adults were thrashed with the buckles of their leather belts. Other Red Guards ransacked the house, upending trunks and boxes, slicing open mattresses and drilling holes in walls, looking for "restoration records" (any item from the KMT days). But nothing was found. In their frustration, the Red Guards busted up all the furniture.

It all happened because Teacher Woo had married into a wealthy family. They owned some real estate in the Xidan district of Beijing. When her father-in-law died, her mother-in-law took

156

over the business. After the Communists came to Beijing in 1949, her mother-in-law gradually handed over their housing to the government, keeping only one small courtyard house.

I had once visited their home and found a traditional northern Chinese courtyard house — three bedrooms facing south, flanked by a living room and study on one side, the kitchen and the rest of the house on the other. In one corner of the yard was a flush toilet. A lilac tree grew in the center of the courtyard, filling the air with its lovely fragrance in spring. It was a nice and quiet home with a gray brick wall around the house and courtyard.

Not long after my visit, Woo and her family were ordered to vacate the side rooms to let more families move in. Each family erected a small kitchen outside of its doorway.

As an old Chinese saying goes: "One monk shoulders two buckets of water with a pole; two monks carry one bucket of water with a pole; and three monks carry no water at all." And so with three families living there, everyone thought the others would clean the toilet. But nobody did the cleaning and the resulting smell was repellent. A couple of months later, the toilet was torn down to make room for a fourth family, who also built their own kitchen. The once quiet courtyard house became noisy, crowded and disheveled.

Eventually the lilac tree was chopped down. No place for it and nobody cared for it anymore.

After the night of the ransacking and disfiguring, Woo pleaded with the Red Guards that she and her children be allowed to return to their room at the institute. She said, "Since all the Red Guards are making revolution under Chairman Mao's direction, there is no difference whether I'm struggled against here or in my school." They let her come back to our school.

I returned to my room, wondering what — or who — would be next.

The madness continued, spreading into primary schools, where "Little Red Guards" began to struggle against their teachers. There was a primary school close to our institute that consistently received the highest test scores in the district. Now such achievements were considered wrong-doings. The principal of that school was a lady over fifty with decades of teaching experience. Regardless, the Red Guards gave her the dreaded "*yin-yang*" haircut. They then hung a heavy signboard over her neck. Scribbled in childish handwriting were the characters "cow, devil, snake and demon." The principal was ordered to beat a broken washbasin like a drum and repeat, "I am a bad egg. I have committed crimes against the people. I deserve capital punishment."

She was forced to parade through the streets, a group of Little Red Guards following behind her. When she paused for breath, they beat her with leather belts. They even forced her to drink ink. For days, then weeks, this went on, until the poor woman had become so thin that she was hardly recognizable. Her replacement was a fat middle-aged woman worker from a textile factory who had been promoted to the rank of a cadre during the Cultural Revolution.

The husband of the tortured woman was the Deputy Dean of the French Department at our institute. He was in a "cowshed" himself, unable to come to his wife's aid. (In our school, basement rooms were used as "cowsheds." They were guarded by the Red Guards.)

The woman eventually suffered a breakdown. Whenever she saw a "Little Red Guard," she would halt and robotically mutter, "I am a cow, ghost, snake, and demon. I am a bad egg. I have committed crimes against the people…"

When the Cultural Revolution ended ten years later, that poor woman finally recovered from her mental disorder. But she could no longer teach. And the primary school never returned to the scholastic heights it had attained when she was principal.

As the months of 1966 passed, the bizarre became commonplace. The center of it all remained Beijing. Red Guards from around the country poured into the capital for "exchange of revolutionary experience." As guests of Chairman Mao, Red Guards could hop on a train or bus, certain they would never be asked for a ticket.

All the *danwei* in Beijing were ordered to form reception centers — makeshift dormitories to accommodate the hundreds of thousands of Red Guards flowing into the capital. Most of our students had gone elsewhere for "exchange of revolutionary experience." So, with many classrooms empty, we shoved desks and chairs to the side and brought in straw mattresses for the visitors to sleep on.

Red Guards ate for free too. Those of us teachers deemed unqualified for exchange of revolutionary experience. were assigned kitchen duty. My job was serving the meals. Many of the Red Guards were arrogant and rude. If the food did not agree with them, you could hear them complain yards away in the canteen. I had to bite my tongue and apologize, explaining that the sudden influx of visitors meant some teachers were doing the cooking, so standards may have slipped. And I was surprised to find that some female Red Guards cut their *mantou* (steamed rolls) into pieces to dry on a string. Perhaps they intended to bring them home so their family could enjoy free food too.

We also had to clean the kitchen, canteen, hallways, and toilets — the Red Guards were far too busy making revolution. I felt utterly exhausted. I wasn't a vigorous teenager brimming with the excitement of revolution; I was a thirty-something mother of three, separated from my family.

Other than menial labor, there was political study. It may seem impossible that you can fill up the day studying politics, but believe me, you can. Especially if it includes memorizing three articles by Mao, word for word. The articles were "Serve the People," "In Memory of Norman Bethune" and "The Foolish Old Man Who Removed the Mountains."

Every day there was a quotation from Chairman Mao on the top right side of the front page of *People's Daily* — which became our focus for the day. If Mao was quoted in any of the other articles in the paper, his words jumped out in bold print. Whenever Mao said something new, we were expected to write those words on banners for a march. Mao was a night owl of sorts, many times the Red Guards would get his latest pronouncement late at night. They were not permitted to keep the supreme directives from the people overnight. Therefore, we were summoned from our rooms, whatever the hour, to listen to the latest from the Chairman and march around the neighborhood, waving banners and shouting slogans. It was really funny, especially late at night, since we were doing the waving and shouting by ourselves. There were no pedestrians around.

In my school, we followed the routine that all people in China followed. Every morning, the entire staff would assemble before Mao's portrait and recite his quotations. We did it again in the evening. These gatherings were called: "asking directions from the Great Leader in the morning and reporting to the Great Leader in the evening."

After several days of this, I couldn't help thinking to myself: this was no different from morning and evening prayers in a church. I had been to Christian schools as a student, so I knew the routine. And deeper down, I remembered how my mother, a devout Buddhist, would burn incense before a Buddha inside the house at dawn and dusk. (But this is where parallels with organized religion ended. For religious and historic sites were under attack during the Cultural Revolution, even the stone tablets in a Confucian shrine at his birthplace in Qufu were knocked down.)

The moment this idea popped into my head, I stopped myself short and reproached myself for bourgeois thinking. It turned out I wasn't alone. When the chaos of the Cultural Revolution was over and the paranoia subsided, many people admitted having the same kind of feelings about the morning and evening gatherings. Nobody had dared to voice them though.

Now, over thirty years later, with the worst of the Cultural Revolution far in the past, we can see the absurdity. At the time, however, you had little choice but to go along. One middle-school teacher, I recall, made the mistake of speaking his mind. He was promptly branded an "active counter-revolutionary" and sent to a labor farm.

One day someone noticed that Teacher Han of Room 208 was missing. Her teenage daughter didn't know where her mother was either. Our department sent people to search the city. She was one of our best teachers. Her class liked her teaching.

What we didn't know was that all of a sudden she had been denounced by her class. They claimed her boyfriend before marriage had been a KMT spy. So, in their simplistic logic, it naturally followed that Han was a KMT spy too. They forced her to admit that. And then they made her stand on a desk in the center of the room for hours and beat her. Han could not put up with such humiliations.

Teacher Han's body was finally found a few days later in a deserted freight car at a suburban train station. Empty bottles of DDV (a pesticide similar to DDT) were found near her body, which had begun to decompose. Han had committed suicide. A talented linguist, she ended her life without leaving any message.

Such suicides were not seen as the sad result of overzealous persecution. They were evidence of guilt and crime against the Communist Party and the people. They were the dregs of society, and their families were no better. Sympathy was not permitted.

Mao Zedong's portraits were in all the homes all over the country. In every *danwei* and in the center of every town and city, there also stood a statue of him.

In the countryside, every village had loud speakers that broadcast quotations from Chairman Mao and the "Red Sun" songs all day long. The lyrics of the songs were from Mao's quotations. Mao was regarded as the Red Sun in people's hearts.

～

A couple of years ago as I was walking down a busy Beijing sidewalk, I heard buses and taxis competing with the chatter of voices and the thumping of music coming from a store. I stopped short. That music — what was it? My eyes opened wide in recognition.

The melody was the same, but the beat was quicker. The lyrics and the music were the same, but instead of a chorus of reverent voices, it was a woman singing what sounded like a love song.

Disco Mao! It was one of the "Red Sun" songs. The entire series of songs from the days of the Cultural Revolution have made a comeback recently, hopped-up with a dance beat. I had a friend whose teenage daughter played the cassette over and over. It eventually got on the mother's nerves. She told her daughter to stop playing it, but for the girl, born after the Cultural Revolution — who listened to Taiwanese, Hong Kong and foreign love songs over the radio every day — it was a fresh new sound.

Times have changed. I look around Beijing now and re-calling the days of blue, gray and military green, marvel at the difference. I see girls with make-up and stylish hairdos. Their hair dyed brown or red. Fingernails and toenails painted in red, pink, silver or even green. They wear mini-skirts or tight pants. They usually follow the latest fashion from Hong Kong.

A little flashy, but it looks nice on them.

It may not sound like much of a change, but it is.

We can chuckle now at the ironies of life. I look around now at the young people of China and find it almost amusing that young girls are watching their weight, exercising to keep the pounds off. A lot of them are faithful followers of Jane Fonda.

I envy them. They live in good times.

我们有一了甜蜜的家

18

Pretty Apricot

———————————— 〰 ————————————

Despite the troubles that were affecting the entire country, we tried to maintain a semblance of calm in our family life at home in Beijing. Our daughters were still kids and I wanted to protect them from the tumult outside of our residential compound. One Sunday in 1967, we were all at home enjoying a rare day together. The girls, as usual, were pestering their father to tell them a story. They got their wish, for just then I heard a knock on the door. I opened it and saw a young woman standing there — tall, slim, with short hair and big eyes. She smiled, revealing white, even teeth.

"I am May, Auntie. Don't you remember me?"

My goodness! It was my niece, the daughter of my brother Hai-ching. When I first met her after returning to China in 1957, she was but a chubby primary-school pupil, too bashful to speak to me. I brought her into the living room. "Look who's here!" The girls gathered around her cheerfully and she affectionately greeted Tung-ping as "Uncle."

Her father, my second brother, had been a teenager when I was born. I still remember fondly how Hai-ching let me ride on his shoulders so I could have a better view of the dragon boats racing. A few years later he went off to Huang Pu Military Academy (the West Point of China), graduated, and then fought against the Japanese. After retiring from the army in 1946, he tried his hand at business. He became a co-owner of a cement factory. I was in America at that time but didn't write to him. Those were the years of McCarthyism. I was afraid to write to anyone in Communist China.

When I returned to China, I discovered that my brother, his wife and their children were in Hangzhou, crowded into one room. He was suffering for his past. He told me that during a political movement in the early 1950s, he had been branded a "reactionary Kuomintang officer" on account of his service in the KMT army. The cement factory was confiscated and he was sent to a labor farm to be "remolded" through hard labor. He had been discharged and had returned to Hangzhou shortly before I came back to China.

Jobless, my brother and several other men who had shared the same fate put their heads together. They figured the government would not assign them jobs. They came up with a plan for running a small boiler factory, and got approval from the Neighborhood Residents' Committee. But they'd have to raise the start-up money themselves. Seeing my brother in such straits, I helped him out with all the money I had.

A relative warned me not to do it. He said someone with my brother's political history would never be allowed to operate a boiler factory. He suggested my brother stay on the farm. "It's a labor farm, I know," the relative said, "but at least they won't let your brother starve. Anywhere else, he'll suffer at the hands of whatever political campaign comes along."

That prediction came true, unfortunately. A year later, Hangzhou mobilized some of its residents to settle in the countryside. In a big ceremony, the leaders of the Neighborhood Residents' Committee pinned red paper flowers on the breasts of my brother and his friends and sent them off with drums beating and cymbals clanging.

It was now time for my relative to say, "Didn't I tell you? I knew the cadres would not let people like your brother run a factory."

I countered, "But they settled down in the countryside out of their own free will. I was told that they voluntarily entered their names. It was precisely on that basis that the Neighborhood Residents' Committee approved their application and took over the boiler factory."

My relative muttered, "Voluntarily or involuntarily, who knows." He thought I was naive. In retrospect, I probably was.

My brother Hai-ching had six children: Four sons and two daughters. The last son was given away to a worker's family soon after he was born. This way, the baby would become a worker's son instead of the son of a reactionary KMT officer. That left my brother with five kids: Bing, May, Fang, June and Yan-yan.

Bing was the only one in the family who had finished middle school. He was bright and had excellent grades in all his courses. But he didn't take the college entrance exams because all applicants had to be cleared politically first. Bing said that no college would accept him, the son of a former Kuomintang officer.

Bing managed to get a job as a clerk in a tricycle pedicab business. Due to lack of buses, pedicabs had become a popular form of transportation. One man pedaled in the front, with a seat in the back for two passengers. There was also a cover to keep the sunshine or raindrops off them. Tourists especially liked to take these pedicabs. They could have a good view of the scenery and still have some privacy for themselves.

Pedaling a tricycle was, of course, a heavier job than being a clerk. Some of the workers protested, saying that the son of a

KMT officer shouldn't have such "an easy job" as clerk. Thereafter, Bing was ordered to pedal a tricycle. Bing eventually married a seamstress. He told me his children would at least have half of their blood "red" from their mother's side. (Being the son of a KMT officer, his blood was considered "black" by some people.)

May's younger brother Fang helped Bing with his work after finishing primary school. Like Bing, he was tall and good-looking. When he went to a commune to help with the harvesting one summer, the daughter of a brigade leader of that commune fell in love with him. They eventually got married and decided to settle down in that people's commune. Fang was well-liked by other commune members for two reasons: he was a nice young man and his father-in-law was the brigade leader.

After Fang left for the commune, Yan-yan, the youngest son of the family, replaced Fang in helping Bing with his work. In the 1980s, when China opened her doors, the government began to change its policy toward the descendants of former KMT officers. Yan-yan got a job as a taxi-driver. Sadly, he was killed in a robbery a few years later.

As soon as May turned sixteen, she went to work in a textile factory to help the family make ends meet. But this was not her passion in life. As a child, she loved Yue opera, always humming familiar tunes. One year, an opera troupe from Jiangxi province held a tryout and the director was impressed by May's tall, slim figure, pretty face and sonorous voice. Even though she wasn't from a desirable class, he made an exception and put her in the troupe. May took the stage name Pretty Apricot and became quite a star in that region.

Now here she was in our living room. I knew she was a singer, but was unaware of her considerable popularity. She looked healthy and beautiful... but why was she in Beijing?

May told us that the director of her troupe had been de-

nounced and savagely beaten for having lost proper "class stance."
The rebels accused him of training May, the daughter of a reactionary KMT officer. May herself was put under separate interrogation and was severely beaten, too. They even ordered her to kneel on broken glass.

"If they beat you, who performed the operas?"

"The troupe had already been dissolved. Comrade Jiang Qing (Madame Mao) had declared the Yue opera decadent. Who would dare to perform these days? The troupe simply lays idle. Auntie, look at the bruises on me." I stopped her. "Not now, I'll get a room ready for you first." I was easily excitable in those days; I knew the bruises would upset me.

I led her to a bedroom. May sat down and finished her story. She said armed fighting had flared up where the troupe was based. She was beaten every day and feared for her life. One night, May slipped away. Changing into an old military uniform, she disguised herself as a Red Guard, stole onto a train and made her way to Beijing.

Now she would stay with us for a while. Any houseguest had to be officially registered with the police, so we applied for a temporary residence permit for May for three months. Her ordeal had clearly tired her. Being twenty-one years old though proved a big help. After a few days of rest, she was back to her normal lively self.

Our *ayi* was from Shanghai. When she heard that May was a Yue opera singer, she asked her to sing something for us.

"No! Please don't," I put a stop to that immediately. I was afraid her voice might carry into the next apartment, or outside. Madame Mao had given the final word on which operas were politically acceptable. (Only four Beijing operas and two ballets were allowed to be staged during the entire ten years of the Cultural Revolution.) If someone heard a traditional Yue opera being sung, we'd all be in trouble.

I bought May a monthly bus pass so she could see the sights. Tiananmen Square, the Palace Museum, the Summer Palace, the Great Wall. We went to Beijing University to read the big-character posters — such was the entertainment in those days. I brought her to my school as well. Her beauty drew many admiring glances from the boys.

During her stay, May filled me in on her family's fate. My brother Hai-ching had become too old and weak to work on the labor farm. During holidays, such as May 1 (Labor Day) and October 1 (National Day), production brigade cadres would round up him and some others from the five contempt-ible black categories for verbal and physical abuse.

Fortunately, China changed its policy toward KMT army veterans in the 1980s. An association of Huang Pu Military Academy graduates was established to help them out. Due to their help my brother was provided with new housing in Hangzhou, and he began to receive a small monthly pension. Sadly he remained in poor health. In 1994 he had a bad fall and died that year in Hangzhou.

May's temporary residence permit ran out all too soon. Since things were now getting tense in Beijing also, we figured it was just as well that we send her back south on a train. May said she would go back to her mother's place in Hangzhou and stay away from the opera troupe. She eventually chose — from many suitors — a college graduate from a revolutionary cadre family to be her husband. He had been a fan of hers when she was a performer. But for the rest of that chaotic decade 1966–1976, she had to keep a low profile, working in a warehouse at her husband's factory. After the Cultural Revolution, the Yue opera was performed once again on stage, but her prime sing-ing years were past. May had to give up her career.

"I chose a man of good class origin for my husband," she explained to me later. "My children would be of good class origin and would not have to put up with the snubbing and insults as my brothers, sisters and I had to."

When her sister June finished primary school, May invited her to stay at her house. She made sure that June married one of the workers in her husband's factory.

This was the fate of my brother's family! Even though my brother Hai-ching had fought against the Japanese for eight years (1937–1945), had retired from the KMT army after the war, and had never fought against the Communists during the Chinese civil war, he was still branded "a reactionary KMT officer" after the Communists took over in 1949. For the rest of his life, all his family members suffered on account of that.

However, for propaganda purposes, the government treated some top war criminals much better, including the last emperor Pu Yi. In fact, quite a few Kuomintang generals who had fought the Communists in the battlefields as well as a leading official from KMT intelligence. They were paroled after serving some time in prison and were free to go abroad or stay in China as they wished. If they chose to stay, they were provided with housing and living expenses. This was definitely not an offer extended to my brother and his family.

19

Stop! Stop! No More Reciting

———⌇———

Sometime after my niece May's visit, embroidery became a big craze in China. It wasn't the traditional intricate artwork you see for sale in China now. This was sewing as devotion — creating portraits of Mao Zedong in embroidery. The girls bought some curtain cloth and with cross-stitching created a vivid needlework of Mao. They asked Tung-ping to write "Long Live Chairman Mao" on the handkerchief, then sewed the characters with colored thread.

There were many ways to show loyalty to Chairman Mao. Nearly everyone wore a Mao badge with Mao's head or full-length portrait on it. Initially made of metal, badge materials later became more exotic: bamboo, porcelain, and even plexiglass for forward-looking citizens.

Badge making was an activity for which Institute 703 — where missile making had been suspended anyway — was ideally suited. After all, it was a research institute for materials technology. Metals, non-metals, you name it, they had it. And they had the best in manufacturing equipment. The wide variety of badges that came out of 703 were very nice indeed. Mine was as big as a saucer, with Mao's profile in relief against a background of Tiananmen. It never failed to draw envious glances.

One day our *ayi* took Little Buddha with her to buy vegetables. As usual, she pinned a beautiful crimson-and-gold Mao badge on the girl's clothing. The *ayi* set little Buddha on a stone stool outside while she waited in a long queue. When she emerged, the badge was gone.

Oh was she mad! She stamped her feet. "How dare someone steal a Chairman Mao badge from a child in broad daylight."

I tried to calm her down. "Don't be so angry," I said. "It might well be that the thief acted out of love for Chairman Mao. Just accept it as if you had given it away as a gift."

It was possible. People did love Chairman Mao. They loved those badges too.

After June 1966, the president of our school and the deans of the various departments were removed from their posts. Students started to run the school.

It was not just our school. All the schools in China — primary, secondary as well as universities — stopped classes in order to "make revolution." Some students rebelled against former landlords, former capitalists and counter-revolutionaries. Others stayed on campus to rebel against the teachers and staff, especially those who had been educated in foreign countries or in China before 1949 when the Communists established a new government. That certainly described me.

As a woman who had lived in the United States, someone who could speak English, and a teacher, I was considered one of the "stinking ninth elements." So were middle-school and primary-school teachers, writers, engineers, scientists, doctors, actors — anyone with an education.

In such an upside-down world, a teacher had to obey orders from any student. One weekday in May of 1968, at dusk I was going out the school gate to head for home. It would be a journey of two to three hours by bus to the other side of the city — if buses were running. Service was spotty during the Cultural Revolution. As often as possible, I tried to get home to my family's apartment in the far southern suburbs of the city. I heard a voice shouting:

"Hey you!"

It was Fang, one of my students, who was now the head of the Revolutionary Committee of the English Department. "Where do you think you're going?"

Teachers had become nameless to the students. It was always "Hey you" or "Hey there."

"If you are talking to me," I replied curtly, "I'm going home."

"Going home?" Fang raised his voice. "It's not Saturday. You are not allowed to go home on weekdays."

"I wasn't informed about that," I said. "Could you tell me who made this rule?"

"I did. From now on, you are not to go home on weekdays, you hear?"

I turned back without uttering a word. I was furious. I went straight to the office of the Chairman of our College Revolutionary Committee, a man named Li. He was rather tall, square-faced and always wore a mask of indifference. Though we worked in the same college, we seldom talked to each other.

On entering his office, I immediately asked: "Comrade Li, why can't I go home on weekdays?" Am I under political investigation? Am I a counter-revolutionary or something? Why am I not allowed to go home?"

Instead of answering my question, Li asked, "Who told you that?"

"Fang did."

"Comrade Fang is the Number One Hand in the Revolutionary Committee of the English Department. You must abide by his orders." Li said flatly and turned to his work without paying any more attention to me.

That was the Great Proletarian Cultural Revolution! No rules, no regulations, no law and order. Whoever was in power, his word was the law. Fang's spur-of-the-moment decision prevented me from seeing my family for the entire week.

Whenever I was away, Tung-ping watched over the girls with help from our *ayi*. Because I came home only on weekends, many family duties fell to him, such as attending the parents' meetings or taking the children to the doctor. All this was on top of his endless work hours. In fact, he often worked through the dinner hour, making sure the engineers and technicians were following the meticulous research requirements he insisted upon.

When he arrived home, our children would run to him, chattering happily. No matter how fatiguing his workload was or how heavy the political pressure at his workplace was during those tense months in 1968, the girls could always cheer him up.

Rebellious organizations were popping up everywhere in China during the first years of the Cultural Revolution — in every school, factory and government office. As might be expected in a climate where political fervor was rewarded, there was competition to demonstrate which group was most loyal to Chairman Mao. This sometimes led to splits within rebellious organizations, with each side claiming to be truer in spirit to Mao's revolutionary line.

Such was the situation at the Seventh Machine Building Ministry, of which Tung-ping's institute was a part. The two major factions in the Ministry were 915 and 916, named after the dates they were formed (September 15 and September 16,

1966). The 915 group, mostly bureaucrats, was formed to show their loyalty to Minister Wang Bingzhang. The 916 faction, mostly technical people, sprung up the next day in opposition. The conflict escalated from initially giving cold shoulders to one another, to the posting of big-character posters, to public arguments and finally fist fights. As time went on, the differences deepened. Most people simply did not go to work.

In the spring of 1968, the conflict at the Seventh Ministry got worse as these two factions vied for control. Tung-ping continued going to his office every day. "I feel ashamed getting paid without working," he confided to me.

Because I spent most nights across town at the college, I was unaware of all this turmoil within his Ministry. But I realized something was going on when a 9 p.m. curfew was imposed by faction 915 in our neighborhood in early June. Fighting between 915 and 916 had now escalated into major physical confrontation. Both sides were arming themselves with sharpened lengths of pipes. I urged Tung-ping to leave town. But he stayed put, loyal to his work and his family.

Now with the new rules at my school, I could only be together with the family on weekends. I was allowed to leave on Saturday but had to return by Monday morning. I had been counting the days, tearing off the pages of a calendar with mounting excitement. When I thought of Tung-ping back home, my heart constricted with love and longing. I knew he was waiting for me.

A week is a long time!

By the summer of 1968, the Cultural Revolution was entering the next phase: finding and denouncing "capitalist-roaders." At our school, the Red Guards held meeting after meeting to denounce the president. They charged him with recruiting a large number of bourgeois intellectuals as teachers.

But Comrade Wei — a man who always wore his Mao cap proudly — would not submit. He stubbornly refused to admit he had pursued a "revisionist line" in education.

To be fair, how could anyone put together a staff of foreign-language teachers without drawing from the ranks of so-called "bourgeois intellectuals"?

I started watching my back.

One day at a denunciation meeting, the students prepared a dunce cap for him with the characters "capitalist-roader" on it. Then they walked up to the president and knocked off his Mao cap. The man was bald. Forget the politics, the struggle, the bitter accusations and denials; this was what struck me. No wonder Comrade Wei always had his Mao cap on. Evidently the Red Guards were using this "exposure" to further embarrass him. Then they ordered him to assume the "jet plane" posture — bending over and keeping his head inches off the ground while straining to keep his arms straight up skyward, like a jet. He was forced to hold this pose as he listened to their accusations. Every now and then they'd kick and beat him.

As I watched this at the meeting, standing next to me was the president's wife. She was on the school's staff. Tears welled up in her eyes, but she fought to keep them off her cheeks. What a sad lot, I thought: to watch her husband insulted, and not to have the right to cry.

Suddenly, a Party member from the administrative office stepped forward. He could not bear it any longer. Coming from a poor peasant family background, he felt confident in arguing against the students.

"Comrade Wei," he declared, "is not a capitalist-roader."

The Red Guards were astonished. They never expected, probably had never heard of anyone challenging them. A mob rushed forward, pushing the man into the center of the room. Some pasted paper on him while others took a broom and used it as a brush to write in huge Chinese characters "petty reptile." They had no dunce cap ready, so someone grabbed a wastebasket and put it on his head. They started to shove him toward the president but he resisted. The Red Guards descended on him and beat him.

The head of the Red Guards then turned to the crowd and exhorted us to recite Mao's quotation:

"A revolution is not a dinner party or writing an essay, or painting a picture, or doing embroidery; it cannot be so refined, so leisurely and gentle, so temperate, kind, cautious, restrained or magnanimous. A revolution is an insurrection, an act of violence by which one class overthrows another." He then led the audience in shouting:

"Down with the capitalist-roader!"

"Down with the petty reptile!"

Aside from the school-wide denunciation meetings, there were numerous smaller sessions for criticism and repudiation. One took place in the faculty dining hall, where a young girl named Li accused the president of persecution. Specifically, he had assigned her, a coal miner's daughter, to clean offices, while bourgeois intellectuals gave lectures. She hooted what kind of class awareness did this demonstrate? Then she vehemently invoked the words of Mao:

"The length of schooling should be shortened. Education should be revolutionized. We can't let bourgeois intellectuals keep on dominating our schools any longer."

Li scanned the crowd. "All of you stinking ninth elements are guilty! Come over and kneel down before Chairman Mao's portrait and say, 'I am guilty'."

Intellectuals with bourgeois family origin were branded as one of the nine categories of class enemies. The other eight were: landlords, rich farmers, counter-revolutionaries, bad elements, rightists, traitors, spies and capitalist-roaders.

I hesitated, looking around at my colleagues, who were doing the same. Slowly, uncertainly, we all stood, but nobody moved toward the Mao portrait. After all, you would not expect someone to admit to himself that he stinks. So Li produced a list of names, then announced the first one, a woman.

She walked forward, stopped and lowered herself to her knees. Li called out the next name, and so on, until kneeling teachers filled the clearing in the center of the room. There were still more names, and those people were told to kneel where they were.

As yet, my name hadn't been announced. I cast a glance around the room and found far more people kneeling than standing. Li walked toward a few people including me who were still standing.

"Who is Woo?" she shouted.

"Me," came the reply from my neighbor in our school dorm, the woman whose hair had been cut *yin-yang* style. She was standing near me.

"Kneel down!" Teacher Woo obeyed.

Li walked up to me.

"What's your name?" she asked sharply.

I was about to reply when a male Red Guard interrupted, asking Li to step outside. What was going on? The two talked for a while. When they returned, the young man announced to everyone: "Comrade Li has asked you to plead guilty before Chairman Mao's portrait out of her instinctive class feeling," he said. "It is altogether correct and proper. However, as we proletarians have taken upon ourselves the responsibility of freeing the whole of mankind, we can surely remold you bourgeois intellectuals. You must remold yourself solidly with Mao Zedong Thought and be led by the working class."

It seemed to me the Red Guard had decided that Li's singling out of each teacher had gone far enough, and now he was trying to save face for all concerned.

He asked all the people present to stand up and sing "Sailing the Seas Depends on the Helmsman":

"Sailing on the seas depends on the helmsman,
All things rely on the sun for their growth…"

Since this song was the customary ending to a meeting, there was a collective sigh of relief.

The indoctrination was ceaseless, and it was aimed at all generations. One day at home, I had asked the children to help clean the windows and sweep the floors. As they worked, they recited in unison, "Be determined, fear no sacrifice, and surmount difficulties to win victory."

Well, this seemed a bit of an overreaction to a little house cleaning. "Why do you all recite that quotation?" I asked.

One of my daughters replied, "Our teachers told us that whenever we meet with difficulties, we can draw extra strength from reciting this quotation of Chairman Mao."

"What is the 'difficulty' in doing cleaning at home? Do you feel you have to recite that quotation?"

They shrugged, then said, "Let's recite Chairman Mao's latest instruction: 'Fear neither hardship, nor death, nor fatigue'."

What was this? That wasn't right. Those weren't the exact words! There was nothing in that quotation about fatigue. But here were my girls, even Little Buddha, shouting it out. These kids — how could they tamper with Chairman Mao's instructions? I panicked.

"Stop! Stop!" I ordered. "No more reciting!"

I was truly frightened. Had anybody heard them? I looked around. My outburst frightened the children. Tung-ping hurried in from the next room to see what the matter was. I explained what had happened.

Tung-ping turned to the children, patting them on the heads. He spoke to them slowly and gently. "Chairman Mao's original wording is 'Fear neither hardship nor death'." he said. "Since you Little Red Guards all love Chairman Mao, you should not change his instructions. See that? Be careful next time."

The children nodded obediently. Then Tung-ping looked around the room and praised them for their cleaning. He said they all loved to do labor and were good kids.

In our bedroom, Tung-ping took me to task, saying I was too severe with the children. I argued, "You know people are being sent to jail just because of mistakes they made when copying a quotation from Chairman Mao."

"You could tell them the reason. Don't panic yourself or they'll get scared," Tung-ping advised.

That week, Tung-ping was on doctor-ordered rest at home due to severe hay fever. Because there had been some fights between the factions lately — resulting in the 9 p.m. curfew imposed in our neighborhood by faction 915, I proposed that he take his rest at my college. It was near the Hospital of Chinese Traditional Medicine and he could try some Chinese herb medicine for his hay fever there.

He thanked me but rejected the idea.

"There's an important meeting next month and I must be there. I have to prepare for it," he said.

After a couple of days of rest, Tung-ping got up as usual for work. He took a lot of extra handkerchiefs (paper tissues weren't available in China until the 1980s) and headed to the office, sniffling as he went.

20

Open the Door!

———————————— ❧ ————————————

AFTER SPENDING Monday through Friday at my college, I was anxious to get home on Saturdays. I missed Tung-ping and the kids so. June 8, 1968 was such a Saturday. As soon as I woke up, I started counting the hours — though I knew I couldn't leave until after lunch.

I had another reason for going home that day. I had to pack for a full day of "doing labor" at a people's commune on June 10. The whole school was headed out to help with the summer harvest. This "field trip" was in keeping with Mao Zedong Thought, which declared that everyone should learn from poor and lower-middle peasants. Just like the previous year, we would form a double line and march out of town in the predawn darkness, behind two students carrying red flags, the stars still overhead. As we marched, students would shout such slogans as "Long Live Chairman Mao" and "Learn from the poor and lower-middle peasants."

In the fields, it was a remarkable sight: students and young teachers cutting wheat, women and older teachers tying it into bundles and carrying it off, primary school pupils fanning out across the field to pick up any overlooked stalks. I carried bundles of wheat with great difficulty. I had never performed heavy manual labor before. The high June sun was relentless and there was no breeze or shade. We wore long pants, long-sleeve shirts and wide-brimmed straw hats to protect us from the sun. We worked, with only a lunch break, until sunset. Then we formed the two lines again and marched back to our school. On the way back, nobody shouted slogans or carried the red flags high.

Every *danwei* was scheduled to spend some time helping the commune members with the harvest. Now another trip to a people's commune was looming. I spent the morning of June 8th in typical fashion, reading and discussing the articles in *People's Daily*, taking special note of that day's quotation from Mao in the upper right corner. I hurried back to my dormitory room to cook up some lunch on the coal-fired stove in the hallway when I heard the news — Typist Ling had committed suicide.

I was shocked. The Cultural Revolution had claimed another innocent victim. I immediately thought of her teenager daughter. We all knew Typist Ling, a petite woman with fine features. She and her husband Teacher Chan had lived for years in Paris — where their home became an informal salon for overseas Chinese. They returned to China in the early 1950s, flush with enthusiasm for the new People's Republic.

Once settled in Beijing, they found a world of difference from Paris, not the least of which was the expectation that Ling would work outside their home. (At the time she was a highly capable homemaker whose sewing skills helped turn their apartment into a cozy home.) Not having any formal professional training, Ling came to be a typist at our school.

Ten years prior, in 1957, her husband Teacher Chan had been one of thousands who voiced criticism of the Communist Party. When the "Anti-Rightist Campaign" came down hard on those who had spoken out, Chan was put under extreme pressure to "name names" of those who shared his opinions. If he cooperated, he was promised, he wouldn't be branded a "rightist." He gave in to the pressure and gave out names. He wasn't labeled a rightist, but he was looked down upon by those he had named, who indeed were branded rightists and sent to labor camps.

When the Cultural Revolution began, Chan's past came back to haunt him. On June 1, 1966, *People's Daily* carried that pivotal editorial, calling upon the revolutionary masses to "sweep away all cows, devils, snakes and demons." The Red Guards branded Chan a counter-revolutionary, so they shut him up in a "cowshed." He was forbidden to go home and visitors were not permitted.

Chan was treated terribly. The Red Guards plucked his eyebrows and ordered him to lick the soles of their shoes and beat him afterwards. Ling was ordered to reveal her husband's counter-revolutionary deeds. She kept silent and was herself severely criticized.

Now in the middle of 1968, Ling herself had been mentioned again in a number of posters. The accusation: giving shelter to her rightist husband. Then on Friday, June 7, a poster appeared on the wall of Building 7 where her apartment was, charging her with an illicit love affair with a political cadre. She stopped reading and ran up to her home.

A friend told me her daughter found her hanging from a ceiling pipe in the bathroom.

Those of us in the English and French departments were shocked and deeply saddened. It was the sixth suicide at our small college of about sixty faculty members and staff since the Cultural Revolution had begun two years earlier. And we didn't know how many more would be forced to do so.

In this case, all of us — parents especially — thought about the daughter of the Chans. Her father was in the "cowshed," her mother was dead. Who would take care of her?

I had often wondered the same about our children should something befall me or Tung-ping… We talked about it once, but didn't dwell on it.

I remember one Mid-Autumn Festival when Tung-ping and I sat on our balcony gazing up at the gorgeous full moon. The children were asleep and we sat quietly, in peaceful bliss.

"Darling," I said. "How I wish that we could be husband and wife in the next life, for eternity!"

My scientist husband said tenderly, "Now, now, my dear girl, I wish so too, but there is no next life."

"But Mother always taught me to be good when I was little. She said a good child would be reincarnated into a human being and not a beast or anything else in the next life. Or if I were really good, I'd go to heaven. A well-behaved girl might even go to the highest heaven, the Ninth Heaven, Mother said."

"Your mother was a Buddhist," Tung-ping said. "She believed in reincarnation, the next life and heaven, but how could you think so too?"

Maybe I wasn't sure about the next life. But I could wish, couldn't I? Tung-ping took me by the arm and we went back inside, moving slowly toward the bedroom, our warm home illuminated by the pale moonlight.

At that time, death seemed so remote that it was hardly worth thinking about. Now, as the tension of the Cultural Revolution erupted more frequently into violence, more and more people were cracking under the pressure and even dying from mistreatment or cruelty. Death seemed closer around us.

At Tung-ping's institute, the struggle between those two factions 915 and 916 continued to escalate in the late spring of 1968. So much so that work was now virtually halted at the institute. Nonetheless, Tung-ping continued to show up for work, telling me that he felt guilty otherwise. Even rumors of violence at other places didn't dissuade him.

As the director of Institute 703, Tung-ping thought it important to stay out of the factional fighting. To him, keeping the work going was paramount. Members of 915 and 916 would come to him, sometimes even to our home, to try to persuade him to side with them. He always thanked them but declined. He — and I — figured if he stayed out of the dispute, he would be safe. He had never harmed anyone in his life and he tried his best to stay out of the growing struggle.

A few weeks prior, we'd been in bed, talking seriously late into the night. "You know," I said, "the situation is pretty bad. I hear people are being beaten to death in Beijing now. Don't you think you should go away some place to hide for a while?"

Tung-ping shook his head. "I hear that outside of Beijing is even more chaotic. In some cities they're using guns and cannons."

He held me close and tried to comfort me. "Don't worry." he said. "We haven't done anything wrong since we returned nor in the past. What's to be afraid of? Besides, we live in the capital, right under the very eyes of Chairman Mao. Do you think people would dare to do any killings here?"

"I guess you're right," I agreed.

His words put me at ease. They made sense. But part of me still felt that what was going on outside was utterly senseless. Why should we have had any confidence that logic would prevail?

The split in the Seventh Ministry was growing much wider and deeper than Tung-ping had expected. This dismayed him, but he tried to keep a clear head. However, he did get upset over the posters about Marshal Nie such as "Down with Nie Rongzhen" and "Deep-fry Nie Rongzhen." Nie was the man in overall charge of the space program in China, and the man who had presided over the conference in Guangzhou in 1961 which defended the role of intellectuals.

The prior spring, in March of 1967, Nie had again made a speech encouraging more scientific research, unimpaired by political interference. Technical matters should be decided by technical personnel, he said, not by political directors. Tung-ping (just as in 1961) was heartened by Marshal Nie's words and relayed them to the staff of Institute 703. Pausing at times to control himself, Tung-ping concluded with determination "So long as our research blossoms, I would give up my life for it, if it is needed! Comrades, let's do our utmost!"

An engineer present later recalled that my husband's speech had prompted great applause — "Director Yao had voiced what was in the depth of the hearts of us technical personnel."

As the battle between the two factions raged on, Tung-ping carried on his work as best he could. But it was beginning to wear him down.

One early morning in May of 1968, we were standing in front of the bathroom mirror of our apartment. He was washing his eyeglasses as he did every day and I was combing my hair. We caught each other's eyes in the reflection and smiled. I suddenly discovered that he had some gray hairs.

"Eeee — you have some gray hair?" I said. "I never noticed that before." Then I looked at myself in the mirror… and found some wrinkles around my eyes.

"Look," I said, "I'm getting old too. I have some wrinkles. See? Here, here and here." I pointed to my forehead and the corners of my eyes.

Tung-ping gently touched my face, "Getting old? We are not old at all. I'm forty-five and you're eight years younger. We have a long sweet life ahead of us and we'll have many years together to work for our country."

That's how Tung-ping saw things — as an open-ended

opportunity to spend his life with the ones he loved, doing the work he loved, in the country he loved.

A month later, on June 8, 1968 here I was at my school putting away the lunch dishes. I had a bus to catch and hurried out the college gate. I squeezed onto the bus, which lurched away from campus. My mind wandered back to Typist Ling and the horror her daughter must have felt. Then I turned my thoughts to my home, my husband and my daughters.

That same morning, Tung-ping had risen early as usual, taken his thermos bottle with boiled water from the kitchen, put the bottle in a gray plastic bag and hopped on his bike for the short ride to his office, carrying the bag in one hand while steering with the other. When he arrived at work, he arranged the papers on his desk, swept the floor, and poured himself a cup of tea.

He spent the morning going over a technical paper, examining it with a practiced eye for any mistakes or inconsistencies. He signed the corrected version about noon, stacked the books and papers he was using and prepared to head home for lunch. There were very few people in the institute that day. The fighting between the factions of the Seventh Ministry, 915 and 916, had become violent in recent days, with rumors of people being injured. Two engineers saw him getting ready to leave and approached him.

"Director, there's some fighting going on in our compound, not far away," one of them urged. "You had better wait for a while. Don't go home yet."

Tung-ping thanked them for their concern. "I have to go on with my work in the afternoon. Besides, we are not involved in this conflict. I don't think it has got anything to do with us," he said.

So he got on his bike, avoiding what trouble there was outside, and arrived at our apartment twenty minutes later.

"*Baba, Baba*!" The girls called out, surrounding Tung-ping when he came in the door. He smiled, patted them on their heads, and went to wash his hands. Little Buddha followed him. He bent down to give her a kiss, scooped her up and carried her into the dining room.

The girls took their places at the *baxian* table. Tung-ping sat down in his usual place. He had just picked up his chopsticks when there was a sudden banging and shouting.

"Open the door!"

21

"Good-bye! My Darling"

———— ✄ ————

THAT SATURDAY, June 8, was a hot humid day. After two hours riding buses, I squeezed onto a southbound bus for the final leg of the trip home. It was packed; I felt elbows and arms and warm, sweaty backs all around me. But the crowded bus didn't bother me, I was used to it. I just wanted it to run faster.

About three stops from home, the bus stopped for no apparent reason. We wondered what was wrong. Some passengers politely asked the ticket collector, a young girl sitting on a specially elevated seat. "You all are asking me? How should I know?" she shot back. "Get off the bus and walk!"

Her answer was not too rude — none of the profanity we'd come to expect from many young people, who thought swearing was how members of the proletariat should talk. We filed off the bus, walking to our destinations.

I was perspiring after a couple of minutes from my brisk walk. And it felt like it was going to rain. I was almost out of breath, but the thought of entering our sweet home — my girls running up to me, everyone jabbering at once, above all, my husband's dark handsome face with a sun-shine smile when

I entered — kept me going. With these happy thoughts, tiredness left me. I picked up my pace.

Our three-bedroom apartment was on the top floor of a three-story building. The apartment door faced north. As you crossed the threshold, you entered a hallway which led into the living room. There were two sofas, a couch and a walnut coffee table. Since the furniture was provided by Tung-ping's *danwei,* I had no choice of color. The sofas and couch had olive green covers and our Oriental rug was a deep wine! The couch was against the bay window; it was Tung-ping's favorite spot. He usually left the living room door open. This way, he could see me the minute I stepped into our home.

The master bedroom was off the living room, to its west. We had a bathroom with a tub and a walk-in closet all to ourselves. Tung-ping's study was to the east of the living room. From his big desk there by the window, Tung-ping could see the green plants and flowers on our balcony whenever his eyes got tired. One wall there was covered with bookcases. I told the kids not to go into *Baba*'s room. In case they did, Tung-ping always locked his desk drawers.

The *ayi* and our youngest daughter, Little Buddha, lived in the room next to the study. Our other two daughters lived in the room across the hall from the *ayi.* They all shared a bathroom in their section. The kitchen was also on the north, with a porch and a back door. We kept our "beehive" coal cakes on the back porch. The dining room was next to the kitchen. We still had our *baxian* table with eight chairs a shade lighter than walnut. Light color furniture always appealed to me because it made a room look brighter. I usually sat on the side closest to the kitchen. Tung-ping's seat was across from mine. He wanted to sit next to the living room so that he could answer the phone and the door.

When I was nearing our home, I looked up and saw our

apartment building. "Today is Saturday," I said to myself. "Maybe by chance Tung-ping is waiting for me at home. Maybe he is at his favorite place, sitting on the couch." I longed to see him the minute I opened the door.

We had snowy white curtains on the bay windows behind the couch. Through these windows, we used to see lovely red and yellow Chinese tulips that I had planted in the flower box since they were one of Tung-ping's favorite flowers. Inside, we had green plants everywhere giving life to the room. One wall had built-in shelves which used to display the souvenirs Tung-ping and I had brought back from around the world. On another wall was a picture of Aachen University where Tung-ping had worked for four years.

All of that — anything allegedly "bourgeois" — had been smashed or burned by the Red Guards or, ironically, by Tung-ping and me. Even the tulips outside the windows were dug up and thrown away.

"It was a shame," I thought. But then I comforted myself. "I still have Tung-ping and the kids. They are my most precious darlings." I knew I would be greeted by their kisses and hugs soon. I started to walk even faster towards our home.

As I climbed the final flight of stairs, thinking about my dear ones, the door of our apartment suddenly opened. There stood the *ayi*. She was weeping.

"Director Yao," she said, then stopped. She regained control and stammered out, "He was beaten to death."

What was the woman saying? Is she out of her mind? My feet were stuck to the floor, unable to move. My handbag slipped out from my hand.

"What?" I managed to ask, "What did you say?"

I could not understand her words. This isn't happening, I thought. It can't be true. Oh, God, it must be a nightmare. This isn't happening.

Our three girls ran over to me, crying and shaking. They led me by the hand into the living room.

I saw Tung-ping. He was on his favorite spot, the couch. But he was lying stiffly. His white shirt horribly red with bloodstains. His gray trousers were smeared with blood and dirt. His feet stuck out over the end of the couch. One foot was bare. His face was puffed and swollen, covered with black and blue marks. His glasses were gone.

Tung-ping was dead. My husband, my love, my life and the father of these three crying children, had been cruelly beaten to death.

I tried to collect myself. The girls retreated to their bedroom. I sat in the living room near the body of my husband and listened to our *ayi* stammer out the appalling details. Her words had an unreal quality. Yet right next to me was the stark painful reality.

The *ayi* said that upon hearing the pounding at the door, my husband put down his chopsticks and told the children: "Girls, I'd like you to go to your room for a minute." He nodded at the *ayi*, who quickly herded the girls into their room and closed the door. The pounding continued.

"Why don't you open the door?" roared a man outside. There were other angry voices. As Tung-ping approached the door, the men busted through it, splintering the wood. The attackers were wearing green army trousers and red armbands with "915" in yellow characters on them. Each had a helmet on. And many of them had metal pipes or spears in their hands.

Tung-ping eyed them. "Who are you looking for?" he asked calmly.

"Damn it! We're looking for you!" shouted one. "Why didn't you open the door right away? What were you doing?"

One of them stepped forward and slapped Tung-ping across the face. Then again and again.

They kept slapping at Tung-ping's face… Tung-ping had seen face-slapping before. In his hometown of Wuxi when he was a teenager, Tung-ping saw the Japanese aggressors slapping his compatriots' faces. Those sights enraged him. He soon made up his mind to study hard, become a scientist some day, and dedicate himself to his motherland. Tung-ping had also seen some traitors slapping the faces of Chinese citizens. Those incidents also made a deep impression on young Tung-ping. He started to read books on communism and in 1956 joined the Chinese Communist Party. He thought communism was the ideal system for China.

Today was the third time he witnessed face-slapping, but this time by the hands of his "comrades" — and at his own face.

They grabbed Tung-ping and pushed him out past the broken door and then shoved and dragged him down the stairs to the building door, kicking him along the way.

Outside our building were standing more 915 Revolutionaries. When they saw Tung-ping, they rushed forward. One of the men stepped up and slapped him hard across the face again. He grabbed Tung-ping's eyeglasses and dashed them on the ground and stomped on them.

At that time, eyeglasses were symbols of intellectuals, of book-readers, of the "stinking ninth elements." Children were taught that intellectuals, being unable to carry a heavy load or build a house, were inferior to the workers. Since intellectuals didn't know how to plow the fields or use a shoulder pole to carry the harvest, they were also inferior to the peasants. This contempt for the intellectual was nurtured from an early age.

For Tung-ping, his glasses were part of his identity, and in a very practical sense, indispensable. And so, the eyeglasses that Tung-ping had used to read journals, look through microscopes, peer into steel furnaces — and just an hour earlier, to inspect a document about China's first satellite — were crushed into the pavement.

The commotion attracted more people. Tung-ping's face began to swell. Some heartless "915 Proletarian Revolutionaries" continued to hit him. Blood came out from his nose and mouth. One of the 915 men kicked Tung-ping in the groin.

Then a 915 man named Yu, an electrician from the Second Academy of the Seventh Ministry located in the western part of Beijing, approached with an iron pipe (the kind used to route water to room radiators). He raised the pipe and swung it down on Tung-ping's head with a sickening thud. Blood spurted. Tung-ping crumpled to the pavement. He struggled to stand up.

Another 915 man named Gao came along. Gao was a cook in a factory nearby, Factory 211 run by the Seventh Ministry. He used his right hand every day to chop pork bones. Now, that very hand knocked Tung-ping down. Tung-ping stopped moving.

For forty-five years, Tung-ping's brain had never stopped working. From primary school, through middle school and then university, he had always finished at the top of his class. Working abroad, his colleagues marveled at this erudite, witty Chinese scientist who could charm people in several languages.

For forty-five years, Tung-ping's brain kept on reading and learning. He concentrated his time on science and knowledge; he also valued justice and love. He loved his work. He loved science. He loved China and the people in this land. He had bright hopes for the future.

"We'll have a lot of work to do when the Cultural Revolution is over, Comrades, let's do our utmost!" That's what he had told the engineers of Institute 703 in May.

"Chieh-ching, we'll have a long and sweet life ahead of us.

We'll have many years to work for our country." That's how he was looking forward to the future.

But, at that very moment, ignorance and brutality were taking the light out of a most precious jewel, the life of a scientist and a patriot!

The "revolutionaries" lifted Tung-ping by the arms and shoulders and dragged him away. A shoe and sock came off. Nobody paid any attention. He was dragged to the headquarters of 915 for questioning.

Tung-ping was propped up on a bench, leaning against a wall, a vacant look on his face. Their leader tried to question him. By then, Tung-ping could not talk. He could not see his tormentors nor could he hear their absurd accusations. He collapsed onto the floor.

Seeing this, the 915 commander ordered: "Get Yao Tung-ping out of here. Don't let him die in our headquarters."

The men dragged Tung-ping outside and back to our building. They gave him a few more kicks.

"Get up!" They shouted. Go back to your home. Do you expect us to carry you home?" Those words just hung there in the air.

A neighbor saw Tung-ping on the ground. He ran up and got our *ayi*, and they found that though Tung-ping was unconscious, he was still taking shallow breaths. Hospital 711 was only a couple of blocks away. It was one of the Seventh Ministry's hospitals.

But there was a cruel hitch: a permit was required from 915 men to take Tung-ping to the hospital. Our neighbor and the *ayi* had to request the permit from the very men who were responsible for the beating. The answer was a loud "No."

Our neighbors carried Tung-ping upstairs to our living room and laid him on the couch. He never regained consciousness.

My husband stopped breathing at 3 o'clock.

The *ayi* kept wiping her tears as she told the story. My grief was so intense that I literally wanted to die, to leave this cauldron of pain and join my husband. I couldn't help scolding myself for not being at Tung-ping's side when this attack happened. I could at least have shielded him with my body. Oh, why did I go to work? When he was beaten to death, I was standing on a packed bus working its way slowly across town. I'd rather have died with him.

Did he feel pain when he lost consciousness? In his last moments, did he realize he was leaving his wife and daughters forever? Was he calling my name and trying to get hold of my hands? I've been asking myself these questions thousands of times since that bloody day in June of 1968.

It was only five days prior that I had seen him last. I had awoken at 5 a.m. that morning. Tung-ping and I had quietly eaten our breakfast, not wanting to wake the *ayi* and the kids. He insisted on walking with me to the bus stop a few blocks away, as he always did.

"Darling, you need the sleep. Please don't get up so early."

"Hey, my dear girl," he said, "aren't you the one who's always complaining that I am away too much? Don't you think I want to be with you too? Let's try to be with each other when I am in Beijing. I also treasure every little bit of time we are together."

At the stop, I squeezed his hand gently and stepped on the bus. "Good-bye, Chieh-ching," he said.

I found a seat by the window, and as I did every time, I said with my lips, "Good-bye, my darling."

Through the window, I could see him smiling and waving at me. I never dreamed that this would be the last time I would see my husband alive.

22

Rage of the Heavens

———————————— 🙠 ————————————

Tung-ping's body lay on the couch. His absence — an irreversible emptiness — weighed on me. It seemed impossible that the husband I had seen so lively on Monday morning was now gone forever.

I sat down on the floor next to him. A white band on his left arm caught my eye. It was the mark left by his watch, which was now gone. Some thought came into my mind like lightning. I went over to one of the armchairs and reached my hands under the cushion and immediately found the watch. I couldn't hold back my tears. I turned to Tung-ping and said "Darling, you thought those thugs came to rob you; you never suspected what they really wanted was your life."

Outside, the weather was changing. Thunder shook the windows and a hard rain fell. It was as if the heavens were angry about the brutality.

When the rain quieted down, the *ayi* tried to talk to me. She had trouble getting the words out. Finally, she said, "Could I stay somewhere else for the night, Comrade Peng?"

I agreed right away. I asked her to take a note for me to inform those outside our apartment compound that Tung-ping had been killed. Our phone line had been cut a that morning by some 915 Proletarian Revolutionaries before they came up to our house. But the *ayi* was too frightened to take the note. I couldn't take it myself and leave my girls alone. I had no choice but to send my oldest daughter to take the note to a friend's house. In the note, I asked this friend to escort her to a military representative to report her father's murder. I carefully folded the note, put it in her shoe and told her to give it to the military man personally. I watched her leave.

Time passed. Our apartment, once a sweet, warm, and wonderful home, was now an eerie morgue. I sat, limp and quiet, holding my young ones, aged three and eight, in my arms.

Soon after the Cultural Revolution had begun two years earlier, two other families had been moved into our apartment, which the 916 Revolutionaries considered far too large. But those families, like the *ayi*, had fled after the violence of the afternoon.

I waited for my daughter to return. The rain had stopped. When dusk fell and she hadn't returned, I became frightened. Had someone grabbed her? Had something horrible happened to her as well? I had to go look for her. I turned to my two young ones and told them to stay in the bedroom and not open the door for anyone.

I walked through the living room, past the still body, out the door and down the steps into the evening air. I headed for a canteen about one hundred meters away. It had been turned into a "headquarters" by the 915 faction. It was the very place to which my dying husband had been dragged earlier that afternoon.

As I neared the headquarters, I saw a man in his thirties, tall and broad-shouldered, wearing a helmet, white shirt and green trousers — the unofficial uniform of the Proletarian Revolutionaries. His red armband with yellow characters identified him as belonging to the 915 faction. I walked right up to him. "Why did you beat my husband Yao Tung-ping to death?" I demanded to know.

"We did not beat him to death," the man replied dismissively. "When we sent him home, he was alive."

"Sent him home alive?" I sputtered. "Your men threw him on the pavement in front of our building. You didn't care if he was alive or dead. When people asked to send him to the hospital for emergency treatment, you didn't allow it."

The man stood there. I forged on.

"Didn't Chairman Mao teach you that you should have revolutionary humanitarianism?" I said. "And you claim you are Chairman Mao's revolutionaries. Then how come you were so cruel to Yao Tung-ping? Is that the proletarian way to treat a dying man?"

My face turned hotter and hotter. I no longer cared if my words got me in trouble. The worst had happened; what else could they do to me?

"Who gave you the right to take my husband away? Who gave you the right to beat him?"

"And now my daughter hasn't come home. Did you take her away? Did you beat her too?"

The man scoffed. "What's the matter with you? How should I know where your daughter is? If you can't find her, what concern is that to us?" He turned and walked into their "headquarters."

I turned back for home. When I entered our apartment, I saw my two little girls standing by the door of the living room. Their father's lifeless body was right behind them. They came to me and we embraced, each trying to comfort the others by not showing grief. We wept silently.

That night, the three of us crammed into one bed. The same bed where Tung-ping and I had slept for years. The girls cried themselves to sleep. But how could I go to sleep? Tung-ping was in the next room. Right there. But the distance was immense — the distance between life and death.

泅

A few weeks earlier, Tung-ping and I had been in this very same bed, talking seriously after the children had gone to sleep. I had been unable to convince Tung-ping that he should move somewhere else until the situation at the Seventh Ministry cooled down. He had said that Chairman Mao would never allow anything truly bad to happen here in the capital.

What a fatal mistake it was!

Tung-ping and I were too naive, too trustful of others. We underestimated the chaos, violence and brutality of the Great Proletarian Cultural Revolution. We paid for it dearly. Now he was gone, our family broken. Forever.

The long night passed slowly. My husband was in the next room, my oldest daughter was missing.

At long last, the sky began to lighten. Strips of sunshine came through the window. It was June 9. Two military representatives — one short, one tall — came to the door. With them was my daughter. She ran through the door into my open arms.

I looked up from our embrace to see several PLA soldiers coming through the door, carrying buckets of ice. The officers directed them to the bathroom across the hall from the master bedroom. What was going on? This couldn't be…

But it was true. They put the blocks of ice in the bathtub, returned to the living room, lifted Tung-ping's body off the couch and carried it into the bathroom and placed it in the tub. They closed the windows and doors tight, creating a kind of freezer.

The PLA officer turned to me. He explained that the night before, my daughter had arrived at their office and delivered the note I had written. It became late, and they were afraid it wasn't safe to send her home, so they let her sleep on a bunk they had in their office.

"Why didn't you send somebody to accompany her home?" I said. "I was crazy with worry and fear."

He tried to soothe me. "Yesterday," he began, "when Premier Zhou heard that Comrade Yao Tung-ping was killed, he became so enraged that he sent Comrade Su Yu here in a helicopter to investigate what had happened."

The Premier knew? Comrade Su Yu came? Su was a four-star general, a former Minister of Defense. I continued to listen.

"At that time," he was saying, "your daughter walked into the office. So we asked the little girl to tell everything to Comrade Su. By the time she had finished, it was too late."

I guess I was supposed to be impressed, but still I asked, "Did you really expect a nine-year-old girl would get the entire story straight? You comrades have been at the Seventh Ministry for some time now. You know that my husband had no political stains, and that his history was clean and clear. You know what a good comrade he was."

The PLA officers admitted that Tung-ping was a good comrade, devoted to his work. And they admitted that his killing was unexpected. The tall PLA officer said he was in the middle of a haircut when he got the word. "I was so shocked that I jumped from my seat and my face was almost cut," he said.

His tone became serious and he tried to console me: "Our great leader, Chairman Mao, personally initiated this Great Proletarian Cultural Revolution. Our beloved leader vowed to guard our country from imperialism and revisionism and prevent her from changing color from red to white."

I kept silent. The other officer squared his shoulders and said solemnly: "Chairman Mao taught us, 'Where there is revolution, there is sacrifice.' Since this Cultural Revolution is the biggest and most important event that has ever taken place in our Party's history, sacrifice is inevitable. Comrade Peng, please put the nation's interest above personal grief."

The tall one made another attempt. "Chairman Mao's closest comrade-in-arms, Vice Chairman Lin Biao, made it clear that 'the gains of the Cultural Revolution are the greatest, the greatest and the greatest, while the losses are minimal, minimal and minimal.' So please attach greater weight to the overall situation and try not to be so sad."

It was easy for them to recite the words of Mao and Lin. They probably thought I would be comforted. But no one, nobody's words could lessen the pain and sorrow I was feeling.

I lost my dearest. Three children lost their precious father. Can anything make up for such losses?

And our country lost a well-educated, hard-working, selfless and devoted scientist. Tung-ping was only forty-five years old, in the prime years for a scientist. Was this a "minimal" loss?

I thought all these things, but didn't say them aloud. Hearing no response, the military men said they had to go.

"You are going?" I asked. "Are you just going to leave my husband's body in the tub in such hot weather?"

"We'll do our best to handle this event," one of them replied. "We've already contacted several hospitals. There just wasn't any room in any of the morgues."

"Too many killings?" I asked bluntly. "That's why there is no place for the bodies, right?"

"Now, now, Comrade Peng, we think you need a rest. The soldiers will come here twice a day with fresh ice. Please do take care of yourself." With that, they left quickly and ran downstairs, leaving my three children and me in the apartment, with my husband's body on ice, in the bathtub.

Tung-ping's death was one of hundreds of thousands during the Cultural Revolution. But this one made an impact at the highest levels of the government.

When Premier Zhou Enlai was told of my husband's death, he was shocked. So shocked that his tea cup slipped out from his hand. He instructed the Ministry of Public Security to thoroughly investigate the case. Two days later, on June 10, the Premier issued a statement:

"A grave case occurred on June 8 in the compound of the research institute where Comrade Yao Tung-ping, the Director of Institute 703, lived. He was beaten to death. This act will not be tolerated by state law or Party discipline. It must be dealt with severely. The criminals who have committed the crime shall be punished."

Beyond this pronouncement, Premier Zhou made an important decision to protect other scientists from harm. A list of scientists (especially those working on atomic research, missiles and satellites) was drawn up, and they were protected — with force when necessary.

It was too late for Tung-ping. But for the sake of others, it was one bit of good that came out of this tragedy.

天憤人怒

23

Where Are You?

———————⟋⟍———————

THE DOOR CLOSED behind the PLA officers. The three girls and I were left with a deep sadness that physically weighed us down. We didn't know how to console one another. The youngest, three-year-old Little Buddha, was on my lap. She reached up with her little hand and tried to wipe the tears from my face.

I looked around the living room. It seemed so very large, so empty. After we moved here in 1960, it was a lovely home. Then came the Cultural Revolution, and with it the orders to be rid of the "four olds." Our apartment, filled with plants, art and objects from around the world, never had a chance.

Now the only thing on the wall was a picture of Mao Zedong.

The room was also deadly quiet now. Before the Cultural Revolution began, my daughters were always talking and singing; laughter filled this room. It was the very sound of a happy home. If Tung-ping's work allowed him to come home at a reasonable hour, it felt like a holiday.

I could just hear them, "*Baba, Baba…!*" Everyone trying to talk to him, everyone trying to get him to tell stories. Little Buddha was especially attached to him. She'd climb up onto his knees and try to get her father to tell her a story or give her a kiss. Whenever he came home, she would run to set his slippers by the door. "*Baba*, your slippers!"

"Oh, *Baobei*," Tung-ping would say. It meant "Precious one." He would pick her up, kiss her, and lift her up and down. The others would chime in, "*Baba*, I'd like that also." "Me too, *Baba*." Tung-ping would shower the other two girls with kisses as well. When bedtime came, the girls always tried to stay in the living room with us. The *ayi* had to come into the room several times before they would finally relent.

Tung-ping knew it was difficult for all of us when he was away. Once, while out of town, he sent me a letter with a sketch inside. It showed a mother hen shielding three little chicks, waving good-bye to a strutting rooster. When the kids saw this, they all came over. "The big rooster is *Baba* — with his glasses on too," Little Buddha pointed out. "This one is me." "And this one is me." Her sisters identified themselves in the sketch. "And this is *Mama* — I am holding *Mama*'s wing," Little Buddha said making another discovery. Their chatter made me so happy. I guess that was exactly Tung-ping's intention.

Although trained as an engineer, Tung-ping had widely diverse interests. His Chinese was excellent and he could write poetry. When he wrote to me, he sometimes included a poem. That usually moved me so or made me laugh merrily.

Tung-ping also liked classical music. While I preferred Perry Como and Rogers and Hammerstein, under his influence I gradually learned to like Beethoven, Chopin, and Mozart. Mozart's 39th was his favorite, and it soon became mine. Many a night, we'd sit on the couch, listening to music without exchanging a word. I would rest my head on his shoulder. There was no need for words between us. We were intoxicated by the beauty of the music and by our love for each other.

But now... now I would never again have a chance to

listen to music with him. The girls would never have him to tell them stories. I couldn't hold back the tears.

My daughters shouldn't have such grief or sadness at this age. They should be singing, laughing and playing, as they had been until yesterday. Now those joyful days were gone forever. We Chinese say that the three great sorrows in life are: to lose one's father at an early age; to lose one's husband in middle age; and to lose one's son in old age. Our girls saw their father killed before their very eyes. It was an experience too horrible to forget.

As their mother, I knew I had to protect them, to keep their life as normal as possible. My first task was not of my choosing: I didn't want them to see their father's body constantly. Fortunately, we had two bathrooms, so they could be spared this further torment. I'd try my best to lessen their pain. I wanted to protect them, as a mother hen protects her little chicks.

As for me, I couldn't control myself. When the girls were in the other room, I went into the bathroom and knelt next to the tub. There he was, motionless. I touched his cold face. Tears blurred my vision. I couldn't see if the redness had disappeared from his face.

"Tung-ping, my love, can you hear me?" I said in a hoarse voice. "I long to talk to you. I long to be with you." Every time I walked in, I couldn't help crying.

While I was in college, I read *Wuthering Heights*. When Heathcliff tried to get Catherine out of her tomb and lay her down next to him, I dismissed it as the romantic exaggeration of Emily Brontë, something that could never happen in real life. But now, I fully understood it. When you love a person, you want to be with him, in life and in death. I wanted to follow Tung-ping! To the other world!

How was I going to face the coming days without him? Without seeing his dear face and eyes looking at me lovingly… without hearing his tender voice… without his gentle touch…

without him holding me when I woke up in bed. I would rather die than live without him.

Wait a minute, how did this idea come into my mind? "Could I really do that?" I asked myself. "No!" I shook my head. I had no freedom to take my own life. During those years, suicide was considered traitorous — to the Communist Party, to the people. If I took my life, my children would be branded for the rest of their lives as the "daughter of a traitor." They would be condemned to the most despicable lives. They would never be able to hold up their heads. They would be kicked into Hell, into the Eighteenth Hell.

Oh, God, I don't want to live and yet, I can't die. For the children, I must live. And, to get revenge for Tung-ping's death, I must live on. An old Chinese saying that I had never paid any attention to before now swam into my mind: "One cannot live under the same sky with the murderer of one's husband." I would do everything in my power to find the murderer and see to it that he was punished for his crime.

"*Mama*!" I heard my children's voices. "The PLA soldiers are here."

It was evening already. The soldiers were back with fresh ice. They rearranged the ice and checked the door and window of the bathroom. They suggested I close the windows and draw the curtains in all the rooms to keep the temperature down. There was no air conditioning then.

Shortly thereafter, the *ayi* returned to our home, as did the two couples who shared our apartment. On the day of the murder, the two families had gone away. Now they were back to gather their belongings. They told me that they had found a place to live.

I remembered Tung-ping's amenable reaction when the revolutionaries first declared that we had to share the apartment with others. (With a study, three bedrooms and two baths, our apartment was too big for just one family, some men from faction 916 had decided.) When these couples arrived, Tung-ping said, "Welcome," and asked *ayi* to help prepare their rooms. I put on a smile but didn't say anything. Each family took one of the bedrooms at the far end of the apartment. Our *ayi* and all three girls now crammed into the study and shared a bathroom with the newcomers.

The couples used our kitchen but ate their meals in their rooms. Tung-ping and I still lived in the master bedroom at the west end of the apartment, facing south. I stayed there as much as possible, except when watching television with the kids in the living room. I didn't like it at all. "I don't care for other people living in our house. No privacy," I would complain to Tung-ping. "I'd rather live in a smaller apartment."

He replied quietly, "They won't live here long. Just do this favor for me, OK, my dear girl?" Listening to his words, and seeing him get thinner every day, I had no heart to refuse this latest intrusion into our home life. Besides, it was Tung-ping who had to give up his study.

As the two couples packed their things, they brought word from outside. They told me that the news of Tung-ping's killing was all over the compound. Everyone was saying if a person like Tung-ping was killed, this place must be dangerous. People were moving out of the area to stay with their relatives. Some were even heading out to farm fields to spend the night, as if a war were going on.

They told me a group of 916 young men tried to start a revenge fight.

"Comrade Peng, it was a good thing you sent your daughter to the military representative. He read what you wrote and it calmed people down."

208

I told them I had written just a few lines. I reported that Tung-ping had been killed; I asked them to find the murderer. I further wrote that although Tung-ping had been killed by some thugs from 915, I didn't want this incident to spread violence. I didn't want this tragedy repeated. I didn't want others' hearts to be torn, as mine had been. I didn't want to see more widows and fatherless children.

At that time, false rumors were beginning to spread. Some disreputable people were claiming that we had a radio to communicate with the "outside" (meaning overseas). I became angry. "Those people are really hideous. Beating people to death and then making up lies."

The couples also told me that another rumor had me working for the Voice of America while I was living in the United States. "Work for Voice of America?" I said. "That's ridiculous. I've never listened to VOA. I don't even know where the office of the Voice of America is located!"

The families said good-bye.

A little while later, the *ayi* packed her suitcase. She opened her mouth but nothing came out. She hesitated, and then finally said, "I'm sorry, Comrade Peng, I am too frightened to live here. Please... Can I quit?"

I nodded. I understood. After they all left, I closed the door. With Tung-ping killed, and some people trying to spread a rumor that we were spies, who would dare live under the same roof with us. Although China had become a socialist country in 1949, in many ways, the society remained almost medieval. People knew the age-old risks of association. Throughout Chinese history, if one committed a serious crime, not only the immediate family would be wiped out, but relations up "to the ninth cousin" (*zhu lian jiu zu*) would suffer some kind of punishment.

My girls came to me quietly. "*Mama*, please rest. You can't stay up all the time. You must get some sleep."

"Good girls," I said, "Why don't you go to bed first? I'll go to bed right away."

I lay on the bed. Another night, but again, how could I go to sleep? I thought of our many nights on that bed, our love, our intimacies, our tenderness, and our happiness. I felt as if Tung-ping were close to me again, chatting and hands touching.

"Tung-ping," I used to kid him, "can't you speak faster?"

He replied, slowly as always: "When you talk, you should speak slowly and clearly. You know, when Winston Churchill made a speech, he always enunciated, word by word."

"Ah, Churchill making a speech! But you are talking about love with your wife! Do you have to be that slow?"

"I can't change my habit," he said. "I am unable to talk like you, so fast, just like a machine gun. Whenever you come home, my ears get no rest. 'Tung-ping, do this, Tung-ping, do that.'"

He faked an exaggerated sigh. "There's nothing I can do about it now," he said. "I can only blame myself for marrying a young lady who goes da–da–da all the time." Before I could answer, he sealed my lips with a kiss.

I recalled the various ways that Tung-ping had changed my life. When we returned to China in 1957, I discovered that life here was very different. I didn't think I could fit into this society. But he encouraged me.

"This is our country," he said. "I know you can adjust to a different kind of life easily. Don't worry, you'll get used to it."

When food was scarce during the Great Leap Forward (1959 to 1961), I was weak with hunger, but Tung-ping took care of me. He shared his supply of food with me and the kids. He even left some of his 40 soy beans just for me.

When I had a miscarriage, he comforted me tenderly: "Just

so long as you are alright, my dear girl, nothing else matters."

When the Cultural Revolution began, and my own students became rude and disrespectful, I got real mad. It was Tung-ping who reassured me.

"Chieh-ching," he said, "one word from Chairman Mao, everything will become normal. Don't feel so bad. OK?"

He described how our life would be in the years ahead. He assured me that he would apply to be transferred to "the third line" area after the Cultural Revolution was over, so that we could be together every day. (This was a reference to the hinterlands where Mao had ordered some vital ministries moved, after Sino-Soviet relations became tense. But no one wanted to settle in those remote regions. To amend this, the Seventh Ministry had announced that anyone who was willing to work in "the third line" area could bring his family along — and one's wife would be assigned a job there too.)

Another night loomed with Tung-ping's body stiff and cold in the bathroom, across the hall from our bedroom.

Now, I was completely alone. Now, if I suffer in my heart, whom should I tell? If I have a problem, who will help me?

"Tung-ping," I cried out. "Where are you? I can't go on without you. Tung-ping, darling, where are you?"

我不能没有你，我的爱人

24

Four Days in Purgatory

————————— ◠ —————————

A KNOCK ON THE DOOR made me sit up. It was the morning of June 10th. Another night had passed without any real sleep. I opened the door and saw some PLA soldiers with ice. "Comrades," I asked, "didn't the military representative come with you? Do you know when the burial is going to be?"

"We don't know about that, Comrade," one of them said. "We were ordered to change the ice twice a day, morning and evening."

I tried to contain my frustration. "Would you please ask your officers which day my husband will be buried? It's too hot. To leave the body with the family is not right. I'm sure you know, without the military representative's permit, no place will accept the body. Will you please ask them?"

They said they would report my inquiry to the officers, and went about the grim task of replenishing the ice. Most of the ice blocks had melted and the water drained out of the tub. They dried the tub, put the fresh ice under and around Tung-ping's body.

In the evening, the same two PLA officers came again. They announced as soon as they came in, "Sorry, Comrade

Peng, we couldn't come earlier, we had to tend to something urgent."

The other said, "Director Yang would like to see you, Comrade Peng. We're going right now, OK?"

"Director Yang?"

"Yes, Director Yang of the Military Control Committee of the Seventh Machine Building Ministry. He is a Long March cadre and an admiral in the Navy."

"Just a moment, let me check the girls first."

With the *ayi* gone and the other families having left, the apartment seemed bigger and emptier than ever before. Despite this, the three girls stayed crowded into one room, which had one double bed and one single bed. I opened the door and the single bed was unoccupied! All three were asleep in the large bed, the youngest in the middle. I locked the doors and left with the military representatives.

There was a military jeep parked outside. The driver was a PLA soldier. The roads were dark. During the Cultural Revolution, some people had smashed the bulbs of the streetlights. Nobody had bothered to fix them. The jeep's headlights provided the only light. We drove slowly over the stone-slabbed streets in our compound. We passed tall trees on both sides, dark green in the shadows.

I could glimpse people among the trees, but when they saw the military jeep, they turned away quickly. It seemed as though in our district, the 915 Proletarian Revolutionaries were on duty around the clock because their headquarters was right here. I had heard that the 916 faction was doing the same thing in the vicinity of their headquarters. Tung-ping hadn't told me about this. He was so worried about the slowdown of work at the institute that he probably wasn't paying much attention to the faction fights.

After we left our residential district, we entered the working quarters which had tall brick walls around it. A PLA soldier stood by one side of the gate. Our driver showed a pass and the soldier let us through. Here in the working quarters, the road was wide and lined with beautiful lily-shaped street lights. But these too were broken. It was pitch black.

We arrived at a gray, four-story building, dark except for a few rooms. We walked inside and I could hear our steps reverberate on the bare floor. The two officers led me upstairs to the second floor. In the long corridor, we met nobody. Before entering the office, the men announced, "Reporting."

Someone inside said "Come in." We walked into a big office with a huge desk, an oblong conference table with straight-backed chairs tucked-in neatly under the table.

Admiral Yang came out from behind his desk to shake my hand. "Comrade Peng, I asked you to come because it's quiet here."

The Admiral was a man in his fifties, of medium height with a round jovial face. He spoke with a Sichuan accent. Though he wore a Navy uniform, he didn't look like a military man to me. But I knew he was a veteran of the Long March, the heroic journey that started in 1934, kept the Communist army intact and made possible the ultimate victory in 1949.

Admiral Yang came forward and greeted me, "Premier Zhou has said on different occasions that Comrade Yao Tung-ping was a good comrade. The Premier was shocked and saddened by Comrade Yao's death. As a result, the Premier has ordered us to draw up a list of scientists who are working at the Seventh Machine Building Ministry and have made important contributions to the space industry of our country. Premier Zhou further ordered us to safeguard them. If necessary, with force."

It was my turn to speak. "If the PLA had taken such precautions earlier, my husband wouldn't have been killed," I said. "I hear Premier Zhou has also instructed the Military Control Committee to track down the killers and hand them over to justice.

Has the PLA found anything out yet? It's been three days since my husband was beaten to death — in broad daylight too. I don't think it should be too hard to identity the murderer."

"Not so fast, Comrade Peng," the admiral said. "We know how you feel and we admire your courage and composure. You don't know how complicated the situation is at the Ministry here. That makes it hard to find the killer. Please have trust in the Party, we'll do all we can. Give us more time."

Nodding at the PLA officers, he said, "They reported to me that when some people wanted to take revenge on the culprits from 915, you said, 'No more widows or fatherless children.' Is that the case?"

He was referring to my note. One of the officers nodded. Yang went on, "I said to myself, that comrade is "*liaobuqi*" (outstanding). That's the right spirit. I hope you will keep this spirit. Even during that situation, you kept a cool head, and helped us to prevent a bigger faction fight. This was not easy. Not easy at all, considering what had just happened to your family. As Chairman Mao taught us, 'Wherever there is revolution, there is sacrifice.' Please turn your grief into strength. Rest well, take care of the children and leave everything to the Party."

One of the military representatives stood up, reporting to the admiral, "Officer, the coroner will be going over to Comrade Yao Tung-ping's apartment. We must go now."

Admiral Yang said good-bye and told me again to trust the Party and take care of the kids and myself.

We were quiet as we drove back. The night wind blew through the window and I felt a chill. The shadows of the trees in the wind looked like ghosts clad in dark green leaves, dancing. As we arrived, it was already 10:30 p.m. Another military jeep arrived at the same time and two men emerged, one with a camera. They were from the coroner's office.

We went upstairs. One of the military men directed the coroner to the bathroom while the other stayed in the living room. He said he wanted to keep me company. I knew his real purpose was to keep me away from the bathroom.

"Why did you ask the coroner to come?"

"After Premier Zhou's instructions to find the murderer, there was another rumor saying that Comrade Yao had died of a heart attack. Some people were even saying that he had committed suicide. That's why we wanted the coroner to come and examine the body."

That set me off.

"How can those people stoop so low? To beat people to death, then spread such lies."

I took out a Chinese writing brush and some paper. I wanted to write a big-character poster, the common form of public communication in those days. While they were often used to denounce individuals for perceived counter-revolutionary crimes, in this case I wanted to tell people the truth: my husband had been beaten to death.

The officer got agitated when he realized what I was doing. "Don't write a poster about that," he urged. "If the word gets out, it will smear the Great Proletarian Cultural Revolution."

"Who is it that is smearing the Great Proletarian Cultural Revolution?" I shot back. "Me — or the killers?"

He couldn't answer. He lit a cigarette and smoked quietly.

I started to write, but it would take me several days to finish the poster. It briefly told of Tung-ping's life, and told exactly how he was killed. I asked some comrades to paste copies on the walls in the neighborhood. I hear other people copied it by hand and posted it all over Beijing. Here is a condensed version of my big-character poster:

AN APPEAL FOR JUSTICE
FOR THOSE WHO MURDERED MY HUSBAND IN COLD BLOOD

Revolutionary Comrades:

Let us first of all wish our most beloved great leader, the reddest sun in our hearts, Chairman Mao, longevity. Long Live Chairman Mao!

And wish Chairman Mao's closest comrade-in-arms, Vice Chairman Lin Biao, excellent health forever. Forever!

With grief and indignation, I, in tears of blood, accuse the counter-revolutionary black hands who murdered my husband Comrade Yao Tung-ping in cold blood. I pray that our great leader Chairman Mao and the Central Committee of the Chinese Communist Party make a thorough investigation into the case.

Revolutionary comrades, arise and resolutely track down the criminals and instigators behind them.

Blood must atone for blood!...

Revolutionaries of the Seventh Machine Building Ministry:

I beg you to draw lessons of blood from my husband's death, resolutely carry out Premier Zhou Enlai's June 10 instruction, see through the plot of the class enemy, and get united to face our common foe. We must do all we can to track down and expose those who instigated this from behind, those who directed the beating on site, and those who did the killing. Let us hack off the black hand and clear the way for revolution. I am convinced that Chairman Mao's Revolutionary Line is sure to triumph over the Seventh Machine Building Ministry and the whole nation."

A proletarian cultural revolutionary salute!

Peng Chieh-ching
June 18, 1968

Later, I was told that some people wept as they read my poster. I took some solace in that. I realized that kind and good people outnumbered cruel ones in that tumultuous era.

After a long time, the two coroners and the other PLA officer came out of the bathroom. Each coroner shook my hand without saying a word. But sympathy and compassion were evident on their faces.

One of the PLA officers said, "It's almost midnight. Please have a rest, Comrade Peng. Tomorrow we have to go to the Navy Hospital to have an autopsy."

"Autopsy?" I don't understand.

"This was only a preliminary examination," the coroner explained gently. "Only in the hospital can we perform an autopsy. Then we will be able to do a detailed report."

They left. I sat on the sofa thinking about the past. Tung-ping, I thought, when you were alive, you always put work first. Remember when you proposed to me, you told me you would always put your work first. I told you I could accept that. I only loved you. I had no interest in your work.

So you put your work first, and you never had one day without working. Now, finally, you have time to rest, but you are resting forever.

You will never smile to me again, you will never talk to me again, and you will never love me again. We had love and happiness, but they were taken away by those thugs. Tung-ping, you were too strict with your principles. That was why you antagonized some mean people. That was why you were killed.

Tears flowed down my face. Oh, the heavenly times we'd had.

煉獄四日

25

Sending Charcoal in the Snows

———————— 🐚 ————————

THE LONG DAYS of unspeakable horror stretched on and on, as the girls and I lived in the apartment while Tung-ping's body was kept in the bathtub. The days and nights blurred, soldiers came and went, the trip to meet with the admiral — nothing seemed clear. I tried to get some sleep, but I kept waking, thinking my husband would be coming through the front door any moment, as he had so many other times late at night.

I recalled one such night years before when the children were in bed and I was waiting up for him. I heard his slow, heavy steps on the stairway; I knew he was tired. I got up, warmed his dinner and filled the tub with water. He kept saying, "Thank you, thank you, Chieh-ching, I'll do it myself."

"Oh, darling," I thought now, "if you were alive, I would care for you, no matter how injured you were. Even if you couldn't move, I would still love you."

I didn't know what time it was. I kept staring at Tung-ping's watch — the Omega he brought back from Switzerland and wore every day — on the desk near our double bed.

Finally, the sun rose again. Now I knew what time it was. I figured out it was the 11th of June. The rays came filtering through the leaves of the trees, through the screen door and landed on Mao Zedong's portrait. I immediately thought of the song, "The East is Red." During the Cultural Revolution, you could hear this song all over the country:

> The east is red.
> The sun is rising.
> China has a Mao Zedong.
> He has found happiness for the people.
> He is the great savior of the people!

I looked at the portrait. The music and the lyrics of "The East is Red" seemed to be floating in the air. I cried out: "Chairman Mao, please save us! Please make Tung-ping alive!"

My crying woke the children. They ran into the living room, wearing their pajamas, hair uncombed. They rushed to me crying, "*Baba*! We want our *Baba*, we want our *Baba*."

Suddenly the PLA soldiers were at the door with more ice. I had forgotten to lock the door the night before. They saw us crying, and didn't know what to do. They talked among themselves and left.

I learned soon enough that they had gone to Hospital 711 and requested a doctor to check on me. A woman physician arrived, wearing a white uniform, carrying a doctor's bag. She led me to bed and gave me an injection and some medicine. Then the doctor, a pleasant woman with a round face in her thirties, said to the girls, "Don't cry. If you cry, your *Mama* will not stop crying."

She turned to me: "This tragedy would be awful for any family to endure, Comrade Peng. But it's already happened. You must face the reality. If you become sick, think of the poor children.

They will have no one to turn to."

I said nothing. Her eyes became red.

She told me in a soft voice, "When we heard Director Yao had been beaten to death, we were all shocked. Everybody was sad. When you weren't home, if the children ever became sick, Director Yao always took them to the doctor himself."

"He was so patient and kind. We all envied you, saying you were a lucky comrade to have such a nice husband." She lowered her head slightly. "Oh, who would think such a tragic thing would happen."

She added. "I don't think it's healthy for the children to be kept in the house all the time. I'm going to take the two little ones downstairs and let them go outside. The oldest one can stay here with you."

As she left, she reminded me again, "If you need anything, Comrade Peng, let the military representatives know. Just think, they left you and the children with a dead body for four days. That's a shame."

After the doctor left, I think I must have dozed off. When I woke up, the three girls were in the room.

"Didn't I tell you to go downstairs? How come you don't want to play downstairs?" I asked them.

They started to cry. "*Mama*, there is nobody outside. I took Little Buddha to Ruby's house to play. Before we could even get in the door, Ruby came out, saying her *Baba* would not let her play with us. She said her *Baba* had told her that something was wrong with our family."

I got up to wipe their eyes. "Don't cry. So Ruby didn't play with you today. There are other friends. Didn't Premier Zhou say your *Baba* was a good comrade? I'm sure when Ruby's *Baba* finds out, he'll let her play with you. Now, please don't cry."

Weiming then announced, "*Mama*, dinner is ready." When I walked into the dining room, I was surprised to find, there were several dishes on our *baxian* table.

"Did you make these?"

"Oh no, my sisters brought them back."

They went to sit at their usual places. Tung-ping's place was vacant. I sat at mine, staring at the unoccupied seat, trying not to think of the happy mealtimes our whole family used to have, with everyone trying to say something funny. All the girls angling to get their father's or mother's attention.

The younger ones explained that when they came back from Ruby's house, they saw their friend Star carrying a basket. "She said her *Mama* made some dishes for us."

Star's father had received his Ph.D. from Cornell University in hydraulic engineering. He had been born in 1922, the same year as Tung-ping. Her mother was from Brunei. She looked like an island beauty from Hawaii with sun-tanned skin, big black eyes and raven hair. They had met and gotten married in the United States. They arrived at Yong-An Hostel a few months before we did. Her father also worked at the Seventh Ministry now and their family lived in the apartment building in front of ours.

This gift basket was special in another way. Star's mother had told me that her husband had been repudiated because of his American background. Just a few days earlier, the revolutionaries had subjected him to the "jet plane" punishment. This excruciating position was a common punishment during the Cultural Revolution. Despite the tenuous situation their family was in, they ignored the danger and sent food to us. It was like "*xue zhong song tan*" (sending charcoal in the snows) — sharing something precious. A real act of courage. I was very touched.

Later on, Star's mother told me she had seen from their living-room window how the "915s" beat Tung-ping. She said her family couldn't do anything about it because one of the "commanders" of 915 had moved into their apartment. But what she had seen must have been a horrible sight. She sent Star and Star's brother to the United States for advanced education as soon as China's doors opened.

She herself left China in the early 1980s. Her husband later went to join them. They never returned. They are now retired and living in a small town in New Jersey.

Later that night, after I put the children to bed and locked the door, several PLA soldiers arrived, along with some officers. They came to remove Tung-ping's body from the bathroom. Together we all went to the morgue that was at the Navy Hospital. I wanted to accompany Tung-ping's body to the hospital but they wouldn't let me. One of the officers stayed with me in the car to make sure I wouldn't go into the hospital. He smoked one cigarette after another while waiting with me.

As I sat in the car, watching his cigarette glowing in the darkness, I thought back to ten years earlier, when Tung-ping and I were married and moving into our apartment next door to this same Navy Hospital.

"How do you like our new home, Tung-ping? Next door to a hospital," I said. "Pretty convenient if one of us ever gets sick."

"But that's a Navy Hospital," he pointed out. "We're civilians. I don't think we can go in. But of course, in an emergency I think they would accept us."

Who would have thought that Tung-ping would eventually be admitted to the hospital — not to see a doctor, but for an autopsy.

Anger welled up inside me. I looked up at the sky and cried to heaven, "I swear to God, I will track down the killers! I swear they will get punished!"

It was left to me to notify Tung-ping's relatives. Since our phone had been cut off, I had to send a letter to Tung-ping's brother, who was still working as an editor in Beijing. Another to his younger sister and her husband, who were university teachers in Chengdu. They traveled up to Beijing and stayed at our house, helping to look after the children. They sorted through Tung-ping's things, finding only clothes and books.

His sister heaved a sigh. "He worked for so many years and yet he remained the same person he was in his university days, keeping a simple lifestyle." Tears streamed down her face. "Dear brother! You were such a nice person. Why did those heartless thugs kill you?" She told me she had just received his June shipment of sugar and milk powder when they got the news of his death. It made things even more unbelievable; hadn't he just sent them a package?

Our apartment building was only a hundred meters away from 915 headquarters. With their "soldiers" constantly patrolling the vicinity, many of Tung-ping's colleagues dared not stop by. Then came Premier Zhou Enlai's order. The guards disappeared and Tung-ping's colleagues finally came to pay their respects.

An engineer told me of Tung-ping's final acts at work. He had attended a meeting on June 5 about technical matters in the manufacture of China's first satellite *Dong Fang Hong* (The East is Red). Tung-ping volunteered on behalf of Institute 703 to solve the the challange of ultra-high temperature resistent materials in that satellite. He immediately assigned subsidiary tasks to all the departments concerned. Another engineer told me that, while cleaning out Tung-ping's desk, he came across the document that Tung-ping was correcting on the morning of his murder. It was about the heat-proof materials for this satellite.

Then a woman engineer who had cancer spoke up: "Why wasn't it me who died? How I wish I could have died in Director Yao's stead! My death means nothing. But how can we go on with our work now that the director is murdered?"

We were all moved by her words. Our sobbing filled the room.

That week the famous words of a great patriot and scholar, Wen Tianxiang, kept coming into my mind. "No one has ever escaped the clutches of death since time immemorial. But my name will go down in history for the cause for which I shed my blood." Wen Tianxiang (1236-1283) was a high official in the Song dynasty. At the time, the Mongols were occupying North China. Wen donated all of his property to the Song army and fought against the aggressors. Then in a battle, he was captured by the Mongols. Because of his popularity and influence, the Mongols offered Wen a high position in their court if he switched to their side. Wen refused and was executed.

These two verses written after his capture 700 hundred years ago have inspired Chinese from generation to generation and are known to all educated Chinese today. And I recalled from my days in America, similar words of another revolutionary hero, Nathan Hale: "I regret that I have but one life to give for my country."

Tung-ping was like Wen and Hale!

Even though this was "modern" China and the year was 1968, one thing that still remained true was the concept of *zhu lian jiu zu* However unfair, the entire family "up to the ninth cousin" suffered for the sins (or perceived sins) of the individual. In my situation, that meant one thing: I had to clear Tung-ping's name or my daughters would suffer the consequences.

A few days after Tung-ping's body had been removed from our apartment, I asked the Military Control Commission to pursue two things: find out the killer(s) and make a political assessment of Tung-ping. The assessment was crucial, because at that time in China, if someone was determined to be a "class enemy," killing was considered acceptable.

The Ministry's Military Control Commission asked me to wait however. The circumstances were "very complicated," they said.

Weeks, then months began to slip by. I was told Tung-ping's body was still at the morgue, but I was never informed officially. My husband's killers were loose, and my husband's political reputation was unsettled. Neither of these was acceptable.

Finally, some leading cadres from Institute 703 came by. It turned out they only had information about Tung-ping's pension.

Item one: 430 *yuan*, lump sum.
Item two: 20 *yuan* a month for each child until age 16.

That was it. There was little I could say about the lump sum, although it was less than two months of Tung-ping's pay. But as for item two, I gave them a piece of my mind.

"You all know children are not permitted to go to school until they are seven," I began. "Then they have six years of primary school and six years of middle school. That means they will be nineteen years old when they finish. No jobs will be assigned to them while they are still in school. Don't you comrades think item two should be changed to 20 *yuan* for each child until she is assigned a job or graduates from school?"

They nodded their heads. But on the certificate they gave me, it still said 20 *yuan* until age 16.

In early July, about a month after the murder, I was required to return to work. The term "work" was loosely defined. All the schools in China were closed. Our only job was to "make revolution." No winter vacation, no summer vacation. All administration and department heads had been pushed aside and placed under investigation. When I returned to the college, I saw the ex-head of the English Department. She embraced me but didn't say a word; she couldn't. She was under investigation herself.

I was told by a friend of a despicable plan that involved me. A particular "revolutionary" student in my class, a young man from a "red" family, was now the Number One Hand of the Revolutionary Committee of our department. Reportedly this fellow told his classmates, "How come Peng hasn't shed a tear since her husband was killed?"

Incredibly, he tried to place me under suspicion. "Maybe she's a spy," he said. "Maybe she had been planning to murder an outstanding scientist of our Party, so she married him. I think we should go and investigate her."

None of his classmates said anything. He had to drop it.

I couldn't help wondering if others were entertaining such thoughts. After all, Red Guards had been taught that those of us educated abroad were spies or class enemies. No matter that we had given up good jobs, comfortable living conditions, foreign residence permits and in some cases citizenship.

I remember one spirited Red Guard from a well-known university in Beijing who came to our school. This girl of about twenty was wearing the typical Red Guard army-green uniform, tight belt and red armband with the Chinese characters for Red Guard on it. She stood there, with her Little Red Book in hand, "First of all, we wish our great leader Chairman Mao a long life!" We all raised our little red books and shouted after her, "Long live Chairman Mao!"

Then she shouted, "Rebellion is justified" and we repeated, "Rebellion is justified!"

She started talking about her revolutionary experiences at

her university. I don't remember it all, but one thing she said still gives me goose bumps thirty years later: "Those old 'stinking ninth elements' are die-hard people. When dealing with them, you must not be soft-hearted. You should treat them with the proletarian iron fist." She raised her fist for emphasis.

She continued, "So when they didn't confess what they had done in the old society, we Red Guards of Chairman Mao used pliers to pull out their teeth. When we pulled out one, they would confess some. Then we would pull another, until we got what we wanted from them."

Even now I still feel terrible thinking about this. That Red Guard reminded me of the character Madame Defarge, in *A Tale of Two Cities* by Charles Dickens. She calmly counted the heads being chopped off as she did her knitting.

As a mother, as a human being, I had to wonder: What would become of this young woman when she stepped into society? What kind of person would she be?

26

A Scarlet "X"

WHEN I returned to school in early July, I brought all my daughters along to live with me. I certainly wasn't going to leave the girls in the same apartment where their father's body had been for those four painful days. And I had to stay at my teaching job, because my salary would now be the family's only income. Life would be much harder now.

I still lived in Room 204 in Building 6. The room across the hall happened to be vacant, so I applied for that one for the girls. Parenting would also be harder now. Tung-ping used to help the girls with their homework and handle other parental duties, as I was so far away across town. Now, that too was my responsibility. During the day, I tried my best to keep the girls' spirits up by keeping them distracted and busy.

I became constantly haunted by a foreboding that some tragedy would again befall our family. I worried day and night about the past, about how the children were coping with it at present, and always about the future. How would these horrendous events affect them? Were they doomed to be second-class citizens, even in this socialist society?

I became very strict. There would be no ideological slip-ups in our household. I kept them in the dormitory rooms after school. There were some handwritten books being passed around — nothing subversive, but unapproved. I forbade my girls from reading them. I was as watchful and protective as any mother hen.

A friend said to me, "Chieh-ching, you may think your life is over. But your daughters are still kids. Let them go out and play, let them go to the movies." So I did. I let them go see the one movie being shown then every Saturday night, "Underground Warfare," a movie about the war with the Japanese. My girls saw it so often that they could recite the dialogue before the actors did. They would play war games afterwards and everyone wanted to be in the role of the Communist soldiers.

Nights were difficult. I had trouble sleeping, something that had always been a challenge. Sometimes I sensed Tung-ping close to me, touching my face as he used to. "Don't worry, darling," I'd murmur, "I will bring our children up. Please don't worry."

In those days, school children generally wore cotton trousers and shirts — even shoes were made of cloth. I bought clothing a size larger, so the child could grow into it, then pass it along to the next girl. Eventually the clothes were all patched at the knees and elbows. I tried my best to find cloth to match; sometimes I had to make the patches in contrasting colors. Little did I know patched jeans or even holes at the knees were the fashion in other countries.

As for food, there were ways to cut corners without cutting nutrition. I bought a lot of carrots instead of more expensive apples. In summer, tomatoes were $\frac{1}{10}$ the price of watermelons. So I'd buy the tomatoes, cool them in water, and they were as good as watermelons. I bought fish heads, which were always sold cheaply, and made soup with bok choy and tofu. The kids loved it. Pork bones were available for pennies a pound, and by hacking them up to get the marrow, I could make a tasty soup with rice noodles. "*Mama*, the soup is great!" "Yes, *Mama* it's delicious!"

We tried to have a festival during the Chinese New Year. I usually made "Lion's-head," "Pearl-balls," red-cooked fish and green vegetables. I would buy a pound of hard candy that had bright colored wrappings, an ounce of each kind. We would spread the candy on our *baxian* table after the New Year's Eve dinner. Then we started our game. I would count: "one, two, three," each girl would pick out one piece of candy. Then I would count again, and they would pick out another until all the candy was gone. I bought hard candy because it lasted longer. The girls would save the candy for the whole holiday season and collect the paper wrappings to show their friends.

The tragedy made my daughters grow up overnight. They knew it was difficult for me to support them. There were odd jobs available through the Neighborhood Residents' Committee, such as pasting together paper boxes. They came to me one day and suggested that they apply for the job. I was touched by their thoughtfulness. I told them. "Girls, all you have to do is to study hard. Let *Mama* take care of the family budget."

Tung-ping's brother offered to adopt one of the girls. I thanked him for his kindness but I wanted to keep the whole family together. I was in need of money badly, yet I didn't want to accept charity, not even from the government. So I had to sell Tung-ping's camera, his wristwatch and some of his clothes. I felt pain doing this but I am sure Tung-ping would understand. I used the money to buy textbooks and other things they needed in school.

I let the girls have some money to spend, 5 *fen* a week when they were in primary school, 10 *fen* a week in middle school and one *yuan* a week in college. (100 *fen* make one *yuan*.) I wanted them to have some pocket money no matter how little they were. They usually saved their money in piggy banks. Once in a while, Weiming would take out some of her coins to buy a popsicle (3 *fen*) for Little Buddha, who was not in school yet and thus got no pocket money.

Every day after school, the girls tried to help me with the housework. Even Little Buddha would follow her older sisters around, trying to help. "Little Buddha, your help just makes more work," they'd say. "Please go away and play."

We lived at the college during the week. But on Saturday afternoons, we'd file onto the bus and head back to our old home in the southern suburbs to spend what was left of the weekend, just as I had for all those years.

Why return to those gruesome memories? If we didn't return, it would have fed the rumors that I was a spy, or that I had been shut up in a "cowshed." Certain people were trying to fuel such rumors, figuring the murder of my husband would then be justified and those responsible would not be punished. So, no matter how tired we were, or what the weather was, we would return home to show the world — or at least that insular world of the Seventh Ministry — that we were still around.

My unconscious mind still refused to accept Tung-ping's death. He was only on a business trip I thought to myself. One of these days, I'd open the door and he'd be sitting on the couch and we would run to each other's arms.

Several years earlier, as I was changing buses near the Beijing Zoo on my way home, I unexpectedly met Tung-ping. "Hi, Tung-ping! How come you're here?" I was so surprised I was actually shouting — and didn't even notice he was with some associates.

"So, Lao Yao," one of them said to Tung-ping, "I guess this is Comrade Peng, right?" Tung-ping introduced me to them. They were scientists attending a conference on their way home. I forgot about the bus, and Tung-ping's driver took us home in the institute's car.

Now, whenever the bus arrived at the zoo, I would reflexively look around for Tung-ping. Maybe I would accidentally meet him again, take a ride in his car, and we'd go home together.

In December 1968, all the papers carried the following news from the Xinhua News Agency: Chairman Mao called on the Red Guards to go to the countryside. Tens of thousands of Red Guards were sent to rural areas and remote regions of China. They were to be re-educated by the poor and lower-middle peasants. Hence, the Proletarian Revolutionaries, generally older, were taking their place as the shock troops of the revolution.

Almost every *danwei* had more than one revolutionary group, and each group declared they were the true rebels. (Each claimed the support of the Central Cultural Revolution Group.) Naturally there were conflicts between them — which sometime turned violent. In some parts of the country, it was essentially a state of civil war, with guns and cannons. The antagonism between the rebel factions in a way was greater than their common anger toward the capitalist-roaders. The rebels knew that they were in large part fighting for power, since in their eyes, most of the capitalist-roaders were "dead tigers" already.

Now the faction fighting was becoming more frequent. Chairman Mao had to send Mao Zedong Thought Propaganda Teams to quell the jousting that escalating all over the city. Each Thought Team was led by the People's Liberation Army with some workers as team members.

A Mao Thought Propaganda Team arrived on our campus. First, they announced there would be some class education — to recall the bitterness of the past and appreciate the sweetness of today. We were told to get some grass, weeds and leaves and boil them together. Naturally, it tasted awful. That was the point. The Thought Team members announced: this kind of "bitter meal" was what people in the old society had to eat. They hammered home the idea that life was unbearably miserable before the Communists took over in 1949.

Then we were asked to talk about the bitter old days… and the sweet present days. One worker said his pay was so low pre-1949 that he had to eat leaves and weeds. Now he got wheat flour and rice, thanks to our Great Savior, Chairman Mao.

Another man pulled up his pant leg to show us his scars. "Comrades, look at this! This scar was made by a landlord's dog. I was a little beggar in the old society. When I went to a landlord's back door to beg, instead of giving me some leftovers, he let out his dog to bite me. Now, I am a worker. It was Chairman Mao who saved me. So we should always follow Chairman Mao. We must crush those capitalist-roaders to make sure our country will not turn back to the old society." Then, he wished a long life to Chairman Mao! We all shouted the same.

After this, there was a "Mao Loyalty Dance." Everyone across the country, from small toddlers to the elderly had to do the dance. The teachers of the English Department were ordered to put on a performance. We wore Mao badges on our dark blue jackets and held the Little Red Books in our hands. We did our simple back-and-forth dance, singing these lyrics as an accordion played:

> Beloved Chairman Mao,
> The red sun in our hearts.
> We have so much in our hearts to tell you.
> We have so many songs to sing to you.…

Whenever the red sun was mentioned in the lyrics, we held our Little Red Books close to our hearts. And when Mao was mentioned, we'd turn around and look up at his portrait on the wall. The steps were simple, but one elderly teacher would make mistakes. When we went to the right, he'd step to the left, and vice-versa. He'd never danced before, so he was reluctant to do the "Loyalty Dance." But the Mao Thought team members told him, "To dance or not to dance is a way of showing your loyalty to Chairman Mao, while to dance well is only a question of skill." Hearing those words, the elderly teacher had no choice but went up on stage.

I guess it was a surprise for the students to see us teachers dancing. Everyone applauded. My girls loved it, they went around telling everyone: "Did you see it? Our *Mama* danced on the stage!"

In the autumn of 1968 another campaign began: Clean the Class Ranks Movement. Every one of us who had lived abroad had to be investigated once more. We had to write another autobiography, starting from the age of seven. This time we were told to concentrate on the details of our lives, especially before returning to China. This autobiography was put in our dossier, the file that follows every Chinese through every step of his or her life.

The Mao Zedong Thought Propaganda Team did the investigating along with the students. So the students, now with access to fresh files on cadres and teachers, found more "class enemies."

This phase of the Cultural Revolution reached all the way into our dormitory. One Monday morning when I returned to school from home, I saw a notice on the door of Room 203, where Teacher Yuan lived with her two primary-school daughters. The sign declared that she was a spy from Taiwan. A big scarlet 'X' was written across her name.

Here was some irony — these modern revolutionaries were falling back on a feudal practice of the emperors. Long ago, criminals were sent to their beheadings with a wooden board tied behind their backs, with their names written on the board crossed out with a big 'X' in red ink.

Teacher Yuan was ordered to stay in her room until she confessed her "crimes." Her girls, nine and ten, did the grocery shopping, fetched water and emptied the toilet. Because Yuan was charged as a spy, her daughters were expelled from the "Little Red Guards" at the primary school.

Yuan did not deserve this treatment. Born in Taiwan, she had fled to Japan to avoid becoming a high KMT official's concubine. When the official sent someone to get her in Japan, she again fled, this time to mainland China. In a college in Beijing, she met and married a half-Japanese man who, it turned out later, would beat her if she didn't obey his wishes. She divorced him and now supported their two daughters. (Her husband and mother-in-law had left China just before the Cultural Revolution started.)

In 1974 Yuan was able to get her daughters out of China. They went to live with their father and grandmother in Tokyo. They continued with their education in Japan. Later on, one daughter became a nurse, the other worked in a TV station. Both of them married Japanese and settled down in Tokyo. Yuan herself later met someone she loved and remarried. She is now living in Beijing. An investigation cleared her of the spy charges.

One day as I passed the college gatehouse, I picked up a couple of letters for my neighbor in Room 202. Teacher Lee was a jovial ethnic Korean whose English classes used to resound with laughter. When I dropped them off at his room, he was somber. Lee told me he had been put under house arrest by the Red Guards and was forbidden to communicate with anyone. I handed him the letters and turned away without uttering a single word. I knew better than to hang around.

In those days, one could be a comrade today and a class enemy tomorrow. From hero to prisoner, Communist general to warlord, one's situation could change in a day. I had seen so many cases like that, I wasn't surprised to see Lee shut up in his room.

My demands for an investigation into Tung-ping's murder had kept me pretty distracted. I had no idea why Lee was under house arrest so I went outside to read the poster. I found it and read it. It was quite a serious charge. I tried to hide my shock.

Lee stood accused by one of his friends, a student named Jong, who was a fellow ethnic Korean from the Japanese Department. Jong claimed he and Lee had listened to "enemy" (foreign) broadcasts. More shocking was the claim that Lee, had criticized Mao. Lee allegedly said Mao started the Cultural Revolution to get rid of veteran cadres who didn't agree with some of his policies. The poster said Lee had compared Mao's behavior with that of the emperors. Lee even used an old saying:

"When hares are hunted out, the hounds are killed and eaten.
When there are no birds to be shot, the bows are relegated.
When the enemy country surrenders, the meritorious
    generals are put to death."

I could almost hear my heart pounding as I read this, I hurried away. I would not dare to think such things, let alone utter them. But Lee denied that he ever said that. He accused Jong of having made up the charges to save his own neck. As more information came to light, Lee's defense was plausible, and Jong had a credibility problem. Jong had been caught fleeing the country, crossing the border into North Korea with the intention of getting to Japan. But he was sent back to China by the North Koreans.

Teacher Lee claimed — and it made sense — that Jong made things up to curry favor with the authorities. And Lee argued, even if he had such thoughts, was he stupid enough to say them out loud? And who was it that had been caught by the North Koreans? Wasn't it more plausible that Jong had invented these things to save his neck? But it was Lee's word against Jong's, former friend against former friend.

The result was a sign of those divisive times: Lee was put into the "cowshed" for daily hard labor; Jong was sentenced to twenty years in prison.

27

My Letter to Premier Zhou Enlai

ONE DAY in March of 1969, the Red Guards in our school announced over the loud speaker that Soviet soldiers had skirmished with Chinese soldiers over Zhenbao (Treasure) Island and occupied this island. (This island, which belonged to China, sits in the Wusuli River which forms part of the northern border between the two countries.) The Red Guards called on the whole school to gather in the sportsground. We all went there, even the elderly teachers. We then marched around the Soviet Embassy, shouting slogans: "Down with the Soviet social imperialism!" and "Down with the new Czar!" We all shouted these slogans from the bottom of our hearts.

People of my generation could not forget what the Soviet Union had done at the start and finish of the War Against Japanese Aggression. When Japan invaded China in 1937, the Soviet Union signed a no-war treaty with Japan. Then on August 6, 1945, the day the Americans dropped an atomic bomb on Hiroshima, the Soviet Union declared war on Japan and sent 1.5 million soldiers into China and North Korea. The Soviets occupied China's Inner Mongolia and three provinces in the northeast of China. Thus, when the Japanese surrendered on August 15, the Soviet troops already held a large section of Chinese territory. (Their troops remained stationed at Port Arthur till 1954.) Now, they were trying to occupy our island. Naturally we were all outraged by this.

That same year of 1969, Mao issued the order: Dig tunnels deep, save much grain and never be in hegemony. The government made it seem war was imminent. The movie "Underground Warfare" — about digging tunnels to outwit the Japanese invaders — was shown over and over. (This was the film my daughters and other youngsters knew all the lines to.) Tunnels were dug everywhere under schools, shops, and hospitals. Some people even started selling their belongings, including books, furniture and clothing. A colleague of mine, a Ph.D. from Great Britain, sold his British-made suit in haste for 5 *yuan* — less than a dollar.

In October 1969, Lin Biao ordered our country into a state of war. This order was known as "the First Order of Vice-Chairman Lin." His motives were largely political: he sent many disgraced top leaders out of Beijing in the name of "evacuation." Among the senior officials ordered to leave were Liu Shaoqi, "the Number One Capitalist-Roader," and Deng Xiaoping, "the Number Two Capitalist-Roader."

At the same time, all *danwei* were "sending down" their cadres to the countryside to "May 7th Cadre Schools." These "schools" took their name from Mao's letter to Lin Biao back on May 7, 1966 as the Cultural Revolution was just beginning. To carry out Mao's order in late 1968, every *danwei* set up a "May 7th Cadre School" in rural areas, so intellectuals and cadres would live among the peasants and be "re-educated" by them. Mao once said that although peasants had dirty hands and cow manure on their feet, they were much cleaner than intellectuals.

As a result, our school was ordered shut down and moved

to a little village in Hebei province in 1970. Everyone — students, faculty, and administrators — had to leave. (But not the workers; as the 'leading class,' they were simply transferred to some factories in Beijing.) There weren't enough trucks to carry everything, so books were sold for scrap paper, three *fen* a pound. If you are going to be on a farm, the reasoning went, there was no need for books.

Just then, Little Buddha got sick. She came down with hepatitis and ended up in the hospital. I reported this to the PLA officer in charge.

"Could we go later?" I asked.

"No, you have to go with everyone else," he replied.

"What about my child in the hospital?"

"Well, you can go away with your other two girls first, then when your younger girl is released from the hospital, you can come to Beijing to get her."

"But the child is only five years old, and a girl!" I pleaded. "I can't leave her in the hospital, with no one to visit her."

The PLA officer ignored me. I got quite mad. "Don't you have any kids?" I grumbled as I walked away.

I then went to the hospital and asked the doctor about releasing Little Buddha. He raised his eyebrows in surprise, saying, "How can we let her out of the hospital while she has a contagious disease? You want other people to get sick?"

I didn't know what to do, so I went home and started packing. I couldn't talk any sense into the PLA officer, and didn't know whom else to turn to for help.

Then it hit me. Premier Zhou Enlai.

That's right, the Premier of the People's Republic of China. He had known Tung-ping; he had been outraged by his murder.

It was worth trying. I sat down and wrote the following letter:

Beloved Premier Zhou:

My husband, Yao Tung-ping, the director of Institute 703 of the Seventh Machine Building Ministry, was murdered on June 8, 1968. Since then, I have had to raise our three children single-handedly. Now the Institute of Foreign Affairs, where I work, is going to be dissolved and we have been ordered to settle down in a village in Hebei province. But there are some insurmountable difficulties for my family. Hence, I am writing to you for help.

All of our three children are girls. The youngest one is only five years old. She suffered from jaundiced hepatitis suddenly and has been hospitalized. It is very difficult for me to live in the countryside with the other two girls and leave the youngest in the hospital. Comrades such as Dr. Qian Xuesen and Admiral Yang Guoyu, the army representative of the Seventh Machine Building Ministry, know all about this and have shown some concern.

I graduated from a middle school in Nanjing in 1947 and then was awarded a full scholarship to take up college studies in the United States. I also worked there for some years after graduation. I returned to our motherland in late 1957 and have been teaching English in the Chinese Science and Technology University and at this institute.

Neither Comrade Tung-ping nor myself have any close relations in Beijing. I have to shoulder the responsibilities of sustaining my daughters alone. Premier Zhou, please consider my difficulties.

Revolutionary Salute!

Respectfully yours,

Peng Chieh-ching
March 24, 1970

I wrote this letter because I had no other recourse. A friend of mine, a veteran cadre, delivered it to Premier Zhou's office. I didn't know and never expected that the Premier, who had to take care of the entire country, would respond. But he did. And within a week! The Premier wrote the following in the margin of my letter:

> I am asking Comrade Peng Shaohui to inform the military representatives in the Institute of Foreign Affairs not to ask Comrade Peng Chieh-ching to settle down in the countryside. Please contact Comrade Yang Guoyu and Comrade Qian Xuesen for details of the death of Comrade Yao Tung-ping; see where things stand with the investigation into the killing and how to help Comrade Yao's family. Please investigate this matter and make suggestions and report to me.
>
> Zhou Enlai,
> March 30, 1970

General Peng promptly relayed Premier Zhou's orders to the officials at the Seventh Machine Building Ministry. Dr. Qian and Admiral Yang reported the following facts back to General Peng on April 4:

1. The former director of Institute 703, Comrade Yao Tung-ping was beaten to death after he came home for lunch on June 8, 1968. We reported the incident to the Premier instantly. One of the killers is in the detention house under the Public Security Bureau of Beijing. We are investigating Comrade Yao Tung-ping's case.

2. After the death of Comrade Yao Tung-ping, according to the rules and regulations of the state, we made sure each

child received 20 *yuan* a month. We also gave a pension of 650 *yuan* [in actuality, the lump sum paid was 430 *yuan*] based on the rank of division commander in the army.

3. Regarding Comrade Peng, we understand she has difficulty moving to the countryside to settle down there. We have already notified her college not to move her now. As for her work, we suggest that the Beijing Revolutionary Committee arrange for it, if possible.

At the time, I didn't know about the Premier's personal intervention; all I knew was that less than ten days after sending my letter, I was notified that I wouldn't have to go to the countryside.

Soon Little Buddha recovered. The PLA officer had not told me what kind of work I should do, so I decided to go directly to General Peng to find out for myself. The prospect was rather nerve-wracking; I'd never met such a high-ranking official before. (General Peng was the Deputy Chief of the General Staff.) A friend who had been General Peng's Russian interpreter told me not to be nervous. She said the general was a kind man who did not put on airs and his wife was very nice too. I felt relieved after hearing this.

I took a bus to General Peng's residence deep in a lovely *hutong* (lane), near Jingshan Park. I couldn't see any buildings from the gray walls outside. After I rang the bell, a PLA Soldier opened the gate. When I told him my name, he let me in. I was escorted to a two-story building hidden among a lot of tall elm trees.

General Peng was rather thin, not too tall, with salt and pepper hair. There was nothing inside of his left sleeve. The general had lost his left arm fighting in the battlefields.

Madame Peng was of the same height as her husband. She was very fair, with a round face and a pair of smiling eyes. I heard she used to be a doctor of Chinese traditional medicine. She sat there listening to me talking to the general and put in a sentence or two.

General Peng seemed to know a lot about me and my family. He even inquired about Little Buddha, how she was getting along in the hospital. And he told me not to worry. "If you take care of her, she'll get well soon." As for a job — preferably something that utilized my English skills — he said, "Don't worry, wait till your daughter gets well." General Peng urged me to make my daughters' welfare my priority. And he invited me to stay for lunch.

Their dining room was simply furnished with a round wood table. A delicious hot-pot was served, with mutton sliced as thin as paper. Some charcoal underneath kept the broth boiling. The pot was divided into many sections; you dipped the mutton into your section of the pot and added any sauce you liked. There were about ten different kinds of sauces. I told General Peng I had never liked mutton. He said, "It's really good, why don't you have a try?" So, I did. Believe me, it was delicious. After fruit and tea, General Peng walked me to the door, and Madame Peng took me to the gate. They treated me just as warmly and kindly every time I went to their house thereafter.

General Peng tried to arrange several jobs for me, but all the schools were closed and most of the research institutes had been moved to the countryside. So I stayed at home and awaited instructions.

上書周恩来

28

My Ninth Cousin

By 1970, primary and middle schools had re-opened, but not colleges. Mao had decided children should attend class, while "making revolution." Mao believed all students should learn from more than just books. My second daughter Jibin was in the fifth grade. She and her classmates now started working in a shoe factory near their school to learn from the workers. The kids were happy to do anything other than go to class. Mostly they swept floors and cleaned windows. They didn't run any machines.

The school children were pressed into service for tunnel-digging as well. Some had to dig, others pulled carts for long distances to get rid of the dirt. On the way back, they pulled sand, which was used in cement. They were doing more physical labor than school work. The parents started to complain. One parent raised the issue. "How come the school asks them to do so much physical labor?" I agreed with her, but had learned not to voice any contrary opinions. As we say in China, "The bird that flies first will get shot at first."

Jibin was taller than all the other girls in her class, and consequently walked a little stooped out of embarrassment. I wanted her to move up a grade, so I devised a plan. It was a variation of the plan that had worked for Weiming five years earlier.

Back in 1965, Weiming was nearly seven, but her October birthday would just miss the school's cut-off date of September 1. Tung-ping wrote to his elder brother in Wuxi, who wrote back saying Weiming could enter first grade there. We accepted his offer and accompanied her down to the train station in Beijing. But saying good-bye was traumatic. She was fine until the whistle blew and she saw us getting off the train. She wanted to get off the train with us and started to cry. The attendant comforted her. She assured me that Weiming could sleep in her berth, and she would personally hand my daughter over to her uncle.

Tung-ping and I stood on the platform, watching the train pull away and slowly gather speed, its smoke finally disappearing into the sky. Tung-ping looked at my face and asked in a mischievous voice, "Hey, how come it has started raining on such a bright sunny day?"

I hit him lightly on his back. "You jerk, you know I feel bad about this, and you're still joking."

"Who's the one who was asking me every day to send Weiming away? Who kept insisting that Weiming is old enough to start primary school? Who's the one telling me day and night that to enter school at seven is not reasonable? Now that she's gone, you regret it?" He was grinning. I knew he was diverting my attention so I wouldn't cry.

Weiming spent one semester in Wuxi, then her uncle brought her back to Beijing, where she was allowed to continue first grade.

Now I decided to try the same thing with Jibin and Little Buddha, but in Hangzhou, where my brother and sister lived, instead of Wuxi. In Hangzhou, as in many parts of the country, primary school had been cut to five years. This was done to follow Mao's edict: "The studying period should be shortened, the educational method revolutionized…"

If Jibin, who was completing fifth grade, lived in Hangzhou, she would be considered a primary school graduate and could start middle school. Similarly, Little Buddha who was turning six could start primary school. Other cities weren't as strict as Beijing about age requirements. So I bought train tickets for the three of us to Hangzhou.

This time, I bought two hard seats for the girls and one hard sleeping berth, a lower one, for me. With the attendant's permission, I brought them along with me into my hard-berth car and spread out a quilt on the floor. The other travelers were kidding our girls, "Hey, you kids down there have a better berth than we do, a soft one at that, with more space too."

As the train rolled on through the night, lying partly awake in my berth, I recalled a trip with Tung-ping to Hangzhou in the spring of 1958. Hangzhou is truly gorgeous in spring time: green willows by the famed West Lake, peach and plum trees blossoming on its banks. All the colors drinking in the spring drizzle. It's no wonder people say: "Above, there is paradise; on earth, there are Suzhou and Hangzhou."

The water in West Lake was so clear, you could almost see the bottom. Fish of all colors — gold, red, black and silvery white — swam back and forth. It was like a Chinese painting come to life. Strolling beneath the willows, Tung-ping and I felt like we were on a second honeymoon.

Arriving in Hangzhou this time, in 1970, was entirely different. The scenery was as beautiful as before, but now Tung-ping wasn't with me. The scenery made me miss him all the more.

Jibin was admitted into middle school, Little Buddha started first grade. (In school, she had to use her given name Chenfang.) Both Jibin and Chenfang studied hard, were good in athletics, and spoke authentic Mandarin, which was rare in that school.

Both of them became quite popular.

I discovered that the political atmosphere in Hangzhou wasn't nearly as tense as in Beijing. People seemed more concerned with working hard to buy enough rice to fill their stomachs. Here people pulled carts laden with heavy cargo — bricks, steel pipes, chunks of sandstone, just about anything. A man would use a rope and bend down low, almost to the ground to keep up momentum. Sometimes a boy or girl would help. This sight made me feel depressed; I thought it was demeaning work for humans. In Beijing, we used horses or donkeys to pull carts.

One day a distant cousin and her husband invited me to lunch. She was very strong and dark from doing work in the sun. It turned out that she and her two daughters were pulling carts. The girls had quit school after primary school to go to work.

I politely asked the mother why she didn't let the girls go to middle school.

"What's the use of learning more?" the mother replied. "Look at their father, he's a primary school teacher and his pay is not half as much as our daughters." (I was glad he was hard of hearing and didn't have a hearing-aid.)

"Yes, that's right," one of the girls agreed.

"You know," chimed in the second, "if we graduate from middle school, we have to go to the countryside and do farm labor. Doing farm labor is much harder work than pulling carts. And besides, we are young and strong and can pull this cart once or even twice a day. When you get used to it, it's not that hard. This way, we have enough to eat and even have money to buy some new clothes. Don't you think that's nice?"

I couldn't argue. My college friends had been sent to the countryside to learn from the poor and lower-middle peasants. Didn't Chairman Mao once say that the more books you read, the more stupid you get? How could I blame these girls.

Lunch was quite a spread. After lunch, the mother and two

daughters took us for a stroll along the lake. Now the water looked yellow and muddy.

"What's the matter with the water? When I was here in 1958, the water was clear and blue — so beautiful."

The mother said, "*da yue jin* (the Great Leap Forward) came right after you left, remember? We were ordered to increase production, but we didn't have enough fertilizer. We had to use the mud from the lake as fertilizer. That's why the water became muddy like this. I don't know if the mud from the lake worked, because we had less to eat after that."

I was troubled by this, the pride of Hangzhou sullied like that. I couldn't blame the commune members for taking the mud, because they couldn't get chemical fertilizers. They were also using manure or other natural fertilizers.

The mother continued in a resigned voice: "After liberation, one campaign after another, especially *da yue jin*, brought us three years of famine. And still, the people are as poor as before. Even if the country gets stronger, we the people are poorer."

My heart skipped a beat. What was it with the people down here, saying such things out loud? She was either really brave or stupid to utter such "reactionary" thoughts. It was a good thing my daughters were walking ahead and didn't hear what she was saying.

I thought to myself, "I'd rather my daughters learn less or even be illiterate than be influenced by such talk. Otherwise, who knows what fate will befall them?" As a saying goes: Once you are bitten by a snake, you get jumpy when you see a rope. I guess I was in that frame of mind. So I decided Hangzhou, with its loose-lipped residents, was not safe for my daughters. Thankfully, we now had the proper certificates that would allow the girls to continue in the same grades in Beijing's schools.

We got back on the train and headed home. The clacking

train wheels and the coach's gentle swaying rocked Jibin and Chenfang to sleep. Their lives had been turned upside down by upheaval and violence, but we were still together, and they had embarked on a life of academic achievement that would have made their father proud.

When Jibin, Chenfang and I returned home to Beijing from Hangzhou that fall of 1970, the college campus where I worked was like a ghost town. Everyone was in the countryside. The kids' schools were still open, but there were no formal classes. Schools were still following Mao's teaching: learn from the workers and the poor and lower-middle peasants.

Jibin's middle school now had an arrangement with a small metal factory in another district of Beijing. She and her classmates would go and work there for two weeks. The factory cleared a corner of a workshop for the kids to sleep. At first, the youngsters were asked only to clean the grounds and plant trees. The kids worked so hard they cleaned all the areas in the factory and then helped install a walkway from the front gate to the workshop, planting trees along both sides. It made the factory look neat and clean.

After a few days, the kids were put to work on the machines. They had to work three shifts a day, just like the adult workers. The students were excited to work like real workers. But teenagers need enough sleep. One night the inevitable happened. A boy's finger got caught in a machine. His schoolmates didn't know what to do, but their screams brought some workers over. They sent the boy to a hospital but the doctor could not save the finger.

The parents were infuriated. They demanded some kind of compensation. After several meetings with all parties concerned, this was what was offered: The boy could have a job when he graduated from middle school, at that very factory. In the end, the parents took the deal. After all, it meant a job and not being sent to the countryside. Since the parents went along, the school didn't object either, and the practice of sending the teenagers to the factory continued.

Jibin suffered as well. She got sick during her stint from over-exertion and insufficient nourishment. I only found that out when her girlfriends came to visit our dorm room one day and were chatting. While they were working at the factory, their teacher had told them: "You are here to do labor, not to eat good food and have a good time." Why the teacher told her students that was beyond my comprehension. How could middle-school pupils have a good time working in a factory? The boys played deaf to the teacher, buying whatever dishes they liked. But the girls took the teacher's words literally. My daughter and her girlfriends' meals usually consisted of one steamed roll, a small dish of salted turnips and a bowl of water. Working three shifts on the machines with food like this, it's no wonder some of them got sick and others had accidents.

Shortly after Jibin recovered, her school had to go to the countryside to help with the summer harvest, a duty that was impossible to avoid. She got up at 5 a.m. and worked until dark. After a couple of days her eyes were red and swollen.

"Didn't you put your mosquito net down? How come you got bit on the eyelids?" I asked. Then I realized it couldn't have been mosquito bites on both eyelids. I took her to a hospital. The doctor told me Jibin had a kidney ailment; she was immediately admitted to the hospital. Fortunately, she made a fairly quick and complete recovery.

Since no one was in charge of my campus, we moved from our old dormitory, Building 6, which was virtually empty and a little spooky, and took an apartment in Building 8. It was a two-room apartment on the second floor: I took one room and my three daughters the other. I put the *baxian* dining table in their room. Although Tung-ping wasn't with us any more, I'd always put a bowl, a pair of chop sticks and a plate at his usual place, close to the door. What if a miracle happened, and he was sitting at his seat across the table from me!

Our standard of living here was far below that of the apartment in the southern suburbs, but I didn't mind. All I wanted was an uneventful life for my children. As we Chinese often say, children of the poor mature early. All my girls studied hard; I didn't have to check on their homework or things like that. Once in a while, they'd come to me with some questions. I would try my best to help them. (To relax, all three of them liked drawing, just as their father did.)

One of the few couples left in our dormitory was Teachers Jia and Zhang. They were both instructors of Japanese and lived in a two-room apartment on the fourth floor. They had a teenage girl, Emily, who had cerebral palsy and needed constant care, like a three-year-old. I often went up to visit them.

Teacher Jia was tall and willowy. Her skin was as smooth as ivory, her eyes big and slanting. Although the years had turned some of her hair gray, one could still see why she had been called "the most beautiful girl in Tokyo." Her mother had been Japanese. Her father was Chinese, but had been lovingly adopted by a wealthy British couple who owned a steel company in Japan. They raised him as their son because they had no children, and he ended up working in their steel company.

Teacher Jia showed me a knitting book from Japan and taught me some fancy stitches. I learned quickly — building on the basics that Teacher Yuan had shown me two years earlier. I couldn't sleep at night, and the knitting helped me pass the time. It also reminded me of Tung-ping, and the sweater I had been working on for his forty-sixth birthday. As I sat knitting, I sometimes sensed his presence — just like the times we'd sit close to each other in the bedroom, developing film. "You don't like photography. How come you are so interested in developing pictures?" It seemed only a few days before that Tung-ping had spoken those words to me.

The life of Teacher Jia's husband, Teacher Zhang, was a mirror for many overseas Chinese to look into. He had been born into a wealthy family in Japan and been educated at a top university there. He declined to go into his father's shipping business, deciding to come to China in the late 1950s. He always wore a simple dark blue Mao uniform. In fact, one of my girls mistook him for a carpenter when I sent them to find someone to fix a broken window. Zhang had longed to join the Communist Party, but his applications were never accepted.

In 1970, Teachers Jia and Zhang had also been sent to the countryside with the rest of the faculty. But they were now back in Beijing so Teacher Zhang could get a medical check-up. Jia filled me in on life in the countryside: "If you bring your girls there, you will find out how difficult things are," she said. "Even getting water from a well is not easy. You can't even see the bottom of the well, and men have to help the women pull the buckets up. If you're with the girls, life will be very hard indeed."

I agreed but replied, "If my husband were alive, I wouldn't mind settling in the countryside. I wouldn't even mind going to Xinjiang or Tibet."

In 1972, when diplomatic relations were established with Japan, teacher Zhang got word that his father had died and left him trillions of Japanese yen. Zhang and his wife were going to donate the whole sum to the Chinese government, to help build socialism. Friends convinced them to leave some for Emily's care. They accepted the advice.

Sadly, Zhang was later stricken with nose cancer. Both

teachers' families sent medicine to him from Tokyo. But it was no use. On his deathbed, Zhang was granted his life-long wish: to become a member of the Chinese Communist Party. He was moved to tears. Jia's family invited her to move back to Japan. She declined. She wanted to stay in the country her husband loved.

I sympathized with Jia and understood why she wanted to remain in China. Hadn't my experience been similar to hers? Didn't I choose to stay in China because my husband had loved our motherland so much? If Tung-ping could somehow live once more, I'm convinced he would choose to live in China… Although the road was full of hardship and danger, he loved his motherland so much. And I would follow him, my beloved, to the "corner of the seas and beyond the skies."

29

Ping-Pong Diplomacy

———————— 〰 ————————

THE UNTHINKABLE occurred in October 1971. The National Day Parade (on October 1) in Tiananmen Square was canceled. This would be like canceling the Fourth of July celebration in America or Bastille Day in France. Clearly, something was up. But they didn't tell us the reason for the cancellation. We were only told that from now on, there wouldn't be any National Day Parade in Tiananmen Square. (This ban continued until 1984, after Deng Xiaoping became the top man.)

It wasn't until 1972 that we were officially told the real reason: Lin Biao had conspired to assassinate Mao. Believing that his plot had been discovered, on September 13, 1971, Lin Biao commandeered a British-made Trident at Beidaihe's Shanhaiguan Airport and tried to flee to the Soviet Union. The plane crashed near Undur Khan in Mongolia. Everyone on board, including Lin's wife and son, died in the crash. (His daughter did not flee with them.) After hearing this, we were all shocked.

I recall the first time I saw Lin Biao. It was on China's National Day in 1959 when he appeared in public as the new Minister of Defense. Lin stood on the Tiananmen Square rostrum reviewing the parade. He looked small and thin standing next to Mao Zedong. Although wearing an army uniform, he also looked to be in poor health.

At that time, we heard a lot about Lin's heroic deeds. They said Lin was a military wizard; he had won the battle at Pingxingguan during the War of Resistance against Japan. Now that Lin Biao's plane had crashed in Mongolia, the story about him changed completely. They now said that Lin was an opium smoker. That he had tried to run away during the Long March. And there was even analysis of a placard on the wall of his living room: "A lone horse in the sky, coming and going by itself." They say the placard showed that Lin Biao had always put himself above Mao.

The sayings before and after Lin Biao's death were entirely different. People were confused. Which one was the truth? Which one to believe?

1971 also saw the first volley of "ping-pong diplomacy." That March, China sent ping-pong players to the World Table Tennis Tournament in Nagoya, Japan. Toward the end of the event, several American players approached the Chinese team saying they would like to visit China, and hoped they could be invited. As a result, teams from America and other countries were invited to China.

The U.S. team arrived in April, it was the first time in decades that Chinese people had a chance to see pictures of Americans in the newspapers. After more than twenty years of propaganda against the United States, we were allowed to consider a different image now. Most Chinese seemed thrilled at this glimpse of American youth: the long hair, the carefree manner and the liveliness. When Premier Zhou told the players that they had "turned a page in the relations between China and America," it was indeed true — though the changes wouldn't reach the general public for years.

When word came that President Nixon would be visiting

the following year; we knew times were changing. It was amusing to watch the preparations. All the buildings along the road from the airport to the state guest house were repainted. The Anti-Imperialist Hospital, which had once been called Union Hospital, was renamed yet again: Capital Hospital. (Several years later it resumed its old name, the Union Hospital.) Shoe shops, restaurants, and stores were all spiffed up, and their antagonistic names from the days of the Cultural Revolution were removed.

Nixon arrived on February 21, 1972. The visit went smoothly, starting with the airport handshake with Zhou Enlai, a man who had been snubbed by U.S. Secretary of State John Foster Dulles back in 1954 in Geneva. Nixon met with Mao. Madame Mao invited Mrs. Nixon to a performance of "Red Detachment of Women" — an approved ballet. The newspapers were filled with glowing reports. In our political study groups, naturally we all praised Mao for his brilliance in inviting Nixon.

For ordinary Chinese, the trip was a watershed. We were allowed to resume the study of English. There was even a new policy in a lot of *danwei*: 8 to 9 o'clock in the morning was the time to study English! (That hour had been reserved "even in thunderstorms" for studying Mao's writings.) Gradually, English became the number-one foreign language in China. Nowadays, when you walk down a street in Beijing, you hear local people saying "OK," "Hi!" and "Bye-bye!"

Prime Minister Tanaka of Japan came to visit China in September 1972. He was accorded the same diplomatic courtesies as President Nixon. In our political study sessions, we again praised Mao for his brilliant diplomacy. But, during one session, an elderly teacher told us that every time he saw a Japanese flag, it reminded him of wartime. He had been ordered by the Japanese soldiers to bow to the Japanese flag whenever he passed by it. To avoid doing this, he recalled, he usually took the longer way to get to the college.

In 1974, our college resumed English and French classes for cadres. Several teachers from our school were ordered to return to Beijing from the countryside.

Now that China's doors were opening, a lot of Chinese were hoping to put their foot through. The first one in our college to apply for an exit permit was a French teacher named Fourth Phoenix Yan. She was about thirty, single and rather quiet. She had been brought up in Paris and her craft was making violins. She came to teach in our school in 1964. I remember her as a pretty woman who was always dressed in black. When our school moved to Hebei province, she had to go there too. I can imagine what a hard life she had there. She grabbed the chance to return to Paris and reclaim her citizenship. I hear she now lives in New York and her violin shop is doing a thriving business.

After Nixon's visit, the prospect of leaving China was no longer unthinkable. For years the Chinese were told that "two-thirds of the world's people are living under deep water and hot fire." Some of us knew otherwise, but we didn't dare contradict the official line. Even if we did talk, nobody would have believed us. Now that we were given glimpses of the ping-pong players and of President and Mrs. Nixon, it seemed like an officially sanctioned revision of the previous propaganda. For some who were restless there was now reason to hope.

When the doors swung open a little wider in the mid-1970s, many Chinese tried to go back to their former homes overseas or send their sons and daughters abroad. Remember Mr. Wang from the Yong-An Hostel? The successful engineer from Paris who was assigned to teach French in our college. A couple of years later, he married a friend of mine, a pretty girl from Hong Kong. The Wangs would often have afternoon tea and would invite me. We three would talk about the pastries we had overseas, the movies we had seen —"High Noon," "Rear Window," "All About Eve"— and the places we each had been to — Hong Kong, Paris, Rome and New York. Mr. Wang said, "At least we know what life is like in Western countries." Mrs. Wang, who had come to the mainland with her parents, sighed, "I guess we'll grow old and die in Beijing eventually."

Thanks to Nixon's visit, Mr. Wang was allowed to go back to Paris. He secured a job in an engineering firm. Two years later, he bought a house in the suburbs of Paris. In 1974, Mrs. Wang and her two sons were leaving to join him. I saw them off quietly at her apartment. "Chieh-cheng, do you dare to keep in touch with us?" Mrs. Wang asked. I told her I dared not. In fact, I wasn't even brave enough to see them off at the airport.

At that time, none of us could foresee that Chinese citizens would one day be able to travel freely inside and outside the country. To associate with foreign friends without having to ask permission beforehand and report to the authorities afterwards.

Indeed, China has changed tremendously!

Before, having foreign relatives was an unbearable burden. Hundreds of thousands of people were investigated for having relatives overseas. Now the situation is 180 degrees opposite. People began studying their family trees, looking for overseas relatives who might help them go abroad, to study or to live.

In 1979, when Deng Xiaoping visited the United States, a news documentary about the trip was shown in theaters across the country. I couldn't believe my eyes: there on the screen was my middle-school classmate from Nanjing, Cindy. She was now the chief UN interpreter for the dignitaries — and as pretty as when I saw her last while I was at NYU. Her shoulder-length hair was jet-black and she looked fabulous in a red suit. A couple of years later, Cindy came to Beijing. We met at the Beijing Hotel; indeed it was her in the documentary. Cindy didn't know the whereabouts of our fellow classmate Beatrice, but she told me our other classmate Susan was now a vice-president of a bank in Pennsylvania. In 1994, when I went to the United States, Cindy invited me to her house in Scardsdale, New York and Susan asked me to spend Thanksgiving at her home. So, after thirty years apart, we had a nice mini-reunion.

Many young people went to see the documentary again and again, not to watch the Chinese delegation, but to look at the background — at all the cars, skyscrapers, fancy homes and colorful clothing. A lot of the younger crowd, especially in Shanghai, started to copy the American way of dressing: men's shirts with big collars, trouser legs a foot wide and long hair tied back in a pony tail. These were definitely not Mao uniforms.

30

The Year of the Dragon

———————————— ⌇ ————————————

For many in China, the 1970s were a slow tempering of the excesses of the Cultural Revolution, a slow opening to the rest of the world. For our family, it was a slow recovery from a terrible tragedy. For me personally, there lingered feelings of futility and rage. There was still no word on the fate of the men who had murdered my husband. Until they were tracked down, I could not rest.

I aimed high. I sent letters to everyone I could think of — even Chairman Mao, Madame Mao and Premier Zhou Enlai. I would summarize the case and respectfully ask for justice. Of course, it was highly doubtful that Chairman Mao would ever see my letters, but it was worth trying.

One of my letters was to Li Xiannian, the longtime Vice Premier who later became the President of China. I outlined the facts and said that to my knowledge, the criminals had never been punished. Li took an interest in this case and pushed things along. He forwarded my letter to Wang Hongwen, Vice Chairman of the Party Central and in charge of defense — which included the Seventh Ministry. Li wrote in the margin of my letter:

"How could human life be treated as if it were not worth a straw? Although it happened years ago, it is still necessary to resolutely make a thorough investigation. The killer should be punished according to law. However, the scope should be limited, as some were hoodwinked into it. Please give your opinion on the direction."

Wang in turn jotted his own response in the margin, saying he agreed with Li, signed it and sent it off to the Minister of Public Security. Zhou Enlai and Deng Xiaoping signed off on it as well.

Soon after, one of the two culprits — Yu the electrician — was formally arrested. He was charged with delivering the first blow that sent Tung-ping to the ground. The verdict: guilty. The sentence: fifteen years.

As for the other man — the cook named Gao who had hit Tung-ping the second time, he was already in jail. Apparently, he had been detained shortly after the killing. His arrest occurred after Premier Zhou himself ordered faction 915 to hand over the killer. I had never been told about that. Gao had been sentenced to twelve years.

Some people might think that this news would give me a certain sense of satisfaction. It did not. First of all, I wasn't even informed of these arrests until 1976, and then only by some friends. That meant eight years of living in the dark about the whereabouts of my husband's killers. And I didn't find out these exact sentences until 1979, after contacting my representative in the People's Congress. Moreover, the sentences were too light. Fifteen years for cold-blooded murder?

Finally, there had been no trial to speak of — no testimony, and nobody present when they were sentenced. The Court only contacted some members of the Seventh Ministry leadership prior to sentencing. At their sentencing, both men were given credit for time served. Gao was out of prison by 1980, Yu was released in 1989.

What was even more galling to me was that after serving his sentence, Yu, a convicted murderer, was re-hired as an electrician by the Seventh Ministry. And as for Gao, he not only went back to work, he became a group leader in a workshop. Later Gao was promoted to the rank of cadre at Factory 211 under the Seventh Ministry. They even put Gao's picture on the walls of the factory as a model worker. When some people saw the picture, they got mad, asking, "What was the matter with the leadership? Promoting a killer to cadre, and making him a model worker. Should we all learn from him? Going out and beating people to death?"

(In the early 1980s, Gao was on the verge of being named a member of the Communist Party. When friends told me about this, I went directly to some high officials of the Seventh Ministry to protest. How could this be? The Communist Party claims to be "a great, glorious and correct Party," made up of the country's finest people. And they would consider admitting a murderer? Later, I heard Gao did not become a Party member.)

The sentencing of Yu and Gao, besides being unsatisfactory, did not bring my efforts to an end. The political reputation of Tung-ping was still ambiguous. I doubt anyone who had personal dealings with Tung-ping would suspect any human being could harm as gentle a soul as him. But the fact remained that some people had spread wild lies about him back in 1968. Until those were repudiated, my work wasn't finished.

The year 1976 — a Year of the Dragon — was a critical one in China's history. On the morning of January 8, as the girls and I were eating breakfast and getting ready for school, news came over the radio that made me numb. A man's voice came on trembling. "Our beloved Premier Zhou Enlai passed away after failing

264

to respond to all medical treatment.... According to his last wishes, his ashes will be scattered over the motherland he loved so dearly."

"Please stop talking!" I told the girls, "Listen to the broadcast."

The girls put down their chopsticks and then quietly left for school.

Everyone had known Premier Zhou was seriously ill. Nonetheless, his death triggered an emotional response from people all over the country. As the mourning music came over the old RCA radio I had brought back from the United States, I too wept.

Premier Zhou had been a constant in my life. I had first seen his picture in the newspaper when I was a middle-school student in Nanjing. In 1954, when I was living in America, Zhou represented China in negotiations in Geneva, appearing handsome and urbane. The talks led to prisoner-of-war releases in exchange for the opportunity for Chinese scientists to return to China. It was agreed at the conference that any American in China who wanted to return to the U.S. could contact the Polish Embassy for help and any Chinese in the U.S. who wanted to return to China could do so through the Indian Embassy.

Tung-ping, so strict about state secrets, never told me that it was Premier Zhou who had facilitated his returning to China. Admiral Yang told me this later. "I particularly asked Comrade Yao Tung-ping to come back to China," Premier Zhou said at a meeting shortly after the murder. "Our country needs scientists like him. Now he's beaten to death, and you can't find the murderer. You must find the murderer immediately, or the head of that faction should take the responsibility." Zhou had a keen interest in the work of Tung-ping and Institute 703, which was vital to China's national defense and modernization.

It was also Premier Zhou who had ordered protection for the coroners so they could finally examine the body in the bathtub of our apartment and have it removed to the Navy Hospital. Premier Zhou reportedly asked about the welfare of the children and me during that hard time. And it was his attention that allowed us to get Tung-ping's pension, the first official acknowledgment that Tung-ping's reputation was politically clear.

I asked and was granted permission to view Premier Zhou's body and pay my last respects. The line went all the way around Beijing Hospital and beyond. Each of us wore a black cloth armband on the left arm and a little white paper flower on the chest. Everyone was sobbing and wiping tears. We were told to go in as "foursomes." When it was turn for our group to enter, we saw that Premier Zhou's body was in the regular morgue of the hospital. Was this a proper place for a Premier of our country?

At one end of the long table were some fresh flowers from his wife. Premier Zhou's body looked small and thin under the Communist Party flag. We all bowed to the Premier three times. As soon as we left the room, all of us burst out crying. Later that week, more than one million people of all ages, braving a bitter winter wind, lined the route to *Babaoshan* Cemetery where he was cremated. They stood grief-stricken as the cortege traveled the ten *li* distance.

All my friends regarded Zhou as a great man. Outwardly, Zhou had been Mao's supporter. He had to protect himself in order to save others — and he saved many, including Deng Xiaoping. If it hadn't been for Premier Zhou, the Chinese economy would have collapsed in the early stages of the Cultural Revolution. The Premier had cleverly quoted Mao's words "Grasp Production While Making Revolution."

Premier Zhou had left us. His intention of holding a memorial service for Tung-ping remained unfulfilled. So on July 4, 1976 I decided to write directly to Party Vice-Chairman Wang Hongwen, who was in charge of the Seventh Ministry. I asked for an official pronouncement on Tung-ping's character. Wang jotted the following note on my letter on July 12:

This case should be forwarded to the core team of the Seventh Machine Building Ministry for investigation and for reaching a proper conclusion. In addition, they should help tackle the difficulties met with by the family of the deceased scientist.

Hongwen
July 12, 1976

Later that summer, nature and history intervened. On the 28th of July, I took a couple of sleeping pills and lay down to read a book — my usual routine in trying to fall asleep. I was dozing when the windows began to rattle and the lamps sway. I ran to the girls' room. "It's an earthquake! Get up!" We all ran downstairs. Halfway down, Chenfang (Little Buddha) reminded me, "*Mama!* Our money! The grain coupons!" I ran back and grabbed them.

Outside, in the warm night air, people were standing around terrified, half-naked or covered with sheets. There was no place to get information, nothing on the radio or TV. Before dawn it started to rain and then to pour, but all the people stayed outdoors that night, sitting on chairs. Jibin and Chenfang rested their heads on my knees. I held a plastic sheet above to protect them from the downpour.

Weiming was in the hospital when the earthquake occurred. She had fallen sick earlier that summer. I kept calling the hospital but couldn't get through. And most of the buses had stopped running. When a rumor spread that there would be another earthquake, I became frantic. Thankfully a veteran cadre heard of my difficulties and sent a car for me to go pick up my daughter. When we arrived at Weiming's ward, she wasn't there. I looked in all the rooms, but couldn't find her or anyone else. The doctors had discharged their patients. Finally I came to an auditorium. As I walked in I heard Weiming calling "*Mama, Mama....*" The poor girl was lying on a straw mattress in a corner. She was so happy to see me, and her doctor was only too glad to let her go. So we took her back "home."

Most of the residents of Beijing and some other affected cities spent that summer living outside. By the time September came, the nights began to get chilly. We were prohibited from staying inside our apartments — or in any building two stories or higher. The government provided us with bamboo poles and wooden boards. Using some plastic sheets I had, my friends helped me build a tiny hut for our family on the sports-field of the school. We moved our coal stove and placed it just outside the door of this one-room hut. The room was only big enough for two beds and four stools. During the daytime, the beds served as desks as well as a makeshift dining table.

The girls helped me carry the beehive coal cakes from our apartment, do our laundry, and buy the groceries. Once when a colleague visited our "home" and saw us carrying some coal, he offered to help. As he was leaving, I heard him murmuring to himself shaking his head: "It's not easy, a woman with three kids. Not easy at all."

At the time, the newspaper didn't carry any details about the size or extent of the earthquake. I found out from some PLA officers stationed in our school that the city of Tangshan, ninety miles away from Beijing, had been flattened. It was a coal-mining city, and the officers had been ordered to help the people there. Years later I found the following figures in a book: the quake measured 7.8; the death total was 343,000 with another 160,000 people badly injured.

For millennia, Chinese peasants have considered a natural disaster as an omen for change. In this case, the superstition came true: six weeks after the earthquake, Mao Zedong died.

Now the time had come to crush the "Gang of Four," which

was led by Mao's wife, Jiang Qing. Although people detested her, they wouldn't do anything to her while Mao was still alive. People wanted to "spare the rat to save the jade dish." Also in this group were Wang Hongwen (whom I had written to that July), Zhang Chunqiao, and Yao Wenyuan. All three were high-ranking officials during the Cultural Revolution. The four were arrested on charges of killing tens of thousands of people and persecuting hundreds of thousands more.

The "Gang of Four" were sentenced for their crimes and put into prison. (Madame Mao committed suicide in 1991; Wang Hongwen died in 1992.)

Thus, the Cultural Revolution which started in May 1966 ended in October 1976. A few years later, the government officially declared that the "Cultural Revolution" had been a catastrophe for our nation. During those ten years, one hundred million people were directly affected by it. That is, one out of every nine people in China. This book is the story of what happened to just one family.

31

A Visitor From Germany

In the winter of 1977, the government finally resumed the nationwide college entrance exams. These exams had been cancelled back in 1966. As a result, 5,700,000 people sent in their applications. My eldest daughter Weiming was one of them.

Weiming had graduated from middle school in 1976 at the top of her class. She was dedicated to her schoolwork and, like many first-born, had the benefit of lots of parental attention. For example, when Weiming was in primary school, Tungping taught her to write Chinese characters with a writing brush. He showed her how to hold the brush and how to write the strokes correctly. He was always praising her for any progress she made. And if she didn't do the strokes the right way, he would gently explain and ask her to do them again. I think that's why Weiming's calligraphy is the best in our family.

Though she was very good in math and science, Weiming felt she was not strong enough to review these courses for the college entrance exams. She decided to switch to English, knowing I could help prepare her in this field.

When December 1977 came around, applicants for the nationwide college entrance exams were asked to list three universities as their top choices. If their grades were good enough, they would be admitted to one of these three. Otherwise, the Committee would make the decision based on whichever university the applicant was qualified for. Weiming put down the First Institute of Foreign Languages as her only choice.

The applicants were also required to hand in letters of recommendation from their schools or *danwei*. These letters revealed the applicants' family origin (priority given to the five desirable "red categories") and political standing (priority given to members of the Communist Party or Communist Youth League).

That year, applicants for the foreign-language major had to take exams in Chinese, political science, math, history, and English. When the admission letters started to arrive, Weiming didn't receive any. I knew she had done pretty well; her English oral exam was excellent. So I decided to go to the Beijing College Entrance Examinations Committee to find out what the situation was.

When I arrived at their office, a huge crowd (mostly mothers) was there already. The line stretched from the office on the second floor, down the corridor, down the stairway and into the courtyard. By eleven o'clock I had only moved up to the third step of the stairs. But I didn't dare leave for lunch because I didn't want to start at the back of the line again.

Finally, it was my turn to talk to an official. I asked to know Weiming's total grade. The officer pulled out her file and told me her total grade was high. But her English grades weren't as good as those who had attended foreign-language primary school and started English in the third grade. I acknowledged that that might be true, but I also knew that those students had very little math. Could they do well in that subject? I then asked anxiously, "Would it be possible for the college to add more names to their admission list? Or admit students with a high overall grade?" I added, "As a college English teacher myself, I know from experience that a well-rounded student makes a better foreign-language student in the end." The official seemed to agree with me. He promised to relay my suggestion to the First Institute of Foreign Languages.

Later on, the school admitted more students — those with high total grades. And Weiming was one of them! She was accepted by the English Department of the First Institute of Foreign Languages. Weiming was lucky indeed. That year, out of the fifty-two students in her middle-school class, only two passed the college entrance exams. And of the 5,700,000 people who took the college entrance exams that year, only 273,000 applicants (about 5%) were admitted into colleges.

Classes finally resumed in February 1978. Four years later, Weiming graduated from her Institute with flying colors. She was assigned to work at the Chinese Consulate in Houston for two years. Now, she is completing her Ph.D. program at a university in Pennsylvania.

One afternoon in the fall of 1979, my phone rang. I picked up the receiver, a gentleman's voice came into my ear. He introduced himself as Zhang Wei. I recognized the name immediately: Dr. Zhang was the Vice-President of Qinghua University. He told me an old friend of Tung-ping's, Professor D. Boenisch had come to Qinghua to give lectures. The professor had asked to meet with Tung-ping. When told that Tung-ping had passed away, Professor Boenisch requested, "Could I meet Tung-ping's family?"

I asked Dr. Zhang, "What should I tell him?"

"You can tell him the facts."

"If I did, wouldn't people say that I was smearing the Cultural Revolution?"

Dr. Zhang explained to me. "The Gang of Four has been smashed. Now, we can tell people the truth."

The next day, I brought Chenfang (Little Buddha) along with me to the Friendship Hotel where Professor Boenisch was staying. When the professor opened the door and saw us, he said Chenfang looked just like Tung-ping. He told us that as early as 1977, the President of Aachen University had visited Beijing and tried to contact Tung-ping, but nobody had told him anything.

"This time," Professor Boenisch said, "I was determined to find Tung-ping myself. We had worked on several projects together in Aachen University. I even brought some of Tung-ping's pictures with me for people to identify him."

He showed me pictures of Tung-ping at one of their school dances. Tung-ping was dressed as an American. He had on a red and black check shirt. Another was at Tung-ping's birthday party. He was blowing out the candles while some of his German friends were smiling at him. I had seen those pictures before. It brought back sweet memories of when Tung-ping and I were looking at the pictures together.

Celebrating Tung-ping's 32nd birthday party with his housemates and landlady in Aachen, 1955

Then the professor asked me what really happened to Tung-ping. I told him everything. But the past was still too painful for me. Several times, I had to stop to wipe away the tears. The professor's eyes began to get red too. Chenfang was now fifteen. She had forgotten the details of the tragedy. When she heard it all, she started to cry, the professor kept asking us to pardon him for bringing back those painful memories.

He then asked Chenfang if she would like to study metallurgy at Aachen University when she grew up. Chenfang couldn't talk. Still shaken, she just nodded her head.

What the professor said that afternoon gave me an idea. Maybe some day, I thought, I could send my daughters to study abroad…

By 1978, the Cultural Revolution had been over for two years, but no one could be sure what would come next. It had been an entire decade since the tragedy, and Tung-ping's reputation still wasn't clear. Time was working against me — and my daughters. After twelve years of political campaigns, anti-this or down with that, clean-this and smash that, there was no way to be certain what trouble my daughters might encounter without a written record proclaiming their father's martyrdom.

So in early 1978, I wrote a letter to Minister Song Ren-qiong. He was now head of the Seventh Ministry, in charge of tens of thousands of people. I stated that I realized it would be hard to track down those ultimately responsible for inciting the killers… Even so, could the Seventh Ministry make a political assessment of Comrade Yao Tung-ping?

I carried the letter to the Seventh Ministry and asked to see Minister Song. He was tall and thin, wore black-framed glasses and spoke with a Hunan accent. Song read my letter and listened to me attentively. He was very sympathetic to what I had gone through and promised to forward my letter on to the Party Central. After our talk, he walked me to the stairway.

Minister Song did as he had promised. During the Fifth People's Congress in 1978, he passed my letter to Deng Xiaoping and recommended that, with the Party Central's approval, Comrade Yao Tung-ping be declared a revolutionary martyr. The top leaders agreed and decided a memorial service should be planned to coincide with the National Science and Technology Congress in March.

I was informed about the memorial service three days beforehand. The Seventh Ministry said it was going to be held on March 18. And they told me that I should do the inviting. (Usually the deceased person's *danwei* does the inviting along with the widow.)

Three days. Three days to pull together a memorial service I'd waited ten years for. I decided not to let this bother me. Our time together had been the important thing; the memorial service could never reproduce all its moments. But because of the time constraints, I was unable to notify Tung-ping's overseas friends and their families. I did reach Tung-ping's younger brother Yong-ping in town, but couldn't reach his sister and brothers elsewhere in China. (I felt so bad about this, because Tung-ping's elder sister and two brothers all passed away several years later.)

A friend had a suggestion: Hadn't Marshal Nie shown a direct interest in Tung-ping's case? Perhaps I should inform him? I called up Marshal Nie's office, but he was ailing and unable to come. He did however send an arrangement of flowers. When the memorial committee at the Seventh Ministry saw this, they perked up and paid more attention to the service.

March 18 was a cold day. Before the service, I was asked if the arrangement was satisfactory. Tung-ping's picture hung on the wall, draped in black cloth. The urn with his ashes rested beneath it. There were paper flowers all around. When I looked at the presentation, tears clouded my vision.

Visitors began to arrive. Here was General Peng Shaohui, who had shown me such kindness after my school was moved to the countryside. He praised Tung-ping highly for his service to China and for his upright character. Other figures appeared — old friends, senior officials. Here was Dr. Qian Xuesen, the brilliant missile scientist whose return to China attracted so many others back to the motherland as well.

A *Babaoshan* Cemetery attendant approached me with a telegram. It was from former Minister of Defense Su Yu, the four-star general who had been dispatched by Premier Zhou to initially investigate the murder. General Su had only gotten my message that very morning. He couldn't possibly make it, so he sent a telegram of condolence. The general called Tung-ping an "outstanding scientist."

Weiming carried the urn containing her father's ashes. Jibin carried a large photo of their father. Chenfang, now thirteen, held my arm as we walked alongside. We processed slowly toward the vault where the ashes were to be kept. I finally realized this was the final good-bye, and I couldn't control my crying.

I kept looking at the urn, was my Tung-ping really there? No.

Tung-ping was the tall, dark, handsome man with horn-rimmed glasses who had asked me to dance when we first met. Was my Tung-ping really there? No.

Tung-ping was the bridegroom who had carried me into our wedding room and said the marriage vow together with me in English. Was my Tung-ping really there? No.

Tung-ping was the happy father who had celebrated news of our first-born with his brother while I was still in the hospital.

Tung-ping was the loving *Baba* to these three girls.

And Tung-ping was the hard-working scientist who had been working in his office on the heat-preventing system for our first

276

satellite *Dong Fang Hong* on June 8, 1968, the day he was beaten to death.

I said in my heart, "Farewell my darling. We will meet again in the Ninth Heaven."

Tung-ping's ashes were placed later that day in the mausoleum reserved for revolutionary martyrs. A martyr is defined as someone who sacrifices his life for his country; that was my Tung-ping.

In 1985, seven years later, a certificate from the Ministry of the Interior of our country was finally given to me. It read:

"On June 8, 1968, Martyr Yao Tung-ping was beaten to death by some bad elements and was sacrificed for the revolutionary cause."

I copied the certificate and gave each daughter a copy. This way, they would have lasting proof.

Tung-ping's guiding principle was truth — truth discovered through scientific experimentation and observation, through methods developed since the Enlightenment. It wasn't bourgeois; it was good science. Tung-ping refused to yield to those who didn't understand technology and who put politics first. The absurdity, the unfairness, the pointlessness of it all made me cry out.

In retrospect, I wonder how much of the antagonism shown toward Tung-ping by a few with no college education wasn't merely a kind of resentment. I remember a neighbor telling me a cadre was always bragging, "We are the ones who chased away the KMT, why should those intellectuals enjoy our fruits?" I imagine he didn't realize it was also very difficult to reconstruct a country. Perhaps it was this kind of mindset that made him resent Tung-ping and other intellectuals.

I think there was another reason. Because Tung-ping knew he had done nothing wrong, his confident attitude, his independent way of thinking — even his very existence — may have seemed a challenge to someone else's authority. Tung-ping wouldn't obey blindly; he wanted to put the country's interest ahead of any individual's order. In that sense, perhaps he made an inviting target.

Oh, Tung-ping, my heart fills with pain whenever I think of this. But as the years wear on, I love and respect you even more than before.

32

Crossing Over the Pacific

After China and the United States established diplomatic relations in 1979, we could write to foreigners without asking for permission beforehand and reporting to the *danwei* afterwards. The first letter I sent abroad was to Sister Annecita, who had been President of St. Francis College while I was a student there. I told Sister I just couldn't figure out why I missed St. Francis so much even after I was back in my motherland. I wrote that I hoped I would be able to visit her and the other Sisters one day.

In April 1983, the head of another university in the midwest — Dr. Timothy O'Meara, Provost of Notre Dame University — came to Beijing on business. During his visit, he gave an oral and written examination to Chenfang. (He had read her application before arriving.) Although she was a bit nervous, Chenfang adroitly answered his questions, happy that they both shared an interest in mathematics. Only one question stumped her. She was indeed her father's daughter and was awarded a full scholarship in applied physics for the following fall.

Chenfang went to the United States that October. The following year I was able to visit her. On my way, I stopped over in San Francisco and found it looked as beautiful as when I last saw it in 1957, on my trip back to China. But I found the new buildings were taller. I also found a bigger percentage of "plump" people. It seemed clear that America was a land of abundance and prosperity.

The next day I flew on to Chicago. When I arrived at O'Hare International Airport, I started looking for my daughter Chenfang.

"*Mama*! I am here!"

I didn't recognize her at first. A year earlier, she had been a typical Beijing schoolgirl, in white blouse, navy skirt and her hair in two bunches behind her ears. Now she stood tall in jeans, denim jacket, and Nike sneakers. She looked just like an American co-ed. She even had an American name, Carolyn.

We took the bus to South Bend and onto the verdant Notre Dame Campus. "Carolyn" told me that when she arrived for the first time she was amazed by the green grass everywhere, the cute little squirrels running in and out of the bushes, the many trees and the twin lakes. She was about to ask, "What's the name of this park?" but before the English words came out, she was told they had arrived on campus.

Notre Dame University was truly a serene place.

My daughter's dormitory room reminded me of my own college days at St. Francis College, except she had a Cabbage Patch doll on her bed while I had kept a teddy bear. I looked around. On her dresser was a sign: "Don't pray for an easy life, pray to be a strong person." Carolyn saw me looking at it. She explained that when she had first arrived in America, a month late for the start of classes at Notre Dame University, she had a hard time catching up. And she was very homesick. One of her friends had given her the sign.

Carolyn received her bachelor's degree in applied physics from Notre Dame in 1987. (She was on the national dean's honor list throughout her college years.) She was awarded a scholarship to Yale University and received her M.S. in electrical engineering in 1988. I went to New Haven that year. I was proud to see her standing with some of the finest scholars in the world in the commencement ceremony at Yale University. Now, Carolyn is happily married and living in New York state. She has a boy and a girl. The girl was exactly the same weight at birth as her mother: 9 pounds 6 ounces. Another Little Buddha.

45 yellow roses for Tung-ping from his youngest daughter Little Buddha, shown here with her children and the author

The night after I arrived at Notre Dame, we had dinner with Sister Jean, who had been a student at the College of St. Francis with me and now was working in the Notre Dame administration. Sister Jean was a nun, but she no longer wore a habit. She told me all that had changed years ago. I had no idea until she told me. As a matter of fact, I didn't know what had been going on outside of China since returning to China in 1957. I was like "*jin di zhi wa*," a frog at the bottom of a well. I was only able to see a small piece of the sky above the well.

When Carolyn went to the ladies room, Sister Jean looked in my eyes, patted my hand, and said softly, "Poor, poor Penny."

"Oh, Jean, it's terrible. Although it happened almost twenty years ago, whenever I close my eyes, I can still see my husband lying there in blood."

Sister Jean told me she would remember me in her prayers.

I briefly visited Chicago, my home for five years, and found the downtown district rather deserted. I was told that everyone now did their shopping at the "mall" (a new word to me). I contacted a college friend, Jenny, who now taught Spanish in high school. She drove me down to Joliet so we could visit our alma mater, the College of St. Francis. It was now run by laymen and was co-educational. Somehow I was more attached to the St. Francis I knew before, with the Sisters as teachers and only female students. The three and a half years I spent there were my happiest days!

Now, most of our teachers were retired. They lived in a retirement home. To my great sorrow, Sister Annecita passed away. Sister Beatrice, the English professor, was still there though — and still in her Franciscan habit. She told me she intended to wear her habit all her life. She was very happy to see me. I asked her, "Sister, did I give you a hard time in your English class?" "No, Penny, not at all. All my students were pretty good, though I guess you were the one who had a hard time. *Beowulf* and *Paradise Lost* must be difficult for a Chinese girl."

At this point, several Sisters came up to me and asked, "Penny, do you remember us?" I was embarrassed — I didn't. They reminded me they had worked in the kitchen. They were very kind to me. When I first arrived, they tried to make rice for me, but it didn't turn out quite right. So they offered me chop suey! And I still remembered the brownies they sent me while I was at New York University, which I enjoyed enormously.

Another Sister came over. When she saw me with Jenny, she asked her, "Is Penny a Communist now?" I heard her and answered for myself. "No, Comrade Mary, I am not a Communist."

"What did Penny say, Jenny?"

"She said she was not a Communist, Sister."

It dawned on me that I had made a big mistake by calling a Sister "Comrade." So I answered her question once more. "No, Sister Mary. I am not a Communist."

In China, we addressed each other as "Comrade." But starting in the late 1980s, people began to use "Mr.", "Mrs." and "Miss." When I visited Joliet in 1984, we were still using "Comrade so and so." I had called Sister Mary that by force of habit. But Sister Mary was still not at ease. She took Jenny and me to the chapel and we had a prayer together.

Visiting Shirley, my college friend from St. Francis, at her home on Mother's Day 35 years after graduation on this return trip across the Pacific.

The Sisters invited us to stay for lunch at their retirement house. I had a chance to see more Sisters. I told them how much I missed our college after I went back to China. I missed the green grass in spring, my job at St. Joseph's Hospital in summer, the red maple leaves of our campus in the fall and the Christmas carols in winter. But most of all, I missed my teachers. The Sisters who had shown such kindness to me, and who had taught me to be an upright person, by lesson and by example.

The pleasant lunch was over. Jenny and I said good-bye to the Sisters. I promised that I would visit them again.

On this same visit I again stayed with my college friend Shirley, just as I did when I first came to America to study so many years before.

Sister Jean at Notre Dame University told me a classmate of mine, Sister Mary Kay, was working at the law school of Georgetown University in Washington, D.C., a city I planned to visit anyway. Soon after arriving in Washington, D.C., I looked her up and rang her doorbell. A lady in a simple gray dress with short hair opened the door. I recognized her right away: she still had her baby soft skin.

"Mary Kay, don't you recognize me? I'm Penny!"

"Ah," she exclaimed, hugging me, "Penny, where did you come from?"

I pointed to the ground. "I am from the other side of the earth."

Sister Mary Kay invited me to stay with her. She lived in a two-bedroom townhouse on 37th street, right across from the main entrance of Georgetown University. I filled her in on the past quarter-century, from the tragedy of Tung-ping to the triumph of my daughters. I told her about Jibin, my second daughter, who was now an intern in a hospital in Beijing.

I had heard that Georgetown University had an excellent medical school, and Jibin had expressed an interest in studying in the United States. Sister Mary Kay told me of a Dr. Ramey, Chairman of the Department of Physiology. She said Dr. Ramey was a feminist. Sister Mary Kay promised she would contact Dr. Ramey about my daughter on my behalf.

When I walked into Dr. Ramey's office the next day, I found her to be a charming lady, dressed in a navy suit and white blouse. I noticed a placard on her wall: "I am my sister's keeper." I pointed to it and said, "I am one of those sisters." We both laughed about this.

I told Dr. Ramey of "Pamela" (Jibin's American name), of our life, showed her my daughter's medical school grades and letters of recommendation. Dr. Ramey smiled, and said, "Penny, you remind me of my mother." I was stunned for a moment. I knew it was a compliment, yet I was fairly sure I was younger than she was.

"My mother was a great person," she explained. "She would do anything and make any sacrifice for her children, just like you."

Dr. Ramey told me since it was October already, it was rather late for any financial assistance. Then she said to me, "Wait a minute, I think Paul has an opening." So, I visited one more professor, who happened to have visited China a year before, even visiting Pamela's hospital. After studying the papers, the professor asked me, "How is your daughter's English?" "Almost as good as mine," I said. The professor decided to grant Pamela financial assistance in the Ph.D. program of the Physiology Department.

The next year, Pamela flew to Washington, D.C.

Sister Mary Kay met her at Dulles International Airport. She also arranged for Pamela to stay at the Georgetown Visitation Convent, rent-free. The convent was one block from the church where President John F. Kennedy and his family used to go for Mass. Pamela worked part-time cleaning houses and doing ironing while completing her graduate work. Two years later, with Pamela's help, her boyfriend from Shanghai was able to study at Howard University as a freshman.

After she received her Ph.D. from Georgetown University, Pamela went to Johns Hopkins University in Baltimore to do her post-doctorate work. By that time she and her boyfriend Xiao Zhou were married. Later on, Pamela received several job offers and chose to work at Rochester University, because they also had a job opening for her husband.

During this same visit in 1984, there was someone else special in my heart whom I was going to see. Someone I had not seen for over 30 years. It was my oldest brother Ho-ching — who had been a reporter in World War II. He had seen me off on the docks of Shanghai and we kept waving to each other under the bright morning sun until we disappeared from sight. My brother then went to live in Taiwan in 1949. He was now a professor at the Cultural University in Taipei. He was traveling to America with a religious delegation.

My brother Ho-ching and his family gathering in their house in Taiwan for the wedding of his younger son in 1984

We arranged to meet at the hotel in midtown Manhattan where he was staying. As I walked into the lobby, I saw Ho-ching waiting for me, with a huge suitcase next to him. We embraced each other warmly. My brother hadn't changed much, still thin and dark. He told me that my sister in-law had bought a lot of clothing for me and my daughters. We had breakfast at the hotel and toured Chinatown afterwards, dragging the big suitcase with us all the while.

He told me about his children: his daughter who now works in a bank in Canada, his elder son who owns a factory in Taipei, and his younger son who runs a printing shop in Los Angeles. My brother is a very devoted Baptist. He donates part of his salary to the Church and visits a prison every week to give sermons to the prisoners.

My brother always had a soft spot in his heart for me because I looked just like our mother. He even changed my name from *Manman* to Chieh-ching so that I could share our generation name, "Ching." He was very kind and generous to my daughters as well. When Pamela got married, he helped her out by sending a month's salary as a wedding gift — Pamela and Xiao Zhou used it to buy a nice second-hand car.

While I was also a college teacher, I couldn't afford to send them a gift which cost that much. But after seeing the futon in Pamela's bedroom and realizeing they were living in a basement apartment which was rather damp, I spent six months' pay and bought them a bed with a Simmons mattress. We all wish Pamela and Xiao Zhou happiness!

飞越太平洋

33

Meet in the Ninth Heaven

————————⟨⟩————————

I BOUGHT A United Airlines ticket to fly to America on September 16, 1999. A few days before my departure, as I was doing my last-minute gift shopping at the Friendship Store, my cell phone rang. A young woman's voice said anxiously, "Oh, Professor Peng, I am so glad that I've finally gotten hold of you." She introduced herself as someone from Institute 703 and told me that I was invited to attend an important ceremony on September 18 at the Great Hall of the People. (This building sits on the west side of Tiananmen Square.)

Since I had already paid for the ticket, I hesitated. Then she described the nature of the ceremony and told me the invitation came from the State Council. She said she would contact the travel agency about postponing the trip for me.

On the afternoon of September 18, 1999, the Chinese Communist Party, the Central Military Commission and the State Council all filed into the Great Hall of the People in Beijing. All the high-ranking officials were there. President Jiang Zemin then personally presented the "*Liang-dan-yi-xing* Meritorious Service Medals" (the highest presented so far in China) to 23 distinguished scientists who had made great contributions in the fields of atomic bombs, guided missiles and satellites.* My husband, Dr. Yao Tung-ping, was one of the scientists of our country who had the honor to be awarded these golden medals. I was invited in his absence.

President Jiang gave a speech. He noted that most of these distinguished scientists had held good positions while abroad and given them up out of a sense of patriotism. Jiang called on the whole nation to learn from these scientists: their love for the motherland, their selfless devotion to their work, their self-reliance combined with a spirit of cooperation with other *danwei*. Jiang pointed out that many of these scientists had held good positions abroad. Some of them had even given up their lives.

As I was listening to Jiang's speech, I could hardly control my emotion. How could I keep composed? I thought back over the years.

Back in 1958, when Tung-ping first reported to work, the place had only one microscope and a dozen college graduates. Tung-ping turned it into a space-materials and technology institute, the first of its kind in China. Under the leadership of Marshal Nie, he mobilized labs and factories across the country and established technical cooperation among hundreds of organizations. Tung-ping also formed a network of experts to do research in testing space materials, composite materials, failure analysis, welding, brazing and coating, thereby speeding their development.

From 1960 to 1968, the people at Institute 703 (with cooperation of other *danwei*) successfully trial-produced and completed 2,680 new materials. Among the materials devel-

---

* *Liang-dan-yi-xing* is an abbreviation for "atomic bombs, guided missiles, and satellites." It is a term familiar to all Chinese today as a result of this ceremony.

oped and manufactured were cryogenic stainless steel, high-strength aluminum alloys, and several refractory metals: tungsten, molybdenum, tantalum and niobium. When I asked engineers how much of Tung-ping's research was being used in today's rockets, missiles and satellites, they estimated 80 percent. Some of these materials are also used in the manufacture of consumer products Chinese enjoy now.

The purpose of developing these materials was usually to decrease the weight of the rocket or to help withstand the extremely high temperatures of the rocket's combustion engine. When the weight of a rocket or missile is reduced, its range increases and a heavier satellite can be placed on board. Two good ways of removing weight were honeycomb structures and corrugated metal sheets.

Other times the goal was to develop stronger materials. For example in the late 1950s China licensed a copy of a Soviet P-2 missile. Its fuel tank was made of an aluminum–magnesium alloy with a yield strength of only 98 MPa (a measure of tensile strength). Tung-ping joined his colleagues in Harbin for over a month developing a new aluminum–magnesium alloy, increasing its yield strength to 160 MPa. But still they weren't satisfied with this performance. After many more experiments, Institute 703 succeeded in manufacturing an aluminum-copper alloy with a yield strength of more than 300 MPa. This was a big step for China. It matched the technical level of the U.S. and surpassed that of Europe and the USSR.

During the ten years before he was killed, Tung-ping was in charge of numerous projects in cooperation with other ministries and research institutes across the country. The high-temperature brazing alloy and the porous perspiring materials were two achievements mentioned in earlier chapters. Other projects included: new welding, sealing parts, chemical milling, application of fiber-reinforced plastics and spraying techniques.

In 1962, a rocket engine failed during a trial launching. The broken metal pieces were brought to 703. After careful analysis, the engineers determined the cause was metal fatigue. Later Tung-ping wrote an article about this, noting that since a rocket's life span was relatively short, many assumed that fatigue was not a problem. But he showed that since the metal structures of a rocket worked under dynamic load and different degrees of vibration, this was not the case. Many materials in the combustion engine reached their lifespan during launching. Now when a launching fails, experts from Institute 703 are asked to find out what caused the failure.

Tung-ping didn't just develop materials, he developed people. He considered it crucial to train the next generation of engineers. He sent them to factories to watch their experiments become reality. Upon their return, he would expect a detailed report — written as well as oral — and would quiz them.

Tung-ping put in place an apprentice system, giving engineers hands-on experience at the side of an accomplished scientist. (Commissar Huang called them "black engineers of Yao Tung-ping." These so-called "black engineers" today are in leading posts both at home and abroad.) Many engineers at 703 told me it was Tung-ping who helped them develop a good foundation at the outset of their careers. They now regard Tung-ping as a master of learning and integrity.

People remember him personally as well. One couple told me they had invited Tung-ping to preside at their wedding. Sporting his sunshine smile, he predicted the couple would be bound together by love as well as profession. He asked the guests, "Do you know why?" He paused and went on: "Because the bridegroom's field is metals and the bride is a welding expert — they will be welded into one piece forever." Everyone present roared when hearing that scientific blessing.

Tung-ping, along with Marshal Nie and Dr. Qian, also

stressed the need to plan ahead. After all, the United States and the Soviet Union did their materials research three to five years ahead of any missile or rocket launch. Tung-ping drove this point home many times by using a restaurant analogy: "The [rocket] designers are like customers. When they order a dish, were you to answer, 'I don't know how to do it yet. Besides, I have to go buy meat, vegetables, and wait for the chickens to lay eggs.' How could that be? You, the restaurant owner, must research what the customers want to order. Then you must have the meat, vegetables and eggs on hand ahead of time. And you must know how to cook them. This way when the customers order a dish, you can serve it right away."

In the 1980s Tung-ping's work with other esteemed scientists began to receive recognition through several national awards. As one engineer pointed out, "The first generation plants the trees so that the next generation can have shade to keep the heat away. These awards show how much Director Yao did for us."

In 1985, several space scientists were awarded distinguished achievement awards by the National Science and Technology Progress Awarding Committee for their outstanding achievements in strategic arms. Tung-ping was the only recipient who couldn't be present at the ceremony. The awards gave me some comfort, because they represented peer recognition. On January 26, 1992, *People's Daily* carried a half-page story on Tung-ping — something that would have been unthinkable only a few years earlier. In the article Tung-ping was called the pathfinder and founder of China's space materials and technology. I then wrote a story about him that was published in *People's Daily* overseas edition in 1992. And my Chinese book about Tung-ping was published in 1993; the second Chinese edition was released by Qinghua University Press in 2002.

Tung-ping's alma mater, Jiaotong University, held a big

celebration marking their 100th anniversary in 1996. They unveiled a brass bust of Tung-ping in their alumni hall. On the black marble base were the gold characters: "Martyr Yao Tung-ping 1922–1968" written in the calligraphy of Minister Song Renqiong. On the side of the marble base were the key events of Tung-ping's life.

✎

On September 15, 2000, I was invited to the unveiling ceremony of another bust of Tung-ping, this time by Institute 703. The bust and its base stood two meters tall. On the maroon marble base were the Chinese characters "Yao Tung-ping, the Founder of Space Materials and Technology of Our Country" in General Zhang Aiping's calligraphy. (General Zhang was once the Minister of Defense and in charge of research of atomic bombs, missiles and satellites.)

Due to poor health, Dr. Qian Xuesen couldn't attend the ceremony. But he sent a magnificent note to express his feelings about Tung-ping: "He dedicated his whole life to space work in our country. His moral character will move the sun, the moon, and people after us."

All of the people at Institute 703 now acknowledge that it was Tung-ping who laid the foundation of their institute as well as the space materials field of our country. It was Tung-ping who insisted on doing research the scientific way. And it was Tung-ping who helped develop top space scientists. Although Tung-ping had been killed, what he left was a great treasure to all of them. They all remember his "Methodology In Doing Research Work," which is now a study requirement for every newcomer to 703.

That day, several honorable guests as well as people from 703 spoke of Tung-ping's scientific contributions and integrity. At one point, the present director of 703 was so moved by

Tung-ping's deeds that he had to pause to quiet his emotions. When it was my turn, I told the audience that Tung-ping did what any patriot and true scientist would have done. I said I was very much touched that people still remembered him after so many years, and thanked them all.

During the lunch that followed, the director of the institute, the officials, and the scientists all came to have a toast with me. Suddenly I felt Tung-ping's presence at the table. Did he have a glass in his hand? I poured some wine into my glass, then raised my glass, "Forever in love!"

I heard a clinking sound and "Forever in love!"

我俩相會九重天

证　书

姚桐斌同志为我国研制

"两弹一星"作出突出贡献，

特授予两弹一星功勋奖章。

一九九九年九月十八日

两弹一星功勋奖章

中共中央 国务院 中央军委
1999 年 9 月 18 日

Accompanying 24k-gold medal on plaque showing guided missile launch, atom bomb explosion, and satellite in orbit. Presented by President Zhang Zemin on September 18, 1999 at the Great Hall of the People.

Epilogue

It has been more than thirty years since Tung-ping was killed. Scarcely a day goes by when he is not in my thoughts. The sun rises and sets, the willows turn green in spring, the lotuses bloom each summer, the red maple leaves come out in Autumn Festival time and the white snow flakes dance over the Great Wall in winter — all of nature reminds me of him. When I hear certain music, I recall listening with him to our record player. When I pass Tiantan Park, I think of our moonlit strolls. When I look at a picture of us, I remember the familiar Chinese vow of undying love: "The sea may dry up, the rocks may turn to dust, but our love will live forever."

I recall the time we were invited to Tiananmen Square for the National Day parade, and saw the five yellow stars on the red flag, our national flag. We heard the band playing our national anthem. Tung-ping held my hand tight, his love for me and his love for our country surging through him, and into me. I looked up at him, and saw tears welling up in his eyes when he smiled back. He was so happy that he had returned to his motherland, ready to serve his country. His lifelong wish had been realized. I was seeing the pure happiness of a patriot's heart. This is something I shall always remember.

I still have trouble sleeping. Sometimes I sense Tung-ping is there, gently pushing my hair aside as he always did. Tung-ping, how I miss you. The years have been long, tiring and hard. How I want to enjoy your embrace and forget about the difficult times. And return the look of love in your eyes.

I now have two things written by Tung-ping. One is that letter clarifying the translation work he did for a colleague. The other is his Little Red Book, *Quotations From Chairman Mao Zedong*, whose margins so typically are full of Tung-ping's notes in tiny, flawless handwritten characters. He filled the empty spaces with meditations on Mao's words, bits of history and insights. Here was evidence of a thoughtful, conscientious man devoted to his country. That he should be killed by the hands of people who only dimly understood Mao's teachings is the kind of brutal irony typical of those times.

The years of the Cultural Revolution were unspeakably tragic for millions of Chinese. My story is but one of countless heart-breaking tragedies. Millions were persecuted in one way or another, and historians estimate one hundred million people were directly affected. Deaths could have been in the hundreds of thousands; nobody really knows.

I wrote this book in the hope that such a thing as the "Cultural Revolution" will never happen again. Especially if we can learn from the past. As our forefathers handed it down: "We must draw lessons from what we have done in the past to avoid making the same mistakes in the future."

For that reason, I have also recently written articles about my husband which were published in major magazines. They include: *Zhoujia Wenzhai* (Writers Digest), *Yanhuang Chunjiu* (Spring and Autumn of China), and *Zhonghua Ernu* (Sons and Daughters of China). I was also asked to do presentations about Tung-ping in six universities in China. My first stop was Beijing

University and my last stop was Qinghua University. I also recently spoke at George Washington University in the United States.

I will always have warm feelings toward the Sisters at the College of St. Francis who were so kind to me, just as I have warm feelings for some veteran cadres who helped me in my difficult times in China. (In January 1998, this college became the University of St. Francis.)

I still live in Beijing. I am working as a consultant for some North American high-tech firms who want help doing business in China. I guide them through the proper channels, show them the ropes, so to speak. Being born in China and having been educated in the United States, I try to act as a bridge for people between these two continents. Throughout my life, I have been fortunate to have had a foot in both lands. And to have looked up at the stars and heavens that belong to everyone, no matter how far away.

September 2003